THE DONEGAL AWAKENING

*To Paul
with love from
Dad*

County Donegal
(1st Northern Division)

THE DONEGAL AWAKENING

Donegal & The War of Independence

Liam Ó Duibhir

MERCIER PRESS
Irish Publisher – Irish Story

MERCIER PRESS

Cork

www.mercierpress.ie

Trade enquiries to CMD,
55a Spruce Avenue, Stillorgan Industrial Park,
Blackrock, County Dublin

© Liam Ó Duibhir, 2009

ISBN: 978 1 85635 632 9

10 9 8 7 6 5 4 3 2 1

A CIP record for this title is available from the British Library

This book is sold subject to the condition that it shall not, by way of trade or otherwise, be lent, resold, hired out or otherwise circulated without the publisher's prior consent in any form of binding or cover other than that in which it is published and without a similar condition including this condition being imposed on the subsequent purchaser.

No part of this publication may be reproduced or transmitted in any form or by any means, electronic or mechanical, including photocopying, recording or any information or retrieval system, without the prior permission of the publisher in writing.

Printed and bound in the EU.

'What did you think of Dungloe,
Donegal is awake in earnest now ...'

Quote from letter written by Dr J. P. McGinley in Derry jail, Friday 19 December 1919, to Seán MacLoingsigh, Convoy, referring to first **IRA** *attack on the RIC at Dungloe, 12 December 1919.*

*This book is dedicated to my mother Mary
and to my late father Liam.*

CONTENTS

Acknowledgements		9
Introduction		13
1	The New Political Aspiration Versus the Old	17
2	The Obstacles to Revolution	21
	Howth Gun-running and the Donegal Connection	24
3	Home Rule Suspension and the Birth of the Irish Volunteers	26
4	1916 – Leaders in County Donegal	31
5	Organising the IRB in Donegal	36
6	Donegal and 1916	39
7	1917 - Developing the Military and Political Organisations	45
8	1918 – Sowing the Seeds of Revolution	60
	The Threat of Conscription	70
	The German Plot	75
	The General Election	80
9	1919 – Government and War	93
	The First Dáil and First Blood	97
10	Donegal Engages with the Enemy – December 1919	113
11	1920 – The Guerrilla Soldiers and the Donegal Gun-runner	120
	The Republican Justice System	134
	First Daylight Arms Raid	161
	Raids on Fanad Coastguard Station and Belleek RIC Barracks	168
	Internment Camp	194

12   1921 – THE DONEGAL FLYING COLUMN   201
     Meenbanad and Crolly Ambushes   208
     Doctor Johnston's motor car   227
     Unrest in the Ranks of the 1st Northern Division   238
     The Big British Round-Ups   239
     British Raids and Internal Tension   259
     GHQ Investigates Trouble in the Donegal Ranks   273
     The British Agent   294
     Talks and Truce   298

CONCLUSION   306

APPENDIX 1   1st Ulster Division 1919   311
APPENDIX 2   1st Ulster Division (1st Northern Division) 1920   312
APPENDIX 3   IRA General Headquarters despatch, March 1921   316
APPENDIX 4   Donegal Internees – Ballykinlar Camp 1920–1921   317
NOTES   320
REFERENCES   336
INDEX   338

ACKNOWLEDGEMENTS

THE PUBLICATION OF this book was made possible by the personal accounts of the men and women who played their part in the years following the inception of Sinn Féin policy through to the end of the War of Independence in July 1921. These statements were made available by the Bureau of Military Archives, Cathal Brugha Barracks in Dublin. I would like to thank the staff at the Bureau of Military Archives and in particular Victor Laing and Lisa for assistance when researching and for the interesting conversations on the history of this period. I initially accessed the statements at the Donegal County Library in Letterkenny and have to thank Bernie Campbell and the staff there for all their help. The witness statements from the Bureau of Military History are also available at the Central Library, Letterkenny.

The staff of the Archives Department at UCD, Belfield, Dublin were also very helpful during my research for this book and I would like to thank Seamus Helferty and the staff there for their assistance and generosity. The Archives Department was a source of so many reports and correspondence between the Donegal area and General Headquarters in Dublin and gave a great insight into the incidents and problems experienced by the Donegal brigades during that period.

I am indebted and owe a special thanks to Liam McElhinney, Lifford, County Donegal for all the invaluable assistance, direction and information relating to this period. Liam gave me many original resources on this period and he himself is a great authority on the history of this period generally and more importantly at a local level. Liam was also one of the many people who read drafts of this book and highlighted historical errors and made useful suggestions.

A big thank you to Seamus McCann, College Farm Road, Letterkenny and his son Rory McCann, for the use of his father's diary (Seamus McCann senior), which was a very useful source in drafting this publication and a wonderful insight into the life of a Volunteer in the Flying Column based in Donegal. This diary gave detailed accounts of the many ambushes and activities of the flying column and the general situation during the war days.

I am also indebted to Pat and Mary Dawson, Letterkenny for giving me documentation relating to this period, and for the use of a space to compile and write this publication, which made this process so much easier. Thanks to you both for all your help and for your friendship over the years.

I am very grateful and owe a special word of thanks to Niall McGinley for being so generous with his time, and reading a draft highlighting the many grammatical errors and for the points on local history. I would also like to thank Niall for permission to use certain information from his book *Dr McGinley and his Times* and for the use of images from that book.

I would also like to thank Conal Cunningham, Spiddal, County Galway for permission to use an account published in his book on Glencolmcille and the use of a photograph of the burned out RIC barracks at Carrick.

Thanks to Declan O'Carroll for the use of photographs and for pieces of information that were of great significance. Declan was also very helpful when he read an early draft and gave me practical feedback.

I would like to thank the *Derry Journal* and Editorial Director Graig Harkin for permission to use information from the *Derry Journal* archives, which proved a very useful source when writing this book.

The *Derry People and Tirconaill News* archives were also a useful resource and I would like to thank the staff at the *Donegal News* for bringing the archives from Omagh to Letterkenny for my research.

Acknowledgements

Thanks to the editor Columba Gill and to Harry Walsh for all your help during this time. Thanks to Fr Pádraig, Capuchin Friary, Church Street, Dublin for permission to use information from the Capuchin Archives and images from same.

The following people were also very helpful in many ways and provided me with information photographs, advice and read drafts; Aiden Doherty (Ballybofey) and Paddy Doherty (Carndonagh), in particular for a photograph of their father. John McAteer for reading a very early draft and for the positive feedback in the early stages. Seán Beatty (Culdaff) for reading and permission to use information and images from the *Donegal Annual* 1966. Seán was also very helpful with advice on various aspects of the book. Jonnie Patton, who was another reader of the early drafts, for his feedback. Thanks to May McClintock for a detailed list of town lands in north-west Donegal, which was of great assistance. Paddy McIntyre, Declan Birney, Connie Duffy, Odhran Grimes, Ciaran N. Kelly, Aughlihard and Dublin. Thanks to Rosaleen and Joseph Black for the space to relax and recharge in Rathmullan.

To all my family for their encouragement and support during the writing of this book – thank you.

INTRODUCTION

THE POLITICAL AWAKENING in Ireland in the early part of the twentieth century and the subsequent War of Independence produced many interesting stories of political prowess and heroism. It was a period during which many ordinary young Irish people found themselves propelled into an extraordinary state of affairs. The period in question was, arguably, among the most interesting in Irish history and perhaps the first instance of a mass Irish resistance movement against the British along both political and military lines. From the birth of new republican ideology, the 1916 Rising and subsequent War of Independence to the Truce of July 1921, Ireland was thrust into a vicious war against the might of the British Empire. This book provides a snapshot of the events of this period in County Donegal, from the inception of the Sinn Féin idea in the later years of the nineteenth century through political growth and electoral success to physical resistance.

The national spirit was effectively dead following the Great Hunger of the mid-1800s, though the Home Rule movement had given a brief glimmer of hope that at least a degree of independence from British Rule was possible. However, in 1899 the *United Irishman* newspaper was founded and became the springboard for the new vision of Ireland's future, put forward by Arthur Griffith. In that year Griffith penned the first of a series of articles setting out his vision of Irish autonomy from the English parliament at Westminster. The articles were published as a single booklet in 1904 by the *United Irishman*, called *The Resurrection of Hungary – a Parallel for Ireland*. It was this new political philosophy, which would evolve into the Sinn Féin movement, that became the driving force behind the new political thinking and direction in Ireland. Sinn Féin developed into a mass movement giving a demoralised people the confidence to aspire to an Ireland free and independent from Britain. Like the rest of the country, County Donegal experienced a political awakening through this new movement's separatist and independence ideology.

The growing threat to Home Rule, following the establishment of the Ulster Volunteer Force (UVF) in 1913, firmly introduced the gun into Irish politics and prompted the founding of the Irish Volunteers as a defensive movement in November 1914. The UVF had landed weapons at three locations, including Larne, County Antrim, in 1914 and declared that it would resist the introduction of Home Rule by force of arms. This action gave rise to a reaction from the Irish Volunteers, and weapons were subsequently landed at Howth in County Dublin and Kilcoole in County Wicklow later that year.

The Irish Volunteers subsequently split following the outbreak of war in Europe with the Irish Parliamentary Party (IPP) calling on members to join the British army to fight 'for the freedom of small nations'. The split created two armies – the Irish National Volunteers who followed the Irish Parliamentary Party and the Irish Volunteers who followed the Sinn Féin organisation.

The revolutionaries of the Easter Rising of 1916 were almost defeated before the battle began, with disunity among the leaders, countermanded orders and poor communication resulting in the engagement of only a small number of areas, with Dublin being the main theatre for the insurrection. Although there had been little initial support for the rebels, what happened after the Rising shocked the Irish people and led to mass support for the principles of republicanism, beginning a new era in Irish history. The majority of the men and women who participated in Easter Rising had been arrested in the days and weeks following the insurrection, and were subsequently transported to jails in England and afterwards to the Frongoch internment camp in North Wales. However, by December 1916 the British began releasing the internees and the Irish Volunteers immediately set about regrouping and reorganising throughout 1917, establishing Volunteer companies and Sinn Féin cumainn in many towns, villages and parishes.

The new movement, which garnered huge support from the local population, was now intent on nothing short of total separation and independence. The political and military organisations, although having similar aspirations, were to operate independently of each other; Sinn Féin focused on the political arena while the Volunteers or – as they were later to become known – the Irish Republican Army styled themselves as a physical force organisation. The two were interlinked, however, with many Volunteers being elected to local councils and Dáil Éireann.

The result was political success for Sinn Féin in the general election of 1918. In the months before the election the threat from the new movement prompted the British to concoct the 'German Plot' as a means of arresting prominent members in an effort to suppress its development. Similar to other British miscalculations, however, this manoeuvre only aided Sinn Féin in winning 73 out of 110 seats and signalled the end of IPP and unionist dominance of Irish politics. The principles of separatism were adopted and the first Irish parliament, Dáil Éireann, was inaugurated on 21 January 1919, the day the first official action of the War of Independence took place. What followed was an intense and vicious war against all organs of the British establishment with Ireland effectively operating as an independent 'state within a state'.

This was achieved through the operation of national and local government and the establishment of an independent legal system resurrecting the old Brehon Law.

As a method of further undermining British influence a boycott of British and unionist merchandise was organised, resulting in the seizure and destruction of various goods. Guerrilla warfare was a new experience for the young men and women who joined the ranks of the Irish Volunteers and Cumann na mBan. They were facing a much more superior force both in numbers and experience, meaning that the slightest mistake or negligence could prove disastrous.

County Donegal, like many others throughout the country, experienced the brutality of the British military, Royal Irish Constabulary (RIC) and Black and Tans, with many arrests, murders and killings occurring throughout the war years. The Volunteers of the Donegal brigades had to contend with superior British forces and the RIC, a situation made even more difficult by the large unionist population in many parts of the county. Furthermore, the Donegal brigades were relatively isolated from the main body of the movement, and there were also a number of internal disputes, which only added to the problems experienced by the IRA in this area and distracted it from its primary objective. The Donegal flying columns were introduced to bolster the war effort and certainly served their purpose, but also brought intense British reprisals which put great pressure on the general public, the preferred target of the military and police. The War of Independence ended following secret negotiations between members of Dáil Éireann and the British government, concluding with the Truce in July 1921.

1

THE NEW POLITICAL ASPIRATION VERSUS THE OLD

The Irish Parliamentary Party was the major political force in Ireland in the late nineteenth century and the party was the driving force behind the Home Rule movement. The party was later augmented by the reorganised Ancient Order of Hibernians (AOH) which operated as quasi militant support for the Irish MPs. The AOH was formed in America in response to an increase in violence against Irish emigrants who were, for the most part, Catholic. It was resurrected in the late nineteenth century by IPP MP Joe Devlin and the two organisations worked together until the election successes of Sinn Féin in 1918 led to the demise of the IPP.

The first reference to Sinn Féin in a political speech was made in June 1892 at Letterkenny, County Donegal. The speech was made by Irish MP Tim Healy during an election campaign that year. He said:

> Now they [Parnellites] say against us that we put our hopes in the Liberal Party and that we are bound hand and foot to the Liberal Party. Now, I give you the good old watchword of old Ireland – Sinn Fain [sic] – Ourselves alone.[1]

However, in *The Resurrection of Hungary*, Griffith promoted the establishment of relations with Britain along the lines of the 1867 Austro-Hungarian model of dual monarchy, with a recommendation that the Irish Parliamentary Party MPs abstain from Westminster and sit in an Irish parliament. Not surprisingly, this policy met with fierce opposition from the IPP and the Ancient Order of Hibernians. Griffith proposed the policy at a convention in the Rotunda, Dublin, on 28 November 1905 and the meeting endorsed the Sinn Féin policy of dual monarchy as the policy of the National Council. The National Council was established by Arthur Griffith in 1903 and was composed of separatists opposed to the visit of the British monarch The Council's objective was to promote the merits of separation from British rule and in 1903 forced the Dublin Corporation into a climb down from their proposal to present a loyal address to the visiting king. The proposal was put to a public meeting and was narrowly defeated signalling a minor victory for National Council. However despite this Edward VII received a regal welcome in Dublin.

At the meeting of November 1905, it was emphasised that there was a need to establish Sinn Féin branches throughout the country to challenge the Irish Parliamentary Party and these branches would become the political arm of the Sinn Féin movement. A number of Donegal men were at the centre of the founding of Sinn Féin, including Seamus MacManus from Mountcharles. MacManus was actively involved in the Gaelic League and the GAA in his locality, as well as being instrumental in helping establish Sinn Féin in 1905. MacManus was the descendant of one of the leaders of the 1798 rebellion; his grandfather and great-uncle were involved in the rebellion in Armagh, with both fleeing to Donegal following the rebellion's collapse.[2] He was also a member of the National Council and was later expelled from Ireland in 1915 under the provisions of the Defence of the Realm Act, not returning to the country until May 1922.

The attraction of the Sinn Féin policy, as it came to be known, was the sheer simplicity of its logic, with Griffith viewing the 1800 Act of Union as an illegal instrument. He believed that MPs who sat in the Westminster parliament since 1800 were participating in a misdeed and were actively assisting in perpetuating a crime.[3] Griffith declared that they should withdraw from the imperial parliament and together with the elected representatives of the county councils and local authorities establish a council of 300 to take over the governance of the country and pursue a policy of political and economic self-sufficiency. This same policy had won the Hungarians their independence from Austria.[4]

The only organised group in Donegal at the time was the Ancient Order of Hibernians. However, the AOH, nationally, was showing no desire to acknowledge the rationale of the proposals from the new wave of thinking and saw the Sinn Féin policy as a threat to its very existence. Arthur Griffith, addressing a meeting in 1907, said:

> Our demand is for national independence. If England wants peace with Ireland, she can have it when she takes her left hand from Ireland's throat and her right hand out of Ireland's pocket …

The policy possessed a certain appeal for the members of other societies with separatist aspirations, including Cumann na nGael, the National Council, Maud Gonne's Inghinidhe na hÉireann and the Belfast republicans who had founded the Dungannon Clubs in 1905. These organisations later merged to become Sinn Féin.[5] A Sinn Féin cumann was started in Mountcharles at the beginning of January 1908, as was a Sinn Féin band around the same time. The cumann lapsed shortly afterwards and there is no further evidence of Sinn Féin activities until 1917. Other Sinn Féin branches were set up in the county at that time including Letterkenny, which was established by Michael Dawson, who would later act as a republican justice of the Sinn Féin court.

The British government's promise of Home Rule for Ireland began to filter down to the people, and this became evident with the influx of young Catholic men into the ranks of the Royal Irish Constabulary. However, many of the new recruits would later resign in the 1920s or remain to serve as intelligence agents for the IRA.[6] Moreover, the confidence that the Irish Parliamentary Party and the AOH had in the Home Rule Bill being passed and their willingness to settle for whatever Westminster would offer, had suffered a series of blows by 1914.

The first was the threat from Lord Birkenhead that there would be civil war should Ulster be removed from the United Kingdom. Birkenhead was later involved in the prosecution of Roger Casement in 1916 in his role as attorney general. Then there was the establishment of a unionist resistance movement called the Ulster Volunteer Force (UVF) in January 1913. By April 1914 the UVF had landed arms at Larne, Bangor and Donaghadee. The RIC ignored the landing and some even assisted the gunrunners.

The UVF declared that it was prepared to oppose Home Rule by whatever means. All of this effectively meant that any Home Rule act would certainly have a partition element to it. This action was the catalyst for returning the gun to Irish politics, something that remained as a dominant feature for over ninety years.

2

THE OBSTACLES TO REVOLUTION

ESTABLISHING AND DEVELOPING a fighting force in Donegal was going to prove difficult for a number of reasons, namely the geography of the county, the Royal Irish Constabulary and the large unionist population.

The first problem was the geography; the most northerly county in Ireland, Donegal is surrounded by the sea to the north, west and south-west and the remainder borders counties Derry, Tyrone, Fermanagh, Leitrim and Sligo. The terrain is rugged and mountainous. To the north is Slieve Snaght, the dominant mountain in Inishowen, while the west features the Derryveagh mountains, Errigal, Muckish and Bloody Foreland on the coast. In south Donegal can be found Barnes Mór Gap, the Cliffs of Glencolmcille, the Blue Stacks and Slieve League. The Inishowen and Fanad peninsulas are separated by the Atlantic ocean, which enters Lough Swilly at this point at a stretch of river known as the Lake of Shadows. Although picturesque and captivating, this terrain proved difficult for communications and travel, thus adding to the difficulties of proper organisation.

The second problem was the Royal Irish Constabulary, established in 1836 and made up of recruits from the cadet system, which initially attracted recruits from wealthy Tory backgrounds in England and anti-nationalists in Ireland. From the outset the organisation was a military force, with each member equipped with rifle, bayonet and revolver and trained to act as part of a quasi-army force. This extract from the RIC drill book shows that the force was really just an offshoot of the British army:

> The object of the recruit's course of training at the 'Depot' is to fit men for their general duties in the Force. For this purpose the recruits must be developed by physical exercises, and be trained in squad drill and firing exercises, in the estimation of ranges and in skirmishing. Squad drill should be intermixed with instruction in the handling of the carbine, and with physical training and close order drill with skirmishing ... It will be explained to the recruits that:
>
> (i) Fire is only effective when the mark can be seen, and when it is steadily delivered.
> (ii) It is useless to fire merely for the sake of firing, when no opponents are visible and their position is unknown.
> (iii) Engagements are won mainly by the accurate fire of individuals at decisive range. Long range fire should rarely be opened without special directions from a superior; in the absence of orders, however, it may be directed against large bodies, such as half a battalion in close order ...

The drill book also gave suggestions for gathering intelligence in the local areas:

> (1) When it was thought that members of a family had information which the RIC needed, a constable would be sent on a bicycle to their house. When nearing the house he would deliberately puncture one of his tyres with a pin. Then he would call at the house for a basin of

water to locate the puncture and whilst carrying out the repairs, would enter into conversation with members of the family and gradually lead up to the subject in which he was interested ...

(7) Talking to children, who innocently supplied minute particulars which came to their keen perception of all local happenings.
(8) Children of members of the RIC attending the local schools could not fail to collect all the extremely valuable information that was available in abundance amongst other school children.

Later named the Royal Irish Constabulary (RIC) many members never served in uniform and spent their period of service travelling the country working as blacksmiths, carpenters, etc. This was useful in terms of gathering information, which they then passed to their superiors or directly to headquarters at Dublin Castle. The RIC acquired the title 'Royal' for its successful efforts in dealing with the Fenian movement in 1867. Since its inception it had been used as the defender of evictors, oppressors and coercionists of all kinds. During evictions its members protected the operators of the battering ram and in some cases were operators themselves. Large numbers were drafted in to carry out evictions, and to add insult to injury the bill for the reinforcements fell on the rate payers of the county.[1]

The third problem was a legacy of the Ulster plantations with the eastern side of the Donegal having a strong unionist population, notably the Lagan valley and the south-east, where the nucleus of the Donegal UVF originated. That organisation was established in the county in early 1913 with members actively drilling and preparing to resist Home Rule. In its infancy the militant unionist strength in Donegal was four clubs, with a membership of 365.

This increased in May 1913 to six clubs and 483 members and by September 1913 the UVF strength was 890 in Raphoe, 206 in Ramelton and 82 in Letterkenny, a total of 1,178. This increased to 2,746 by November 1913 and 3,099 by the following March, organised in three battalions and armed with 1,299 weapons of various types. By February 1915 the figure decreased, with four battalions and 2,580 men.[2] In response to the unionist threat the National Volunteers was established and was to be put to use only if an effort was made to prevent the introduction of Home Rule by force. The IRB infiltrated the Volunteers by taking up key positions in the organisation and the scene was set for an uprising. Planning for this rising began in late 1913 and over the next eighteen months men travelled the country, visiting towns, villages and parishes in preparation for a rebellion against the British presence in Ireland. However, to counter the unionist threat the next objective for the Volunteers was to procure sufficient numbers of weapons and ammunition.

HOWTH GUN-RUNNING AND THE DONEGAL CONNECTION

IN THE SUMMER of 1914 while salmon fishing off Downings in north-west Donegal, Patrick McGinley from Gola Island received a telegram from Francis Joseph Bigger, a Belfast solicitor who he had met the previous year while fishing at Ardglass, County Down. The telegram summoned McGinley to Belfast immediately; on arrival he was given a letter and directed to Bangor in Wales, where he would make contact with Erskine Childers. On his arrival in Wales Childers took McGinley to the docks and showed him a large sailing boat moored there, the *Asgard*. The two began loading provisions onto the boat and after a week moved out, anchoring in the bay. Childers then requested that McGinley find another good seafaring man and he sent a wire to another Gola Island fisherman, Charlie Duggan, to come and join the crew, which included Mrs Childers, Mary Montague, daughter of Lord Montague.

Charlie Duggan arrived a week later, just in time to join the others, and it was at this point that McGinley and Duggan were informed that they would be involved in gun-running to Ireland when Childers told them of the plan to transport a cargo of German rifles to aid the Irish cause. At the beginning of July the crew of the *Asgard* set off for the Belgian coast, closely followed by another yacht, the *Kelpie*, owned by Conor O'Brien. The weather was fair, the sea smooth and as they worked their way up the English coast, skirting the rocks of Cornwall and the cliffs of Hampshire, Sussex and Kent, they seemed to onlookers to be part of the fleet of pleasure boats. But on passing the straits of Dover they began to dismantle the cabins and the decks were cleared.[3] This was on Sunday, 12 July 1914; while the Orange drums were beating in Ulster and the toast of the 'glorious, pious and immortal memory' was being honoured and acclaimed and the Ulster Volunteer Force parading, these two yachts were approaching the Belgian coast. They soon met with a tug and it was not long before weapons wrapped in long canvas bales were being passed over to the *Asgard*. As she moved away the second yacht, the *Kelpie*, came into sight and joined the tug.[4] The Kelpie was met later by another yacht, the *Chotah*, off the Welsh coast and weapons were transferred to that boat. On 26 July 1914 over 800 Volunteers marched and cycled to Howth from Dublin and the surrounding areas to meet the gun-runners and help transport the 900 German rifles and 29,000 rounds of ammunition. Six days later the *Chotah* landed at Kilcoole on the Wicklow coast with another 600 rifles.[5]

3

HOME RULE SUSPENSION AND THE BIRTH OF THE IRISH VOLUNTEERS

THE VOLUNTEER MOVEMENT was formed at a meeting in Dublin on 25 November 1913 and subsequently companies were formed in nationalist areas of County Donegal. The Irish Republican Brotherhood (IRB) was heavily involved in the Volunteers from its inception.

The outbreak of the War in Europe 1914 meant the suspension of the Home Rule Bill. On 18 September 1914 the bill received the royal assent but was suspended for the duration of the war. The draft bill contained many restrictions – Ireland would have no control over fiscal matters, policing or the army. The bill was considered a 'whitewash' and was unacceptable to the growing numbers who were aligning themselves to Sinn Féin. About September 1914 a split took place in the National Volunteers over the question of Ireland's attitude towards England's war aims and the policy outlined by the Irish Parliamentary Party's leader, John Redmond. The group under the leadership of Eoin MacNeill became known as the Irish Volunteers and those under Redmond as the National Volunteers. The split in the National Volunteers also affected many parts of County Donegal and in October Daniel Kelly discovered that most of the Cloghaneely Company had signed up with John Redmond's group when he mistakenly received their registration.

An Irish Volunteer company was formed in Dungloe in late 1913 and held regular drill sessions, but as arms were not forthcoming, interest began to wane. Another Volunteer company was organised at Cloghaneely college in 1914 by Daniel Kelly. He made contact with a superintendent on the railway who lived in Letterkenny, James Kearns, who had previously obtained 600 rifles for the National Volunteers and these had been left in his care. Daniel Kelly purchased the weapons, at £3 each, for a number of companies established in the county. Later two prominent Irish Volunteer leaders, Dr MacCartan and Dinny McCullough, arrived in Letterkenny to visit James Kearns and all the rifles were later removed to Tyrone and Belfast. James Kearns was a violinist in a Freemason band and was able to buy revolvers, rifles and ammunition in Derry, Belfast and Britain. The Freemason band was employed for unionist functions, Orange lodge dances, etc. and Kearns availed of the opportunity to purchase weapons in different areas.[1]

A number of Volunteer reviews were held in 1914 and in April that year 400 Volunteers paraded in Letterkenny and 2,000 in Convoy. It was estimated that in June 1914, the Volunteer strength in the county was approximately 5,500 and the British estimated in September that there were 74 units consisting of 10,661 members. Over the next two months Volunteer companies were formed in various parts of the county, including; Ballintra, Donegal town, Killaghtee, Inishowen, Kilmacrenan, Drumbologue, Drumoghill, Moville, Newtowncunningham, Castlehill, Mountcharles, Stranorlar, Creeslough, Raphoe, Fahan, Manorcunningham, Milford, Glenswilly, Foxhall, Breenagh, Carndonagh, Moville, Burt, Castlefinn and Drumkeen. Officers of the Donegal County Board of the Irish Volunteers were appointed on 15 August 1914.[2] By January the following year the numbers had dropped dramatically to under 300 with many answering the call of John Redmond to join the British army.[3] The British recruiting officers preyed on young men at the local hiring fairs and filled their heads with stories of adventure and the lure of financial security. They did this when the young men had a number of drinks taken and offered them money which many accepted. The reality of the situation would only come to light the following day when the RIC would turn up and order the young men to honour the commitment made the previous day.

The war in Europe was to impinge on Donegal in another way with the arrival of ten Belgian families to Letterkenny. On Tuesday 12 January 1915, the evening train arrived from Strabane with forty-eight Belgian refugees who were fleeing German occupation of their country. Deeply gratified at the warmth of their reception from the people of Letterkenny, they were taken to the technical school at Lower Main Street for a dinner and a welcoming reception. Following this they were conveyed to a number of houses that were made available to them for the duration of their stay.[4]

About this time republicans were engaging in anti-recruitment campaigns throughout the county and very often Volunteers were called out to intercept and break up British army recruiting meetings. Republicans took part in this campaign in the legitimate view that the Irish people had a right to resist conscription by every means obtainable. The British army published recruitment advertisements in the local and national press and they employed the services of the IPP to assist with recruitment rallies in many small towns and villages. Those arrested for opposing recruitment were charged under the Defence of the Realm Act (DORA) and on conviction were fined, imprisoned or deported.

In early 1915 Herbert Pim visited the county to address the Volunteers at Cloghaneely, but was prevented from doing so by the local priest Fr Boyle. He refused Pim and Daniel Kelly permission to use the local college and told them that he was 'heart and soul with the Allies'. Pim then addressed the local congregation as they left mass and called on anyone wishing to join the Irish Volunteers to give their names, but due to the presence of RIC men, who were taking notes, no one came forward.[5] Herbert Pim, Denis McCullough and Ernest Blythe were later arrested and charged under the Defence of the Realm Act for failing to comply with an order to leave the country. They were sentenced to three, four and three months respectively, on 24 July, for failing to comply with the order. The three had been initially served notice to leave the country, but defied the order and evaded the police for over six months before being captured. The court described them as leaders of the Irish Volunteer movement.

Later in the year Patrick O'Connor was charged under the Defence of the Realm Act and brought before a magistrate in Rathmullan, but was discharged following protests by a local priest. He was arrested again later in the month in Portadown and was conveyed to Armagh jail. Michael Carberry was charged for making statements liable to prejudice the recruiting of crown forces at a recruiting meeting in Kilmacrenan on 24 July.[6] These meetings were used to bolster the Irish regiments in the British army and the recruits would normally be deployed to the front lines after a short period of training where many would meet their deaths in the trenches of Europe. Meanwhile the Ulster Volunteer division, an exclusively Protestant division of the British army and numbering over 20,000, was still based at home after ten months' training at public expense.

The war had an effect on other aspects of life in the county also with the decline in the number of farm labourers. There was over a million acres of land in Donegal, mostly tillage and pasture, but at the hiring fairs farmers were unable to procure the number of labourers they required, a clear indication of the shortage of young men in the county.

On 1 August 1915 Pádraig Pearse delivered the now famous graveside oration at the funeral of the Fenian Jeremiah O'Donovan Rossa at Glasnevin cemetery. O'Donovan Rossa had died in exile in America in early July. Part of Pearse's oration read:

Life springs from death and from the graves of patriot men and women spring living nations. The defenders of this realm have worked well in secret and in the open. They think that they have pacified Ireland. They think that they have foreseen everything, think they have provided against everything; but the fools, the fools, the fools, they have left us our Fenian dead and while Ireland holds these graves, Ireland unfree shall never be at peace.[7]

The obvious interpretation of this oration was that the time had come to end British rule through physical force resistance.

4

1916 - LEADERS IN COUNTY DONEGAL

DONEGAL PLAYED HOST to several leading figures of the 1916 Rising. Pádraig Pearse, Thomas MacDonagh, Joseph Mary Plunkett, Roger Casement and Willie Pearse all visited the county in the years preceding the Rising.

Roger Casement, who was captured following the failed attempt to smuggle weapons into Tralee Bay on 21 April 1916, was a visitor to the county in 1912. His visit was not for political purposes, but for his love of the Irish language and his desire to learn it. He walked from Ballymoney in County Antrim to Lishally, crossed on the ferry to Culmore, proceeded over the Scalp mountain in Inishowen, along the old road to Buncrana and then through the Gap of Mamore to Uris. He spent six months living among the people of Donegal and visited many areas of the county, including Fanad, Portsalon, Tory Island, Cloghaneely and Glenties. The following is an extract from a letter from Roger Casement to his niece Blanche Constance, sent from Tory Island on 16 October 1912: 'This is a photo of me too – taken on Tory Island away off the far N. West Coast of Ireland – right out in the Atlantic. All the people in it speak Irish! – Not English – except me. They can speak English too – but prefer Irish their own tongue. Lots of the islands speak no English at all. I haste now – as I've things to do. Always your affectionate but lazy uncle. Roger.'[1]

After he left the county Casement maintained friendships he had established. He wrote to his friends regularly and was even writing to them while being held in the Tower of London awaiting his execution in August 1916.[2] Roger Casement was arrested at Banna strand in Kerry after landing from the German submarine the *Aud*. The RIC in Tralee sent a wire through to Dublin Castle that a stranger had been arrested at Banna strand and was being transferred to Kingsbridge station Dublin under escort. The train was met at the station by a detective inspector and a party of detectives and Casement was taken directly to London. The DI was the only one who knew it was Roger Casement, but told the escort at the station that it was someone else. The identity of Casement was not revealed until he was safely secured in a cell in London.[3]

Joseph Mary Plunkett also spent time in west Donegal before the 1916 Rising, for much the same reason as Roger Casement. He spent some time in the Cloghaneely area and on Tory Island learning the Irish language.

Pádraig Pearse, one of the main organisers of the Rising, had an association with Donegal, from 1905 when he represented Niall Mac Giolla Bhríde, Creeslough, on appeal to the Court of King's Bench in Dublin, one of the senior courts. Mhic Giolla Bhríde had been summoned in early 1905 for using a cart which did not bear his name and address in legible characters on the public highway. The cart bore his name and address in the Irish language. He represented himself, lost and was fined, but ignored the fine and carried on with his work before being summoned for a second time. He was found guilty and once again fined. The case was then appealed to the Court of King's Bench where he was defended by Pearse. The decision went against him and this was the last case Pearse ever defended as a barrister. Pearse visited Donegal on several occasions, the first time in 1906 when he visited the Irish college in Cloghaneely to deliver classes on the preservation and promotion of the Irish language.

Pearse wrote a series of articles in *An Claidheamh Soluis* entitled 'Belgium and its Schools'. In these he outlined the success of bilingual education in Belgium and recommended a similar policy for Gaeltacht districts in Ireland. Pearse recognised that few teachers in the Gaeltacht areas had a literary knowledge of the language. While proficient in speaking the language, most did not have a great knowledge of written Irish. To convince teachers of the advantages of bilingualism Pearse visited a number of schools, explaining the new policy and giving demonstrations. On 2 July 1906 he returned to Cloghaneely for the reopening of the Irish college and toured the Gaeltacht areas in the county. In July 1907 he returned once again and visited a number of places, including Gweedore and the Rosses, Dungloe, Glenties, Ardara, Carrick, Kilcar, Killybegs, Croagh, Inver and Donegal town.[4]

Pearse's third visit was part of the campaign to organise the Irish Volunteers. He was invited to the county by John E. Boyle and John Sweeney to address a meeting at Dungloe on 1 February 1914, where Pearse spoke of the British declaration issued against the importation of arms:

> As far as I am concerned this was only waste paper. It was illegal, but whether legal or not it could not prevent the Volunteers getting arms when Volunteers were sufficiently drilled and ready to use them. The British government dare not stop them and if the Tories who had been backing up Carson were in power, did anyone mean to say that in face of Unionist actions now they would dare to prevent Irishmen securing arms? If they did, what would the answer be? It would be such an answer as would become Irishmen's to give. A splendid opportunity was given to Irishmen now to realise themselves as men, and they could not call themselves men if they were not able, if need be, to fight in defence of their manhood, in defence of their homes, their women and children, in defence of their rights

> ... it was their right as it was their duty, to arms in defence of their country.
>
> True, there was only four million of a population, but no power on earth could prevent them arming ... It would be for them to see that no section of Irishmen was oppressed in North East Ulster. They did not want to proscribe Protestants or Unionists in Ireland. We claim freedom and we will accord it to everyone. If the freedom of any one section was threatened by whomever, it would be for the rest of Ireland to rise in the defence of that section.[5]

Thomas MacDonagh, another of the Irish Volunteer leaders, visited Donegal in April 1914 and addressed a meeting on Cruckaughrim Hill, Ballyliffin, in Inishowen. A large crowd travelled from Derry for the meeting and the people of Inishowen were there in their thousands. Speaking about the Volunteer movement, he said:

> ... they could no longer go untrained in the use of arms and unable to defend their own territories in the case of necessity... they must have in Ireland a party trained, disciplined and efficient, necessary to secure and maintain the rights and liberties common to all the people of Ireland ... For the past hundred years the Irish people had not been trained to the use of arms.
>
> For a long time they had been submitting their case to the Imperial Parliament, but they felt that for certain very grave reasons it was time that the Irish people should now be able to enforce their claims if necessary by the use of arms ... when certain things had passed – as they would – they would have a strong citizen army, which would be able to fight on all occasions, not for one party or another, not for one country or another but always for Ireland. It was likely that conscription might become necessary for the British Empire in a very short

time. Thousands left Austria every year to avoid conscription. How many young men would leave Ireland? If any did it would be the worst sort of emigration, but this organisation would prevent both these things happening. The Irish people would be able henceforth to hold their country for Irishmen. By becoming Volunteers they would not be joining the British army in any shape. The Irish Volunteers would be the army of Ireland and would receive commands only from Irishmen.

He was not talking politics, he was not saying what their ultimate national destiny would be – that would be for the people of Ireland to choose. He called on them to insist henceforth on the Irish question being:

> … what is best for Ireland and what amount of interference we shall allow in our affairs … the Volunteers believed that with this weapon in their hands they would be able to do their duty to their country in the best way.[6]

He concluded by giving details of the formation of companies, drill practice, etc. After Thomas MacDonagh and Pádraig Pearse's visit to the county the Volunteer organisation proceeded with more enthusiasm.

Willie Pearse was also associated with the county through his trade as a sculptor and, with his father, was involved in the construction of St Eunan's cathedral in Letterkenny. The two men carved the marble railing, which extends the whole width of the cathedral, the caps, annulets, bases and capitals. They were also responsible for carving the pulpit of the Donegal Masters out of Sicilian marble, which is situated on the right at the front of the main altar. As a child Willie also spent some time in Donegal; when he was eight years old he attended the Ballydesken national school in Fanad for a year.[7]

5

ORGANISING THE IRB IN DONEGAL

IN LATE SEPTEMBER 1914 Ernest Blythe was summoned by Seán McDermott and Denis McCullough to organise on behalf of the Irish Republican Brotherhood in north Ulster. The following letter was received by Blythe confirming his appointment:

> The Irish Volunteers
> Headquarters: 41 Kildare Street
> Dublin
>
> Mr Ernest Blythe
> Magheragall
> Lisburn
> County Antrim
>
> Dear Sir
> I beg to notify you of your appointment as Organiser on behalf of the Provisional Committee of the Irish Volunteers. I trust that you will lose no time in getting as many Companies as possible in Ulster affiliated with this Committee.
>
> With best wishes

Yours faithfully
Bulmer Hobson – Hon. Sec.[1]

Ernest Blythe arrived in Donegal at the beginning of November that year and first paid a visit to Dan Kelly at Cashelnagore in west Donegal and Aodh Ó Dubhthaigh who lived between Cashelnagore and Gortahork. He was introduced to a number of young men and authorised Dan Kelly to induct them into the IRB, if he considered them appropriate candidates. Blythe's next stop was Dungloe, but he failed to recruit anyone there. He next addressed a meeting at Niall Mac Giolla Bhríde's house in Creeslough, but was informed by those present that it would be impossible to establish a Volunteer unit in the area. He left Creeslough and walked to Glen and called on Patrick McFadden, who told Blythe that he could not think of anyone in the area who would be interested in joining the IRB, but that he would continue to source recruits quietly. Blythe had more success in Raphoe; there he made contact with Johnny McShane, who organised a number of young men willing to take the IRB oath.

In Letterkenny he met Conal Carberry and considered him to be the most influential man he had met in the north who presented a number of young men to take the oath. At Donegal town a few more recruits were identified. The next stop was Stranorlar and Ballybofey, where he met John Cassidy; there a number of men were sworn into the IRB. Ernest Blythe worked extensively in Donegal and made contact with every Sinn Féin sympathiser on his list of contacts. However, in the course of four to five weeks he only managed to swear in about twenty men.[2]

In 1915, as the IRB continued to organise in the county, a number of organisers paid a visit. These included Bulmer Hobson, Denis McCullough, Herbert Newman Pim, Seamus Dobbyn and Liam Gaynor. It was difficult for any one person to estimate the local strength of the IRB – the organisation was secret in nature and an ordinary member would only know the small number of members in his circle. In the early years the principal aim of local IRB policy was the disruption and disorganisation of the Hibernian organisation. The AOH did likewise and made every effort to disrupt the IRB, the Volunteers and Sinn Féin.[3]

6

DONEGAL AND 1916

IN FEBRUARY 1916 Daniel Kelly invited Pádraig Pearse to Donegal to address a meeting at Doe Castle, Creeslough. The purpose of the meeting was to improve the morale of Volunteers in the county and encourage new recruits. Pearse replied that he would be happy to renew his acquaintance with the people of the county. The plans for the meeting were well advanced when the Rising took place in Dublin.

Some time before the Rising, James Kearns from Letterkenny was busy setting up arms' deals and had arranged for the purchase of three .75 calibre French machine guns from munitions agents in London. In preparation for their importation to Ireland, Kearns had three life-size statues specially made, inside which the guns would be transported, but when he returned to London the agents informed him that the arms had been handed over to the French government. Some three weeks before the Rising, Kearns had a large consignment of weapons prepared in Belfast, Derry and Strabane. The Derry battalion of the Irish Volunteers received instructions to transport the consignment to Letterkenny.[1]

The Easter Rising began at noon on Monday 24 April when Pádraig Pearse read the proclamation in front of the GPO in Dublin. Approximately 1,600 Volunteers, led by Pearse, and 200 members of the Citizen Army, led by James Connolly, took over a number of strategic sites in Dublin and the battle began soon after.[2] In Donegal on Easter Sunday seven Volunteers mobilised at Cashelnagore and cycled to Creeslough where they met another twenty-six men; all were armed with an assortment of rifles and revolvers. The RIC came out of their barracks but were quickly ordered to go back inside. The men had no direct orders to do anything, and as a result of the countermands were unsure of what to do; by Easter Monday there were still no orders forthcoming. On hearing of the action in Dublin, Daniel Kelly and his brother decided to go there, but were told that there were no trains going beyond Dundalk.[3]

Meanwhile in Dublin, a bloody battle ensued and lasted until the afternoon of Saturday 29 April when Pearse, shocked at the number of civilian casualties, surrendered to the British commander, General Maxwell. The British had been responsible for the majority of the civilian casualties. Pearse had personally witnessed the deaths of civilians including a young family killed by British soldiers as they fled their burning building under a white flag. Some sixty-four Volunteers were killed in the fighting and 120 wounded and as a result of intensive shelling from the gunship *Helga*, over 300 civilians were killed and more than 1,000 wounded.[4]

There were said to be a number of Donegal men who fought in Dublin during the Rising including Eunan McGinley, Conor McGinley and Joseph Sweeney who were all students at UCD at the time. Joseph Sweeney was a former student at Pearse's school, St Enda's, fought in Dublin during Easter Week and later spent several months as an internee at Stafford jail and later at Frongoch prison camp in north Wales. The fact there was no uprising in Donegal was partly due to the confusion sparked by Eoin McNeill's attempt to call off the Rising. He issued a letter to the *Sunday Independent* countermanding the manoeuvres, and in response Pearse sent out messages with orders cancelling the countermand. Not surprisingly, this led to confusion throughout the country, with the result that only a small number of areas outside Dublin rose.[5] A number of Donegal men serving in the British forces were also involved in the fighting in Dublin. A policeman killed outside Dublin Castle on Easter Monday was a native of Inishboffin Island, off the Donegal coast.[6]

Another Donegal man who played a part in the Rising was Donncha McNelis from Malinbeg in Glencolmcille parish. McNelis left Donegal as a young man to take up employment in Cork and joined the Volunteers there in 1913. The Cork companies of the Volunteers mobilised at Macroom on Easter Sunday morning on the assumption that they were to receive a consignment of weapons, due to be landed at Banna strand on the Kerry coast. However, with the failure of that plan the Volunteers were instructed to return home.[7]

Over 2,000 men and women were imprisoned and some ninety death sentences passed by a secret military tribunal, of which seventy-five were commuted. In the following weeks the RIC and military were very active in raiding and arresting people who, it was reported, were associated with Sinn Féin. Over 3,500 people were arrested throughout the country, resulting in the internment of more than 1,800 men.

The British military and police had begun raiding for Republican suspects by the end of Easter week. Raids had been carried out in Donegal, Tyrone and Derry, with fourteen men arrested. They were initially taken to Derry jail before being transferred to Dublin by train. Among them were John Cassidy from Ballybofey and Daniel Kelly from Cashelnagore. Kelly was arrested at his home in Cashelnagore on the Saturday 30 April. He had received a tip-off from the guards on the railway that there had been arrests in Derry the previous day, but as the RIC had not interfered with their activities at the beginning of the week, Kelly did not think his liberty was under threat. He decided to remain at home instead of going into hiding. A police party of seventeen RIC men called to his house. When Kelly opened the door, the district inspector said: 'I arrest you in connection with this Volunteer movement.'

Daniel Kelly was taken to Derry by train in the company of

two sergeants and four policemen. On arrival in Derry they made their way to the car rank. They called over a jarvey, but the driver, a man called English, refused to transport the prisoner saying: 'No, I'll never drive that man with you as an escort.' They secured the service of another and went to Victoria police barracks, and later the prisoner was lodged in Derry jail. There were nine other prisoners there – Louis Smith, who was seventy-five, Joe O'Doherty, Vincent O'Doherty, Paddy Hegarty, Paddy Shiels and Charlie Breslin all from Derry city, Hugh Gribben from Castledawson, Jimmy McGurk from Gullaghduff and Jimmie Grieves from Glenmornan. The men were taken out of the jail at 6.30 a.m. and marched to the Great Northern Railway station. Before the train left the station an officer told the soldiers that if there were any attempt to escape or attempted rescue, the orders were to shoot to kill. They eventually arrived at Amiens Street station in Dublin and were marched to Trinity College. Buildings were smouldering following the week's conflict. From Trinity the prisoners were taken to Richmond barracks. While there a British soldier approached one of the soldiers escorting the men and said: 'All these characters should be shot!' The escorting soldier, named Doherty, replied: 'If you touch a hair on one of their heads, you will be sorry for it. These men have a country to fight for. You men have never been to war. Our battalion (Enniskillen Fusiliers) is only after coming from France and now we are stuck on this dirty job.' From the Saturday to the following Friday, in poor conditions, the prisoners were held in Richmond barracks, from where they could hear the shooting of the Rising leaders at Kilmainham jail. On the Friday morning they were marched to Dun Laoghaire where they boarded a ferry for Holyhead in Wales. On arrival at Holyhead in the early hours of the morning; the soldiers enjoyed refreshments, but there were none for the prisoners.

On arrival in England the prisoners were first taken to Wakefield prison where they were held for over three weeks, before being transferred to Frongoch in Wales. Each prisoner was issued with a typed form which said he was 'detained at His Majesty's pleasure'. Four companies of the Scottish Highlanders escorted them and while waiting on the platform for the train the prisoners sang the 'Soldier's Song', to the delight of the Scottish soldiers. One remarked that it was the best marching air he had ever heard. The prisoners eventually arrived at Frongoch camp – 'The University of Revolution' – in north Wales; they were the first of the prisoners to arrive there. One of the Scottish Highlanders said if there had been a Sinn Féin in Scotland he would not have been in the British army. Shortly after their arrival Dinny McCullough approached Daniel Kelly and said: 'We are reorganising the IRB and you will be representing Donegal. Could you nominate a man to represent Derry?' Paddy Hegarty was selected and a meeting of the IRB was held in the YMCA hall in the camp. The meeting proved to be very productive with men being appointed for reorganising the Volunteers in every county from Donegal to Cork.

At the same time Michael Collins began developing his intelligence network within the camp, grilling every man about various aspects of the British administration and loyalists in their areas. The established network was to prove very useful in the war campaign. The internees made good use of their captivity by organising themselves into military units, drilling, parading and preparing themselves for a new and better-organised offensive.[8]

The Irish people were not overly convinced by the actions of Easter Week and even denounced the leaders and Volunteers, blaming them for the civilian dead and general destruction. However, the actions of the British in the following weeks would soon bring about a change in attitude towards the British. The executions of fifteen leaders of the Rising in Dublin between 5 and 12 May, and the execution of Roger Casement in London on 3 August acted as the catalyst for this change.

In the aftermath of the Rising condemnations of the Volunteers' actions were heard in many parts of County Donegal. At a meeting of the Letterkenny Guardians on Friday 28 April the chairman, P. Carroll, JP, said: 'I think it would be a proper thing to condemn the action of these soreheads.'

The clerk interjected: 'You had better keep your names out of the press.'

'Why should we?' asked the chairman. 'If a man hasn't the courage of his convictions he may keep himself under the table.'[9]

At a meeting of the Donegal Board of Guardians on Saturday 5 May, Edward Melly, vice-chairman, protested in forceful terms against the action of the board at the previous meeting in passing a resolution condemning the Dublin rebellion. It was rare, he said, to find a body of men, who ought to have known better, condemning people and encouraging the British government to shoot Irishmen. John McGlinchey, addressing the meeting, said: 'The resolution does not read that way.' The chairman said the resolution read no other way, adding that the British government was always very good at shooting Irishmen. John McGlinchey replied: 'There is nothing objectionable in the resolution.' The chairman said it should have been left to the absentee chief secretary and there should have been no resolution passed until they ascertained who was to blame. He was not taking the side of the insurrectionists, but the resolution should not have been passed. They should have done what every other board had done – remained silent. When Carson and his men were drilling and threatening civil war, he added, there was no resolution passed. They should have then demanded the arrest of Carson. McGlinchey replied that they were not blaming anybody. John Timoney agreed that the resolution was rather premature.

When a resolution from the New Ross Guardians was read, condemning the actions of Sinn Féin and concluding with an expression of confidence in the Irish Party, the chairman said: 'Throw it in the waste paper basket.' Timoney argued that the resolution deserved consideration, but the discussion ended with McGlinchey remarking that the less said about the matter the better.[10]

7

1917 – DEVELOPING THE MILITARY AND POLITICAL ORGANISATIONS

THE AFTERMATH OF the Rising brought about major changes of opinion, which inspired the Irish people into a sharp sense of patriotism. The attitude of the people changed from revulsion to admiration for the men and women who had ignited the flames of rebellion. The majority of the population would become the invisible force behind the regrouped Volunteers in the next phase of conflict against the old enemy.

It soon became apparent that if the goals of the men and women of 1916 were to be realised, there would have to be a robust political organisation to carry on what they had started.[1] The release of the internees began in late December 1916 and continued through the spring and summer of 1917. In contrast to the time of their arrests the Volunteers returned to scenes of jubilation; the people were now behind them, ready and willing to move into the new phase of struggle. In the months following the Rising many young men in County Donegal who were part of the AOH and the Irish National Volunteers severed their links, instead joining the ranks of Sinn Féin and the Irish Volunteers.

During the parliamentary debates about 1916 at Westminster it was becoming more obvious that the partition of the country would be a fundamental element of the Home Rule Bill. Not surprisingly, this led to much interest in the three so-called excluded counties of Ulster – Donegal, Cavan and Monaghan. The plight of the three excluded counties was raised at a meeting of the Grand Orange Lodge of Monaghan in early January 1917. A resolution was passed at that meeting demanding 'that the whole of Ulster be excluded from an Irish Parliament, or if an Ulster Parliament is established, included in such a Parliament'. The reason these three counties were to be excluded was that the large nationalist population could elect sufficient numbers of republican or nationalist representatives to undermine unionist dominance in whatever assembly was established.[2]

When Daniel Kelly returned to Ireland from Frongoch camp he was sent to Donegal with instructions to organise Volunteer companies and enrol people in the IRB. He started a Sinn Féin cumann in Ballybofey and organised a company of Volunteers shortly afterwards.[3] In early 1917 a number of young Letterkenny men left the National Volunteers and set up an Irish Volunteer company in the area. J. P. McGinley, James Dawson and others established the company of Óglaigh na hÉireann, and a Sinn Féin cumann was later established in the town. In the early stages the Volunteer organisation was established on a parish basis, but this was later changed to battallions and companies, bringing the organisation on to a military footing.[4]

James McNulty from Creeslough was asked to return from America to help organise and establish units of Irish Volunteers in his area and also Sinn Féin cumainn. McNulty, who had been associated with Clan na Gael in America, approached Bernard McGinley to join the Irish Volunteers. McGinley discussed the matter with a number of his friends who also decided to join and before long a Volunteer company was established in Creeslough and soon after a Sinn Féin cumann.[5] Early 1917 saw the first Sinn Féin electoral success when on 5 February Count Plunkett won a seat in the North Roscommon by-election.

1917 - Developing the Military and Political Organisations

Some of the Frongoch internees and those interned in other jails were released between the summer and winter of 1916 and on 18 June the following year the remaining prisoners were released and returned to Ireland. Sinn Féin began a period of reorganising, and although there was a sense of uncertainty among the recently released Volunteers as to what the new policy would be, there was no doubt that the vast majority were now opposed to Griffith's 'dual monarchy' principle.

Count Plunkett summoned a conference in the Mansion House on Thursday 19 April at which he endorsed the claim that Ireland should be represented at the Peace Conference, which was scheduled to be held at the conclusion of the war in Europe. A number of declarations were proposed by Plunkett:

> In your name I make the following declarations, which I ask you to endorse.
> (1) That we proclaim Ireland to be a separate nation.
> (2) That we assert Ireland's right to freedom from all foreign control, denying the authority of any foreign Parliament to make laws for Ireland.
> (3) That we affirm the right of the Irish people to declare their will as law and enforce their decisions in their own land without let or hindrance from any other country.
> (4) That, maintaining the status of Ireland, we demand representation at the coming Peace Conference.
> (5) That it is the duty of the nations taking part in the Peace Conference to guarantee the liberty of the nations calling their intervention and the releasing of the small nations from control of the greater Powers.
> (6) That our claim to complete independence in founded on human right and the law of nations.
> (7) That we declare that Ireland has never yielded to, but has ever fought against, foreign rule.

(8) That we hereby bind ourselves to use every means in our power to attain complete liberty for our country.[6]

On the military side the Volunteers' only activity during the early days was weekly training parades, drilling and raising funds for much-needed armaments. Due to a shortage of arms for instructional purposes, the Volunteers made wooden guns for drilling purposes. Very often Volunteers were called out to intercept and break up recruiting meetings for the British army. British soldiers' wives living in the towns and villages of Donegal who were in receipt of marriage allowance became very antagonistic towards the Volunteers and caused considerable trouble.

Sinn Féin and the Irish Volunteers were actively recruiting throughout the county and the IRB was also seeking recruits. The aims and objectives of the IRB and Volunteers were very similar – to organise a fighting force, to procure arms by any and every means in their power and to use physical force when the opportunity arose to secure the freedom of Ireland from British rule.

The reorganisational activities of Sinn Féin were attracting the attention of many within the British establishment and beyond. An Australian politician, George Reid, made an interesting statement at a British Empire Union meeting in London in late May:

> I have got a sneaking sort of respect for these Sinn Féiners, because although they may be mad and wrong and plunging their country into all sorts of misery they do not sneak; they let you know their meaning.[7]

The growing support could also be seen in different parts of the county with the hoisting of Sinn Féin flags. When a flag was raised on a pole in Donegal town on 15 May 1917, the police made no attempt to remove it. It eventually fell and was taken away by a young boy. Another flag was erected on a pole near the village of Mountcharles, while in Buncrana flags were hoisted near the residences of known loyalists to antagonise them. These flags attracted considerable attention from the local RIC who made unsuccessful attempts to remove them. One of the flags was erected on the lawn of the residence of a unionist magistrate who was greatly perturbed by its presence on his property.

The British government was coming under increasing pressure to solve the Irish question and decided to hold a convention that would involve all the parties from the different political standings. This convention was viewed by Sinn Féin as an opportunity for the British and unionists to push for the division of Ireland, establishing a separate state and government in Ulster. The subject of the convention met with fierce resistance from Sinn Féin and was the topic of many debates at cumann meetings all over the country and among senior Sinn Féin figures. Count Plunkett made the following statement regarding the Lloyd George proposals:

> It is quite evident that in their usual manner, the English government and the so-called Irish Party came to terms on the question of putting the dummy Home Rule Act on its feet … The Convention cannot be a free and representative gathering for without a new register and a General Election neither the Irish Party nor the elected Boards have any claim to speak for the people.[8]

Arthur Griffith responded to the idea of the convention:

> The English government had pledged itself to the Ulster Unionists not to force them to accept the decision of the majority of Irishmen, thus enabling a small minority to render nugatory any decision of the great majority. Failure of the Convention was thus secured beforehand by the English government, which would then be enabled to say to the world

that England had left the Irish question to the Irish themselves, and that the Irish had failed to find a solution.[9]

The Con Colbert Sinn Féin cumann, Castlefinn, held a meeting on Thursday 21 May at which the following resolution was proposed by Sam O'Flaherty and unanimously passed:

    i.   Since it is evident that the forthcoming Convention is merely the latest ruse of the Lloyd George–Carson Cabinet to divert the minds of the people from the Peace Conference – to allay feeling abroad, especially in Russia and also in America – and since it does not in its constitution represent the views of the Irish people, and that the outcome can only be some form of partition, we request Mr William Gallagher, JP (vice-chairman of Donegal County Council) to oppose any attempt to have that body represented at the said convention.

    ii.   That we heartily congratulate and welcome home the men who stood between our country and the degradation of national apostasy.

O'Flaherty concluded by saying: 'The Pale in Dublin has disappeared and the Convention was the English attempting to set another one in Ulster.'[10]

At the meeting of Buncrana Urban Council, the chairman, T. J. Trew Colquhoun, a unionist, said he had received a letter from the Local Government Board requesting him to attend a meeting in Belfast on 27 June for the purpose of appointing delegates to attend the Irish Convention. On the motion of William Doherty, JP, seconded by James Farren, the council instructed their chairman to support no candidate who would entertain the partition of Ireland, declaring: 'We must have Home Rule for all Ireland.'[11]

In mid-June Éamon de Valera was selected as the Sinn Féin candidate for East Clare and was subsequently elected on 10 July 1917 with 5,010 votes. On hearing the result the Termon Sinn Féin cumann burned tar barrels to signal de Valera's victory and fires sprang up simultaneously on the tops of all the most prominent hills in the area. A number of days later a Sinn Féin flag was attached to the chimney of a school in Glenties and the children saluted the flag as they made their way to class, but the flag was later removed by the teacher. Some of the children wore republican badges and when told to remove them by the teacher they all stood and burst into song, singing 'Faith of our Fathers' and 'Ireland All Over'.

At a Sinn Féin meeting in the Mansion House, Dublin, on Monday 16 July, a resolution was adopted calling for Christian burials for the sixteen executed leaders of the Rising. The resolution read 'that the bodies of the sixteen Irish men executed by the English Government in 1916 be given up for Christian burial' and called 'upon our people in Ireland and throughout the world to join in support of this claim until the English Government is forced to surrender the remains of our dead'. The Bishop of Limerick, Dr O'Dwyer, added his voice:

> Only a few days ago they liberated the brave fellows who fought side by side with Pearse, MacDonagh and Colbert and they will not liberate the dead bodies of these men ... Though lying in an English prison, it is the soil of Ireland, every sod of which is sacred and the inhumanity of our rulers will only add fervour to the prayers, which we offer to God for their immortal soul.[12]

Éamon de Valera addressed the meeting and said that the people could not think that the executioners were going to give back the bodies of these men and he did not come there to support the demand, but he attended the meeting to honour their memories and to sympathise with the relatives. What he hoped to see and what they would have to wait for, was the day when a free Ireland would consecrate the spot where those men's bodies lay and erect over them a monument suitable to their memory. The men who died were no dreamers, but were prophets who saw Ireland awakening as de Valera saw it.

On 15 July another recently released prisoner, William T. Cosgrave, was unanimously selected as the Sinn Féin candidate for Kilkenny city and was subsequently elected on 11 August. A flag was hoisted on a telegraph pole that night on the Port Road in Letterkenny. The following day, after considerable difficulty, four members of the RIC eventually removed the flag, which read on one side 'Up Kilkenny – Remember Easter Week' and on the other 'IRB'.[13]

The opening session of the British-constituted 'Irish Convention' took place on 25 July 1917, at Trinity College and was presided over by Sir Horace Plunkett. The attendees were made up of representatives from the Irish Party, unionists and members of Orange lodges, with influential figures from the Catholic and Protestant churches also in attendance but no representatives from Sinn Féin. The convention served little purpose and was only an appeasement to American influences. The British monitored all mail and telegraphic correspondence sent from Trinity and to facilitate this they established a fully staffed post office in the grounds of the college.[14]

The RIC, accompanied by the British military, carried out raids for weapons throughout Donegal on Wednesday morning, 15 August and were reported to have used very provocative and aggressive methods. It was suggested that the raids were carried out to seize any weapons formally belonging to the National Volunteers. A number of premises were raided, including a priest's house in the north of the county where a number of arms were captured. Weapons were also discovered at the Inishowen workhouse. As part of the planned operation the RIC and military in Letterkenny disturbed Fr John McCafferty, parish administrator, in the early hours of that Wednesday morning. The district inspector demanded the keys of the Literary Institute and said he was going to search the premises for arms. The priest stated that he knew nothing about arms and that even if he did he would not cooperate. They left and subsequently entered the building by forcing open the doors, but all they found was a card containing the words 'Better Luck Next Time'.

In response to the raids a meeting was held in the assembly hall of the Literary Institute (county library) in Letterkenny the following day, where Fr McCafferty addressed the gathering:

> The search for arms, the property of the Irish Volunteers, and the outrageous manner in which such search was carried out indicated clearly that the intention was to force peaceful and law-abiding people to acts of violence.

Fr McCafferty then requested the Volunteers to form up and march through the town giving public manifestation of their purpose of protecting the liberty and property of the people. Some 150 Volunteers marched through the town afterwards.[15]

About the same time the IRB organised a Sinn Féin cumann in Dungloe, and a company of Volunteers was formed in the same area by Joseph Sweeney, James McCole, Anthony McNulty and Patrick Breslin. This would later become the 1st battalion area, North-West Donegal brigade.[16]

Throughout 1917 the reorganisation of Sinn Féin developed rapidly, with branches springing up all over Donegal, in Carrigans, St Johnston, Dungloe, Glenfinn, Raphoe, Donegal town, Annagry, Buncrana and Clonmany. By the end of December there were thirty-four Sinn Féin clubs in the county with more than 1,600 members. On 16 September 1917 a public meeting was held near the Literary Institute on Lower Main Street, Letterkenny. Before and after the meeting the Derry Pipers' Band marched through the town playing nationalist airs. The purpose of this meeting was to reorganise in the Irish Volunteers in the Letterkenny area. It was estimated that several hundred people attended. Jim Gibbons, an urban councillor from the Market Square, chaired the meeting and introduced Joseph O'Doherty from Derry who dealt with the aims and objectives of Sinn Féin. A resolution was proposed by John McMonagle and seconded by Johnny Curran. It pledged 'support for the Sinn Féin policy as best calculated to realise the nation's claim to independence'. The local media reported that 130 people signed up as part of the town's Sinn Féin club, which became the Jim Connolly Sinn Féin club.

Another public meeting was held on the same day in the Ballyliffin Hall for the purpose of forming a Sinn Féin club for the Clonmany area. At the meeting Mr J. Doherty proposed the following:

> It is hereby resolved to form a Sinn Féin Club, to be called the Clonmany Sinn Féin Club. That we hereby approve of the policy of Sinn Féin, deeming it not the policy of a party, but the policy of the Irish people, of all those Irishmen who consider Ireland a nation and not a collection of English counties or a mere province of England ...
>
> That we consider the Sinn Féin platform the only platform which can unite not merely the different sections into which Nationalist Irishmen are at present divided, but that a great many of our fellow-countrymen who are scheduled Unionists but are true and patriotic Irishmen can be invited to join Sinn Féin and to do so without sacrificing any principle held by them.[17]

On 5 October some Sinn Féin members who had been imprisoned for their opposition to the British recruitment campaign were transferred from Mountjoy to jails in England. Later that month the IRB cooperated with other organisations in calling together a great assembly of Sinn Féin. This, the tenth Sinn Féin convention, was held in the Mansion House for the purpose of forming a new constitution and electing a president. The annual Sinn Féin convention was given the Irish name 'ard fheis'. The ard fheis would have the task of directing the movement and determining exactly what direction it would take. Under the presidency of Éamon de Valera, the new Sinn Féin concentrated on strengthening the movement through political means. Organisers set to work establishing a Sinn Féin club (cumann) in every parish in the country with a council (comhairle ceantair) of delegates from each cumann in each electoral constituency. By the end of October 1917 there were 1,200 Sinn Féin cumainn in the country, and some 1,700 members assembled at the ard fheis of 25 October. A motion brought forward by Cathal Brugha and seconded by Seán Milroy proposed the adoption of a new constitution for Sinn Féin on entirely republican lines; the motion was unanimously accepted. The name Sinn Féin was retained and it was declared in the Preamble that the organisation:

> ... shall, in the name of the Sovereign Irish People:
> (a) Deny the right and oppose the will of the British Parliament and British Crown or any other foreign government to legislate for Ireland;
> (b) Make use of any and every means available to render impotent the power of England to hold Ireland in subjection by military force or otherwise.[18]

The contesting of local and national elections was also to be pursued and British law was to be disregarded. However, the Volunteers were expected to refrain from any kind of altercations with the British military and police, which would require a very high standard of discipline within the local population, both military and civilian. The movement was to adopt a non-violent resistance to English rule.

Shortly after, Patrick Breslin invited the young men of the local Sinn Féin cumann to join the Dungloe Company of the Irish Volunteers, which had been formed earlier that year. A company was organised at Burtonport and later at Annagry, Lettermacaward, Kincasslagh, Meenacross, Loughanure, Doochary, Mullaghduff, Arranmore and other islands around the coast of the Rosses.[19]

About the same time a Volunteer company was formed in Bundoran, attracting a large number of young men. Joseph Murray, school teacher, was approached to carry out the task of recruiting and organising the Volunteer company, and was assisted by Thomas McShea and Patrick (Pappy) Johnston. Murray decided not to take any rank as he considered his services to be more beneficial as an intelligence officer. He argued that if he was not openly associated with the Volunteers he could make contacts and obtain information from British military officers stationed at Finner camp who frequented the local hotels in Bundoran. He was also in a position to make acquaintances and procure useful information from prominent hotel proprietors, justices of the peace, etc., who were in close contact with high ranking police officers in the area.[20]

In late September the Ballybofey Company deployed Volunteers to survey the residence of a land steward called Bustard, as they had received information from a man who worked for Bustard that he had about forty rifles stacked in the attic. A meeting was called in Letterkenny at which Dr J. P. McGinley, Daniel Kelly and Jim Dawson discussed plans to capture the rifles; they knew that Bustard was a hard man, big and burly, who would not hesitate to shoot. It was therefore decided to have twenty men in the bushes opposite the hall door; Daniel Kelly would knock at the door, ask for Bustard, and produce a revolver and hold him at gunpoint. If he put up any resistance the men in the bushes were to rush to Kelly's rescue. The following day Jim Dawson's father arrived at Daniel Kelly's house and asked if he was 'mad or what? You are a married man with a family and I heard of what you plan to do, and you can rest assured that neither Dr McGinley nor my son will be there.' That ended the matter. Two days later District Inspector Moore sent word to the Letterkenny RIC stating that the rifles that Bustard had been moved to the safety of the Royal School in Raphoe.[21] Some time later Daniel Kelly travelled to Dublin to register a number of Volunteer companies established in the county and while there he acquired a number of rifles, which were used for practice every Sunday at various centres.

Cumann na mBan, which had a branch in Falcarragh, was also actively recruiting and organising in the county. Eithne Coyle, a young girl who was to play a prominent role in the War of Independence, was one of those recruited. The Falcarragh branch fell through after a couple of months and Coyle formed another in Cloghaneely in early 1918, which attracted over twenty members. The local Volunteer commandant Barney O'Donnell was responsible for teaching the Cumann na mBan members first aid, weapons training and drilling, etc.[22]

In late 1917 Sam O'Flaherty organised a Volunteer company in Castlefinn and recruited over twenty members. The Con Colbert Sinn Féin cumann had been established in the area some time in late 1916.

On St Stephen's night 1917, Mrs Pearse, mother of Pádraig and William Pearse attended a ceílí as a guest of the Letterkenny Sinn Féin cumann at a céilí held in the club hall, which was situated at the rear of a building on Lower Main street. She was accompanied by her daughter Miss Pearse and her granddaughter Mrs McGarvey. Club president, Dr J. P. McGinley introduced the three ladies who were accorded an enthusiastic welcome. Mrs Pearse, mother of the two republican leaders executed for their part in the 1916 Rising, gave a moving speech about her two sons and their childhood and manhood adventures. The night's programme consisted of an exhibition of film operated by James Kearns, patriotic songs sung by Mrs McGarvey, Miss C. Gillen, John and Conal Bradley, C. A. Flattery, W. McMenamin, James Langan, Michael Dawson, Éamon Coyle and James O'Donnell and a mandolin solo by Mr J. O'Donnell. The night was stewarded by Jim Dawson and Jim Murphy. A dance commenced after the singing and lasted until 5.30 the next morning; a good time was had by all.[23]

A well attended and very enthusiastic meeting was held in the Foresters' Hall, Killybegs, on Sunday 30 December 1917, to inaugurate the newly established Sinn Féin cumann. Michael Murrin, Croaghlin, presiding, said it was 'both fitting and timely that the people of Killybegs, who were ever to be found in the van of the national movement should have embraced the tenets of Sinn Féin and become attached to the only policy in Ireland which could be termed national and the one which had uplifted the Irish cause from the rut to which weak and designing leaders had reduced it to be a position commanding the attention of all the nations'.[24]

Joe McDevitt, Kilcar, a professor at St Enda's school, also addressed the meeting:

> The Irish question, which had degenerated from a national issue to a mere domestic affair, had through the agency of Sinn Féin again assumed an international importance, so much so that even in Russia the representatives of Britain were met with the question – What about the historic injustice to Ireland? The Lloyd George Convention was specially designed to divert the attention of the Irish people from the substance to the shadow, but Ireland has awakened from its national stupor vigilant and self-reliant and will insist on her national rights, confident alike of the inevitable result and the justice of her claim ...[25]

A well-attended Sinn Féin meeting in the Ballyliffin Hall on New Year's Day was addressed by Fr James Maguire, PP, who said that the coming year would be 'very fruitful of events for Ireland' and people should be 'ready to take their part in the national movement'. Fr Philip O'Doherty added: 'Sinn Féin will sweep the country from Malin Head to Cape Clear. Sinn Féin is a clean movement and is free from all taint of jobbery.' He referred to Sinn Féin as an unsectarian organisation that had attracted several unionists. Although Sinn Féin had been charged with being rash, he added, no honest newspaper could charge them with corruption.[26]

8

1918 – SOWING THE SEEDS OF REVOLUTION

On 3 January 1918 the Volunteers in west Donegal received information that two British army deserters, Jimmy (Susan) Ward, Cloghglass and Jimmy Duffy from Meenbanad, had been arrested at a dance the previous evening. They were being held at Burtonport RIC barracks. The local Volunteers, under the command of Joe Sweeney, decided to organise a rescue operation, not so much to liberate the two men, but to capture a rifle also seized by the RIC. A number of Volunteers carried out the rescue, and Bernie Sweeney secured a couple of revolvers for them with a warning only to use as much force as necessary. Bertie Sweeney then went to Burtonport barracks, posing as a relative, to visit the two prisoners and warn them to be prepared when they were being transferred the next day. The following morning the RIC escort, consisting of one sergeant and three constables, arrived on the first incoming train. Their return train was not due to leave until the afternoon, so the escort decided to pass the time drinking in a local bar. By the time they arrived at the RIC barracks to escort the prisoners to the train at Burtonport station, the four-man escort were intoxicated, but they made it on to the train safely. Meanwhile, the rescue party had gone to Meenbanad railway station where they found the platform crowded with people returning from the Dungloe fair. When the train pulled into Meenbanad, Jim Bonner held up the driver; Paddy Gallagher was the first man to enter the carriage, by the back, and immediately struck one of the RIC, but in the confusion one of the prisoners was also hit. The rifle and bayonet were wrenched from the sergeant's hands by John Bonner and the two deserters were spirited away by the local Volunteers. They were taken to separate locations, a sensible move as the RIC later mounted an exhaustive search of the area but failed to locate either of the two men. This incident has been described as the first official attack on the forces of the crown in the War of Independence without a single shot being fired. The men involved were: John and Jim Bonner, Meenmore; Anthony Sweeney, Meenbanad; James Ward, Upper Keadue; Paddy and Phil Gallagher, Meenbanad, and Joseph Sweeney, Burtonport.[1]

The aggression of the unionist recruits of the British military was observed a few weeks later on Friday 18 January. A large contingent of Sinn Féin members and supporter, returning to Ballyshannon from a meeting in Bundoran, were attacked as they passed Finner camp by soldiers belonging to the Ulster division. Shouts of 'Up Sinn Féin' were met with insults against the Pope. The Sinn Féin members sought cover as the soldiers threw stones and physically attacked them. Some took refuge in a nearby house, but they were pursued and attacked; all the windows in the house were smashed during the incident. Thirteen Sinn Féin members received injuries and one was seriously hurt, while two soldiers were also injured. A young man named Teevan from Ballyshannon later died as a result of injuries sustained.[2]

The winter months were harsh in Donegal and were beginning to impact on the food provision in some parts of the county. The executive committee of the O'Rahilly Sinn Féin cumann, Culdaff, raised the issue at a meeting on Tuesday 22 January. Cumann president James Kelly chaired the meeting, with the secretary John Doherty proposing a resolution calling on farmers and others with an interest in food production to use every means to conserve farm produce for the people of Ireland. The secretary also called on all transport workers at Irish ports not to handle foodstuff that was intended for export. On several occasions during this time Creeslough, Milford, Carrigart and other areas experienced a shortage of flour and bread. Heavy snowfall at the time also added to the food shortage.[3]

The Sinn Féin president, Éamon de Valera, arrived in Donegal on Thursday 7 February accompanied by Seán MacEntee as part of a tour of the north-west. The two men were met on the outskirts of Letterkenny by a torchlight procession comprising some 400 Sinn Féin supporters and were escorted to McCarry's hotel. The following day de Valera and MacEntee addressed a meeting at the Market Square attended by over 800. Dr J. P. McGinley, chairing the event, made the opening address:

> I am truly delighted to see such a vast gathering assembled in support of the policy, which has swept the country like a wave, bearing on its crest – 'Ireland Over All' – a policy which declared that Ireland shall not be a slave state within the British Empire, but shall be maintained as a free and independent republic, a policy which had lifted the Irish Question from a mere domestic squabble with England to one of international importance, which has made the Irish Question as well known in Petrograd and New York today as in Dublin and Cork, a policy which has been vindicated in the recent elections in Longford, Clare and Kilkenny ... Sinn Féin did not stand for conciliation; it would leave that to the kaiser of Germany and his troops. Sinn Féin professed loyalty to Ireland alone and defied England to conscript the young men of Ireland.

MacEntee declared that now – when its ancient enemy was down and out – was Sinn Féin's time. The day of Britain's extreme difficulty was the day of Ireland's greatest opportunity. Unlike those recreant politicians in 1914 who did not use Britain's difficulty as Ireland's opportunity, they were resolved that the men (Irish Party and Unionist MPs) who voiced Ireland's claims at the Peace Conference would be men sitting in an elected assembly in Dublin. He described the Convention as being waked in London, and said instead of giving it a decent Christian wake it should be dumped into the Atlantic and given a suicide's grave. Sinn Féiners were not enemies of the Convention, but viewed it with distrust.

On arriving in Carndonagh on Sunday 10 February 1918 de Valera and MacEntee were welcomed by Sinn Féin members from Clonmany, Malin, Moville and other areas. A fife and drum band travelled from Clonmany and the Carndonagh brass and reed band were also there to greet the two men. As their train was pulling into the station a number of young girls sang the 'Soldier's Song'. Following addresses from the Inishowen Board of Guardians and local Sinn Féin cumainn, de Valera took the platform. He said they were told that the hard-headed men of the north would not join with them, but that the people had shown on that day that the most northerly point was on their side and he was certain that before long they would be marching shoulder to shoulder with every true nationalist in the country, indeed with every man, be he Catholic or Protestant, who loved Ireland first. Nothing gave him greater pleasure, he said, than to see how the Guardians realised so clearly what many people forgot – that there was only one way to settle labour questions and questions relating to the poor and that was by getting rid of alien domination and looking after our affairs for ourselves.

The following day the two men addressed large gatherings in Creeslough and Cloghaneely. At Creeslough Mr Seaghan MacMenamin, DC, Kingarrow addressed the crowd:

> A few years ago no one would imagine that today we would be witnessing such magnificent Sinn Féin meetings in what was always regarded as the great stronghold of the Irish Party …

But today the people of the county are denouncing with one voice the putrid doctrine of parliamentarianism as well as the British connection.

Seán MacEntee warned them that one of the terms of the convention settlement was that a measure of conscription would be introduced. They must turn themselves away from England, think only of Ireland and do nothing except for Ireland.

Dr J. P. McGinley drove the guests to Cloghaneely that evening and they then took a train from Cashelnagore to Dungloe. As the train passed through Gweedore and Kincasslagh stations large crowds were gathered to welcome them, and on arriving at Dungloe they travelled by road to Burtonport where they were met by a torchlight procession and a band. The following morning they returned to Dungloe to be met by over 200 Volunteers and two bands.

The meeting, held near the Dungloe police barracks, attracted about 1,000 people. De Valera said it would be a shame if, in this fight for freedom, Ulster should not be in the forefront and he was sure Ulster would be. It was a legitimate aim, he said, to secure for one's country complete independence. England wanted to exploit them and was striving to keep them in ignorance of their own strength and of their own resources.

After lunch at Sweeneys' hotel the party travelled to Glenties and again received a great welcome. Over a mile outside the town approximately 400 Volunteers carrying sticks and Sinn Féin flags met the visiting party and were led by four men on horseback. De Valera addressed the meeting in Irish and said had the native language been kept alive all over the country as it was there, there would be very little need for them to come to preach the policy of Sinn Féin. The language itself would ensure love of country and would be the best possible means of keeping slavery away from them.[4]

The two men arrived in Raphoe on Wednesday evening, 13 February to a much different scene. Before the meeting a number of men and boys carrying torchlights paraded the town. The police prevented the gathering from entering a certain street where Orangemen resided and from where shouts of 'Down with the Molly Maguires' could be heard. De Valera said he hoped that the day had dawned in Ireland when sectarianism could not be used as a means of keeping the people apart. It was only ignorance that kept one body of Irishmen away from another, when questions concerning the welfare of their country were being discussed on a public platform. Members of the AOH and Unionist Party became hostile and attempted to halt proceedings, and the speakers were attacked by British soldiers home on leave. With the situation becoming precarious, Seán MacEntee sent a telegram to Jim Dawson, captain of the Volunteers in Letterkenny. In a short space of time approximately ninety men were mobilised from there, Castlefinn and Ballybofey, all making their way to Raphoe. The Volunteers under Jim Dawson helped themselves to an array of pickaxe handles, slash hooks, pieces of lead piping and other items when passing by Speers' hardware shop in Letterkenny; an IOU was hastily written and passed under the door. On arrival in Raphoe the Volunteers looked a formidable force. The RIC, under the charge of District Inspector Moore, attempted to stop them from marching through the street, but were brushed aside and quickly withdrew. DI Moore said he would not allow the parade to proceed, but James McMonagle went up to him with an old Queen Anne rifle, bayonet fixed, and ordered him to move off, which he promptly did.

The opposition parties soon withdrew to the Horse Square further up the town and some of the Volunteers were about to pursue them but were called back by de Valera, who told them that they were asked to report for the purpose of protecting the speakers and the people attending the meeting. He then ordered them to form a protective ring around the crowd. A successful meeting was held without any further disturbance and the Volunteers then marched back to Castlefinn, Ballybofey and Letterkenny.[5]

Another meeting was held in Castlefinn that night and then de Valera and MacEntee made their way to Killygordan. The following afternoon they were met outside Stranorlar by two bands and a large number of Volunteers. The procession proceeded to the corner of Navenny Street where the meeting was held. Many in the large attendance carried tricolours, banners and flags with mottos such as 'Sinn Féin Abú' and 'Remember Ashe'. The AOH had issued threats that they would prevent the meeting taking place in Ballybofey on February 15 February. They based this threat on the fact that they did not allow Orangemen to march in Ballybofey and neither would they allow Sinn Féin to do so. Daniel Kelly warned the AOH superiors that, should they cause any trouble, they would only come off second best. In Killybegs later that night de Valera and MacEntee were greeted by a large crowd carrying torchlights. A public meeting was held on Friday morning at which MacEntee said that an olive branch had been thrown out to Sinn Féin by Mr Dillon who asked that Sinn Féin should not contest by-elections. The objective was to leave Dillon and his party in a position where they could continue to misrepresent the Irish people in the most critical period of their country's history. Sinn Féin contested elections to show the world that Home Rule, or colonial Home Rule, within the empire would not satisfy the Irish people, who instead wanted sovereign independence. At a meeting in Ballyshannon the speakers again received Volunteer protection, who had proceeded by back roads to Ballyshannon to avoid passing Finner camp, headquarters of the Bedford Regiment.[6] The RIC collected extracts from de Valera's speeches during his visit to Donegal and sent them to the G division in Dublin, where the most seditious sections were selected and used to secure a warrant for his arrest. The G men in Dublin failed to execute the warrant and, due to some political pressure, it was later withdrawn.[7]

Eithne Coyle had formed two branches of Cumann na mBan in west Donegal in early 1918 before relocating to Roscommon; Cumann na mBan continued to establish branches in the county

1918 - Sowing the Seeds of Revolution

to assist the work of the Volunteers. The principle duties of each local branch was the carrying of arms and ammunition, despatch carrying, intelligence work, organising safe houses for wanted men, looking after the wounded, and raising and collecting funds for the Volunteers, prisoners' families, etc.[8] As part of the drive to establish Cumann na mBan branches in every part of the county a well attended recruitment meeting was held in the Jim Connolly Sinn Féin clubrooms in Letterkenny on Thursday 14 February. A large number of members were enrolled on the night and an officer board was appointed comprising Mrs M. J. Clancy, president; Mrs C. A. Flattery, treasurer; Miss Sarah Gallagher, secretary. A committee was also formed; the members were Susan McGranaghan, Agnes McFadden, Nan Murphy and Aggie Collins.[9]

The momentum of the Sinn Féin movement continued with meetings being held in almost every town, village and parish in the county. On Wednesday 5 March, a Fair Day in Ardara, over 3,000 people attended one such meeting. The gathering was addressed by Sinn Féin organiser P. C. O'Mahony:

> Sinn Féin is a matter of pure business, which enforces the law of every nation to mind its own business. It stands for independence and self reliance, it connotes the highest order of patriotism and personifies in short truth, justice and equality ... We mean to have a happy and prosperous people in the soil of Ireland and we want that people to be free, healthy, wealthy and contented.[10]

Shortly after de Valera and MacEntee's visit new Sinn Féin branches were established in Glenfinn and Gweedore.

Another large Sinn Féin meeting was held at Ballybofey on Sunday 17 March attracting approximately 5,000 people and six bands. The crowd was addressed by Sam O'Flaherty, Castlefinn and Eoin McNeill, founding member of the National Volunteers in

67

1913, who expressed surprise at the large numbers. Ballybofey was selected because it was an AOH stronghold, and a large Sinn Féin crowd walking through the town would have a powerful effect on the local population. When the parade was over Volunteers policed the large crowd. District Inspector Moore ordered the Volunteer officer in charge to remove his men, but was told: 'I am taking no orders from you'. The Volunteer officer consulted with Jim Dawson, who told him to carry on as he was doing.

The district inspector then ordered Sergeant Mooney of the RIC to send out his men from the barracks, but Mooney replied: 'No. I am in charge of the men of the barracks. This picket did good work as they kept any men from getting under the influence of drink and kept everything in order.' At the meeting's conclusion the Letterkenny contingent of Volunteers, under the command of Jim Dawson, formed up in a column to march back to Letterkenny. DI Moore from Raphoe had a strong force of police drawn across the road at the bridge between Ballybofey and Stranorlar. When Dawson's company approached, Moore drew his revolver and called on them to halt. They refused, and Moore fired over their heads; in response Jim Dawson produced a revolver and fired over the heads of the police. The police then withdrew to either side of the road, but marched alongside the parade for some distance.[11]

Jim Dawson was subsequently arrested on the night of Wednesday 27 March. At the time he was secretary of the Sinn Féin East Donegal Executive, secretary of the Jim Connolly Sinn Féin cumann and commandant of the Irish Volunteers. Dawson had been on his way home from the local Sinn Féin club and was arrested at the Market Square. A head constable and a sergeant stationed at No. 2 RIC barracks carried out the arrest and were taking him to the barracks at Lower Main Street when a number of young Volunteers and local girls became aware of the arrest and decided to attempt a rescue. Jim Dawson appealed to the girls and commanded the Volunteers to desist from any action. News of the arrest spread quickly throughout the town and a large body of Volunteers assembled at the Sinn Féin clubrooms. They marched through the streets in military formation carrying hurlies, and were accompanied by large numbers of young boys and girls singing national songs. Several police patrols were despatched and paraded up and down the town for the remainder of the night. The following day a special court was convened in the barracks and Jim Dawson was charged with unlawful assembly and illegal drilling. The public were excluded from the hearing, but Dawson's parents, a lady friend, Dr J. P. McGinley and C. A. Flattery, solicitor were present. The court set bail at a personal surety of £50 and two others of £25 each but this was refused by the prisoner. Jim Dawson said he did not recognise the court's jurisdiction and looked on the proceedings as a farce. He was remanded to Derry jail until 10 April where he was to appear at Donegal town petty sessions.

On the Thursday afternoon as the RIC were preparing to take the prisoner to the train station a large gathering of eighty Volunteers assembled outside the barracks armed with hurlies. The RIC had difficulty arranging for a car to take the prisoner to the station, as all the local drivers refused to do so. A car was eventually acquired and driven by an RIC man. When the prisoner was being put into the car, Volunteers from Cumann na mBan assembled and bid farewell to the popular young man. The police endeavoured to keep the people back and soon batons and hurlies were produced, resulting in a number of injuries on both sides. The car with the prisoner sped off to the station with a number of people following. The Derry train arrived and the prisoner was placed in a carriage under heavy escort. The platform was soon crowded with local people and Volunteers. The prisoner, calling from a window with a tricolour in his hand, told the crowd not to give the police an excuse to use batons and to go home. All obeyed and left the platform singing republican songs.[12] Jim Dawson was further remanded in custody at a special court in Derry on 4 April.

The growth of Sinn Féin was also spreading to the islands around the Donegal coast at this time. On Sunday 28 March a Sinn Féin cumann was inaugurated on Arranmore Island with twenty-five members enrolling.[13]

THE THREAT OF CONSCRIPTION

THE BRITISH WERE suffering heavy losses in the trenches of Europe and attention was directed to Ireland as a means of bolstering the numbers in the British army. Almost as a deliberate ploy the British raised the issue of Home Rule being rolled out at the conclusion of the war in an effort to gain the support of the Irish Parliamentary Party; however, this only served to enrage the Sinn Féin party. The Conscription Bill was subsequently introduced at Westminster on Saturday 9 April 1918 and Lloyd George announced that the full terms of the Conscription Act would be applied to Ireland. All members of the IPP voted against the bill, but despite this it was passed through the House of Commons the following Saturday, 16 April.

The Mansion House Conference followed on Tuesday 18 April and was attended by representatives from Sinn Féin, the IPP, Labour, the All-for-Ireland League and independents. The conference denied the right of the British government to impose military service in Ireland and regarded the threat as a declaration of war on the Irish nation. The Volunteer movement was overwhelmed by applications and most were accepted. However, as time went on and the conscription threat receded, the numbers dropped.[14] Opposition to the bill was to cause the British government much embarrassment, and led to a campaign to undermine Sinn Féin's efforts to oppose it.

While attention was drawn to the conscription issue, Volunteers were being tried in a court in Donegal for the offence of assembly, which was outlawed by the same parliament that now required their services. On Wednesday 10 April the following people appeared before the Ballyshannon court: P. C. O'Mahony, Sinn Féin organiser; Patrick J. Brennan, secretary, South Donegal Executive; Jim Dawson, and Bernard Ryan, commandant of Bundoran Volunteers. They had each been sentenced to three months in prison on charges of unlawful assembly at various locations in March, including Ballybofey and Bundoran. O'Mahony questioned the procedure, quoting from the Crimes Act, and said they considered themselves the victims of inhuman militarism and unjustifiable force. He added that they did not deny they had drilled and please God they would drill again. All refused to recognise the right of any government, except an Irish republican government, to deprive them of their liberty and freedom. They declared that the instrument of militarism and unjust force by which they were held captive was illegal. The court erupted with loud and prolonged cheering by friends and supporters with one man being ejected by the police and sustaining injuries in the struggle.

O'Mahony asked the court to recognise them as political prisoners, and if this was not forthcoming they would adopt every means in their power to enforce their demands for political status. The prisoners and the majority of the people in the court then began singing the 'Soldier's Song'. Jim Dawson's mother was roughly handled by the police as she tried to speak to her son in the dock. She struggled with the captors and then the prisoners stood on the seats of the dock attempting to seize the police. However, when the police realised it was Mrs Dawson they released her. The prisoners were seen off at the station, on their way to Derry jail, by Volunteers with hurlies, while members of Cumann na mBan were also present. The police escort consisted of fifteen armed men and at Donegal there were over a hundred of the Inniskilling Fusiliers from Finner camp, with fifty or sixty police. Despite this, Sinn Féin members again turned up in large numbers.[15]

The following day the first of many anti-conscription meetings was held in the public square in Milford and on Friday another took place in the Glenties Town Hall, with 150 Volunteers marching through the town to attend. On Sunday 14 April a large Sinn Féin anti-conscription meeting was held in Frosses, attended by Sinn Féin cumainn from Ardaghey, Mountcharles, Drimarone, Donegal town, Tawnawully, Killybegs and Killyaghtee, and several branches of Cumann na mBan. It was estimated that between 5,000-6,000 people were present, where a pledge was solemnly taken to resist the application of conscription.

On the motion of Joseph MacManus seconded by Peter Meehan, Ballymacahill, the chair was taken by Seamus Ward, president of the South Donegal Sinn Féin executive. The chairman said Sinn Féin wanted recognition for Ireland's sovereign independence, or, in other words, a free and independent nation. The meeting was addressed by Seaghan MacMenamin, DC, Kingarrow: 'No half measure will satisfy the people of Ireland,' he said. 'Great Britain declared they entered the present war for justice, right and small nationalities, but did her attitude at the present show it? No. If Great Britain were honest there would be no Irish problem. No people could be conscripted against their will. There was nothing so much required in Ireland at the present as unity.'

James N. Dolan, Manorhamilton, then addressed the meeting – his brother Charles J. Dolan was the first member of the Irish Party to abandon the English House of Commons. Dolan said: 'We are not alone fighting for our own lives, but the lives of our mothers and sisters and the life of Ireland, which is threatened with conscription. We will not serve under a foreign government and before we will allow a foreign government to take away the manhood of Ireland we will sacrifice our own lives.'[16]

The anti-conscription pledge was administered to a great gathering of the people of Letterkenny on Sunday evening 21 April. The meeting was held on Sentry Hill, adjacent to St Eunan's cathedral where over

500 Sinn Féin members and 80 students of St Eunan's college marched in military formation to Sentry Hill. It was reported that about 2,500 people had gathered for the meeting. An anti-conscription committee was formed comprising local representatives of the United Irish League, AOH, Sinn Féin and Labour Association.[17] The speeches were heard with little evidence of enthusiasm until Dr McGinley was invited to speak. He began by telling the people that passive resistance would not deter the British government from enforcing conscription: 'There is only one way – that is, the unionists and Ulster Volunteers are all well armed – go out and collect those arms and we will resist this threat at the point of the rifle.' This was met with cheers and applause, to the embarrassment of the parish priest, who presided over the meeting.[18] Similar gatherings took place in Fahan, Burt and Inch on the same day with everyone from sixteen years of age signing up to the pledge against compulsory conscription. Another branch of Cumann na mBan was established in Burtonport on the same day and over thirty members were enrolled.[19]

A number of anti-conscription meetings were also held on the same day in Carrigart, Buncrana, parish of Doe, Killybegs, Arranmore Island, Donegal town, Castlefinn, Rathmullan, Killygordon, Culdaff, Cloghaneely, Glenfinn, Termon, Murlogh and Ardara.[20] In the face of such strong opposition all over the country, the British decided that it would be wise to abandon the conscription idea. After the conscription scare had passed, the large numbers who had rushed to join the Volunteers fell away again.

An organising convention was held in Fanad in late April attracting up to 600 people. This was followed in early May with the founding of a Sinn Féin branch in Glenswilly, located several miles from Letterkenny. Dr J. P. McGinley inaugurated the Glenswilly Sinn Féin cumann and the following officers were appointed: Dan Gallagher, president; Hugh McMonagle, vice-president; Neil Kelly, treasurer; Tom Crossan, secretary and J. P. McMonagle as secretary.[21]

Between 3 and 4 a.m. on Saturday 11 May, three Sinn Féin members were arrested in Letterkenny. Approximately thirty extra police from stations in other areas were drafted into the town to support the local force. James Langan was arrested at his lodgings on the Main Street at 3.15 a.m., Francis Gallagher was detained at his home in Lower Main Street at 3.40 a.m. and Packie Carberry was arrested about 4 a.m. at his mother's house on the Port Road. A special court was held at 6.30 a.m. in No. 1 RIC barracks at Lower Main Street and the three men were charged, under the Crimes Act, with unlawful assembly and the disturbances during the arrest and trial of Jim Dawson in March.

The three were returned for trial on Friday 17 May with extra police being drafted in to the town the evening before. James Langan was ordered to give personal security of £40 and two sureties of £20 each to be of good behaviour for twelve months. Francis Gallagher was sentenced to one month's imprisonment and Patrick Carberry to three months. Both were brought to the railway station escorted by approximately fifty police. There were about a hundred young people on the platform, who cheered the prisoners; there was no disturbance as the train left for Derry.

While the general consensus was opposition to the introduction of conscription, the Volunteer officers at GHQ were making plans in the event of its introduction. A party of Volunteers travelled to England under the command of Cathal Brugha, with directions to shoot members of the British parliament from the public gallery the moment conscription was introduced. The Volunteers were to act in the final reading of the Conscription Act and they were fully aware that they would not leave the House of Commons alive if the operation was to be successfully executed. Cathal Brugha was to target the British Prime Minister, Lloyd George, while the other Volunteers were each allotted a minister. This party remained in England for several months until Brugha eventually cancelled the operation as he considered it impossible to get into the House of Commons undetected.[22]

THE GERMAN PLOT

THE BRITISH GOVERNMENT announced in mid-May that it had uncovered evidence that Sinn Féin leaders were actively involved in a plot with the German military in procuring arms to launch another insurrection. The first arrests were made in what became known as the 'German Plot' on Friday 17 May. Seventy-three Sinn Féin members were arrested, including de Valera, Griffith, Cosgrave, Countess Markievicz and other prominent members. None were charged with any offence, but were taken to Dublin Castle and later to Dun Laoghaire where they were put on the mail boat for Holyhead and on to England, where they were imprisoned in various jails. The following morning the British government published its reasons for the arrests:

> In consequence of the knowledge that certain persons in Ireland have entered into treasonable communication with the German enemy, it is the duty of all loyal subjects to assist his Majesty's Government in the suppression of this treasonable conspiracy.[23]

The Sinn Féin leaders had received prior notice of the arrests through the Dublin Castle agent, Éamon Broy, and decided to use the planned operation to their advantage, allowing the British to walk into what would inevitably become another miscalculated assault on Irish citizens. A hurried meeting of the Sinn Féin executive was held earlier on the day of the arrests to select a new officer board to replace those about to be arrested.

In a blatant example of British hypocrisy Lloyd George referred to the alleged conspiracy during a speech in Edinburgh later that month:

> ... some of them men of great sway and influence among their countrymen, entered into a conspiracy with the military autocracy which is trampling down the liberties of the small

nations of Europe to stab Britain in the back while the whole of her attention and strength was concentrated upon the struggle to deliver those enslaved nationalities ...[24]

In the summer of 1918 instructions were received from GHQ in Dublin to organise the various companies in Donegal on a battalion basis. Joe Sweeney called a meeting of company officers at Dungloe parochial hall, at which the Dungloe, Burtonport, Annagry, Loughanure, Lettermacaward and Doochary companies were formed into the 1st battalion. Subsequently Meenacross, Kincasslagh, Ranafast and the islands were added to this battalion, while a second battalion was formed to cover the combined area of Gweedore and Cloghaneely and a third to encompass the parishes of Termon and Kilmacrenan. James McCole was appointed O/C of the 1st battalion, vice-O/C was Frank O'Donnell, Patrick Breslin was adjutant and the quartermaster was Patrick O'Donnell.[25]

The west Donegal Sinn Féin executive continued to put pressure on its rival, the Irish Parliamentary Party when it published a letter in the *Derry Journal* in June. The letter was addressed to Hugh Law, Irish Party MP for West Donegal, calling on him 'to place his resignation in the hands of his constituents'. The letter went on:

> We assure you that the West Donegal Executive of Sinn Féin is the one body in the constituency that can voice the opinion of nine out of every ten of the people. You will agree with us that it is more honourable for a Member of Parliament to resign his seat when publicly asked by the majority to do so than to stick on and get wiped out in the annihilation that awaits his party at the next General Election.

The letter was signed by Joe Sweeney, Seaghan MacMenamin, James Maguire, James McNulty, Patrick McFadden, Michael McNelis, Hugh McGill and Bernard G. Boyle, dated 12 June 1918.[26]

1918 – Sowing the Seeds of Revolution

The first of those arrested during the so called 'German Plot' round-up was elected in the East Cavan by-election. Sinn Féin vice-president Arthur Griffith won the seat on Friday 21 June with a majority of 1,204. He received 3,785 votes, compared to 2,581 for his opponent, Hugh O'Hanlon, an Irish Party candidate. There was much jubilation at the result in Letterkenny and that night bonfires blazed in the nearby hills. Republican flags were flown and the Sinn Féin band with the local Volunteers paraded through the town. Afterwards the large gathering assembled at the Sinn Féin clubrooms where it was addressed by Dr J. P. McGinley.[27]

In early July a native of the Ballybofey area, Joseph Quinn, returned home on leave from the British army. He had served his time in the Signal Corps during the war in Europe and was considering absconding from the British army at that time. He travelled to Letterkenny where he made contact with Jim Dawson, O/C of the local battalion. Dawson informed him that he was anxious to have someone with military experience to organise and train the Volunteers and persuaded Quinn to go to the Ardara area where he made contact with Brian Monaghan and Michael Dawson, both active members of the Volunteers. Joseph Quinn was tasked with forming and training Volunteer companies in the Mountcharles area. He also trained the local Volunteers in signalling and later organised a signalling squad.[28]

The growing support for Sinn Féin eventually provoked a response from the British establishment in Ireland and a meeting of the Privy Council was held on Wednesday 3 July in the council chamber of Dublin Castle. It was proclaimed that in pursuance and by virtue of the 1887 Criminal Law and Procedure (Ireland) Act, Sinn Féin and other organisations were deemed to be 'dangerous associations'. The wording read: 'Whereas, we are satisfied that there exist in Ireland associations known by the names of the Sinn Féin organisation, the Sinn Féin clubs, the Irish Volunteers, the Cumann na mBan and the Gaelic League … [and] declare from the date hereof the said Associations … to be dangerous.' The following were the terms of the Act:

If the Lord Lieutenant is satisfied that any association; Formed for the commission of crimes; or Carrying on operations for or by the commission of crimes; or Encouraging or aiding persons to commit crimes; or Promoting or inciting to acts of violence or intimidation; or Interfering with the administration of the law or disturbing the maintenance of law and order; exist in any part of Ireland, the Lord Lieutenant, by and with the advice of the Privy Council, may from time to time by proclamation declare to be dangerous any such association or associations named or described in such proclamation.[29]

Despite the proclamation, the East Donegal Sinn Féin executive held a meeting on Sunday 8 July in Raphoe and all cumainn were represented. This was the first meeting since the arrest and deportation of the East Donegal Executive president Sam O'Flaherty, Castlefinn. O'Flaherty had been transported to a jail in England shortly after his arrest as part of the German plot round-ups. The executive entered an emphatic protest against the outrageous action of the English government, which professed to be horrified at the deportation of Belgians from their country by the Germans. If this was England's answer to Ireland's legitimate claim, they were reminded that public opinion could not thus be stifled in the twentieth century. The meeting called on the Irish Parliamentary Party representative for the area, E. J. Kelly, MP, to resign and give the electors of East Donegal an opportunity of returning Sam O'Flaherty at the head of the poll.

A special court was held in Stranorlar on Wednesday 4 August, where further charges of unlawful assembly under the Crimes Act were heard against four Sinn Féin members. Patrick Bogan, Laught, Thomas McGlynn, Carricknashane, Michael Doherty from Scotland and Felix Boyle, Castlefinn were charged in relation to a meeting in the Sinn Féin clubrooms in Castlefinn. The meeting was held on 13 June and the gathering marched up the street afterwards, singing songs and shouting slogans such as 'Up the Rebels'. Prosecuting the case, H. T. Gallagher said: 'The disorderly conduct of the defendants in marching and shouting through the village at midnight was sufficient to put fear and dread into the minds of the respectable inhabitants.' The magistrates ordered the defendants to enter into personal bonds, without other security, for their future good conduct and the men agreed to do so.

In a separate case, Bernard Campbell, Patrick Molloy, James Rutledge and Joseph Gallagher, all from Glenties, were charged with unlawful assembly at Glenties on 21 June. The date in question was the declaration of the poll from the East Cavan election and over 200 people gathered in the street and lit bonfires. It was alleged that some people threw lighted sods of turf and bottles at the police. The four men were identified by members of the RIC as the instigators and were ordered to enter into bail of £50 each with two sureties of £25 each or in default to go to jail for six months. The bail was paid and the men discharged.[30]

The annual meeting of the Sinn Féin Ard Comhairle was held in the Mansion House, Dublin on Tuesday 17 August with delegates present from sixty-five constituencies. Eoin MacNeill entered the following motion:

> That, in view of previous experience of English policy in Ireland and the military measures recently adopted, we warn the Irish public against yielding to any suggestion that the danger of conscription is removed and we urge the people to maintain and perfect preparations to resist conscription by every effective means.

The report of the secretaries, Alderman T. Kelly and Harry Boland, stated that the year had been fruitful in every branch of national endeavour. The position of Sinn Féin stood stronger and more virile than ever, notwithstanding the fact that the leaders were in prison. The number of cumainn affiliated on 17 December 1917 was 1,240, and this had risen to 1,666 by August; the numbers for the provinces were as follows: Leinster: 408; Munster: 554; Connacht: 368; Ulster: 336.

At the meeting the following resolution was adopted:

> That in order to give every Irish voter an opportunity of voting for or against the establishment of an independent Irish Republic, the ard comhairle strongly recommends local Sinn Féin to contest every seat at general election.[31]

When the threat of conscription passed, the focus of the Irish Volunteers was then put on the collection of weapons. In the beginning the Volunteers took weapons from those considered unfriendly, mainly the AOH and unionists. The Volunteers left the weapons with those deemed 'friendly' on the understanding that they would keep them safe and make them available when needed.[32]

The local branches of Cumann na mBan were reformed into semi-military organisations and prominent members were given military positions. Each branch had a captain, first and second lieutenants, an adjutant, a quartermaster, section leaders and squad leaders. This reorganisation meant that Cumann na mBan members were to play a more active role in the war in supporting their local Volunteer companies.[33]

THE GENERAL ELECTION

THE GENERAL ELECTION was announced in September with 14 December 1918 allocated as the day of polling. Sinn Féin were to select four leading figures of the Irish Volunteers as candidates for the four Donegal constituencies. A decision was taken by Sinn Féin to support E. J. Kelly, the nationalist candidate for East

Donegal, while Sam O'Flaherty was selected to stand as a token Sinn Féin candidate in that constituency. This was to prevent a split in the nationalist vote that could lead to the election of a unionist candidate. Sam O'Flaherty had been arrested in May as part of the so-called 'German Plot' round-up and deported to Lincoln jail in England where he was being held at the time of his selection.[34] At a meeting of the West Donegal Executive in Dungloe on Wednesday 4 September, Joe Sweeney, Burtonport, was unanimously selected as the Sinn Féin candidate for the constituency. Sweeney was proposed by Seaghan MacMenamin and seconded by Patrick McFadden from Creeslough.[35]

Following the announcement of the election the young members of Fianna Éireann boy scouts in Letterkenny became very active painting slogans on walls to antagonise the local RIC. On Sunday morning 8 September slogans appeared on the front wall and gate of No. 2 RIC barracks, the courthouse, town clock, a public house and walls of a yard on Lower Main Street in Letterkenny. The slogans read: 'IRA'; 'Don't Join the British Army'; 'Revenge for Easter Week'; 'Join the de Valera IRA'; 'Up the Rebels'; 'Down with the RIC Slaves'.[36]

At the South Donegal Sinn Féin executive selection convention on Sunday 15 September, P. J. Ward, solicitor, Donegal town and Killybegs was selected as the candidate for South Donegal. On the same day a meeting of the North Donegal Sinn Féin executive selected Joseph O'Doherty, a native of Derry, for the North Donegal constituency.[37]

The October edition of *An t-Óglach*, the official newsletter of the Volunteers, carried the following piece confirming the new offensive:

> Passive resistance is no resistance at all. Our active military resistance is the only thing that will tell. Any plans, theories, or doubts tending to distract the minds of the people from

the policy of fierce, ruthless fighting ought to be severely discouraged.

This statement would suggest that the Volunteers were to prepare to engage in physical force resistance against the British establishment in Ireland.[38]

However, the Volunteers in Donegal realised that the impending election would be a very hard fought and close contest requiring all their energy and enthusiasm to ensure success. Therefore the focus of the Volunteers in the county was on the impending election, during which time military actions were to be sidelined. During the course of some election meetings, addressed by speakers on behalf of Sinn Féin, it was found necessary to mobilise a strong force of Volunteers to deal with attempted interference by supporters of the AOH. This kept everyone very busy for the duration of the campaign. The local Cumann na mBan branches were active in canvassing every house in the different parishes.

The North Donegal election campaign opened on Thursday 21 November in Carndonagh where a large and enthusiastic crowd gathered to support Joseph O'Doherty, Sinn Féin candidate for the constituency.[39] The next day a meeting was held at the Market Square in Letterkenny in support of the Sinn Féin candidates for East and West Donegal. Dr J. P. McGinley presided over the meeting, which attracted a large crowd and also the attention of the military and police. A company of soldiers was stationed at the courthouse during the day and, in addition to the local force, over a hundred RIC men were drafted into the town. Despite the presence of the military and police there was no trouble and the meeting was addressed by several speakers. A letter from Rev. James McGlinchey, dean, St Columba's college in Derry was read out. In it he referred to Sam O'Flaherty, the East Donegal candidate:

> He is a man with the genuine Irish spirit and of educational

and personal qualities fitting him to uphold worthily Ireland's banner and Ireland's honour ... He speaks from his forced exile in an English prison to the Irish men and women of East Donegal and he asks their votes not for himself, not for East Donegal alone, but for Ireland.[40]

The Gweedore Sinn Féin cumann held a large meeting in their clubrooms the following Sunday 24 November where Éamon O'Boyle, presiding, welcomed the West Donegal candidate, Joseph Sweeney, to the area. Addressing the gathering, Sweeney said that 'no people appealed to him like those of Gweedore, whose fighting spirit was traditional' and he knew he could rely on them for support. Following the meeting he addressed the overflow of people who had to wait outside the clubrooms.[41]

During this period all schools in the county were closed owing to the serious outbreak of influenza. This afforded many teachers such as Joseph Murray, intelligence officer with the Bundoran Company, the opportunity to work in a full-time capacity for Sinn Féin. The influenza epidemic called 'Spanish Flu' itself was to cost the lives of over 100,000 people nationally, with Donegal having among the highest death rates in the country. Although called the 'Spanish Flu' the origins of this epidemic could be traced to the battlefields of Europe and was spread through the return of soldiers to Ireland and elsewhere. The Spanish were the first to recognise this as an epidemic thus the title 'Spanish Flu'.[42]

A very large meeting in support of Joseph O'Doherty was held at Fanavolty, Fanad, on Sunday 1 December, presided over by Éamon Friel, chairman of the local Sinn Féin cumann. The meeting was addressed by the candidate, as well as P. J. McGoldrick and Manus McCool. Afterwards a meeting in the village of Rosnakill, which was decorated with Sinn Féin flags, was addressed by Manus Shiels, who compared the Irish Party to a rotten potato. Joseph O'Doherty also spoke and it was reported that after his speech several opponents said they had been converted to the Sinn Féin policy. On the same day a series of meetings was held at Meenacross, addressed by the West Donegal candidate, Joe Sweeney. At Dungloe, Annagry, Gweedore and Kincasslagh great enthusiasm was demonstrated, although in Kincasslagh continuous interruptions by a group from the AOH disrupted Seaghan MacMenamin's speech. The meeting at Gweedore chapel was chaired by John Breslin, Bunbeg, and was addressed by John Sweeney, father of the candidate. He said it gave him pleasure to speak from the same spot where in coercion days he stood beside the immortal Fr McFadden. He did not attend the meeting to support Sinn Féin because his son was the candidate. He had been a loyal follower of the Irish Party until they were found wanting. Hugh O'Duffy, Gaelic League organiser, reminded the old men and women that the assertion that voting Sinn Féin meant the end of the pension was nothing more than the last kick of a dying horse. He knew he could depend on the freedom-loving people of Gweedore to cast those rumours aside and strike a blow for freedom.[43]

The political candidates took advantage of any large gatherings to deliver their message and canvas the constituents. This was the case on a fair day in Kilmacrenan, Tuesday 3 December, where representatives of both Sinn Féin and the Irish Party took advantage of the large gathering. During the Irish Party's meeting there were many questions, interruptions, cheers and counter-cheers. Before it had concluded the Sinn Féin supporters moved off and held a meeting a few yards away, at which speeches were delivered by Dr J. P. McGinley, Joseph McDevitt and Seaghan MacMenamin. On the same day at Fintown similar meetings were held, at which a large number of Sinn Féin supporters from the area carried republican flags. A platform was erected in the centre of the road and a number of speeches were made, arousing great enthusiasm.

At the close of the Sinn Féin meeting, the Irish Party representatives addressed the gathering and nearly every word of the speaker was met with shouts of 'Four hundred a year' (the annual salary for

MPs), 'Oath of allegiance' and 'Why haven't you khaki on you?' For some time chaos reigned and the police, fearing that the car that the Irish Party supporters used as a platform would be overturned, formed a cordon across the road. Again and again the crowd surged towards the platform and Sinn Féin flags were waved in the speaker's face. Throughout the week Sinn Féin held meetings in Kilcar, Donegal town, Glencolmcille, Carrick, Ardara, Killybegs, Bruckless, Ballintra, Cashelard, Killymard, Clar and Croagh. A very enthusiastic meeting was held in Ballyshannon and a torchlight procession lent colour to the proceedings.[44]

A similar meeting was organised in Bundoran, but the British had received prior notice and declared the meeting illegal. The town was overrun with extra military drafted in from Finner camp, together with a large force of armed police. In reaction the local Volunteers arranged a large presence in the town with large numbers arriving from other areas, including north Sligo and north Leitrim. As they arrived in the town the military attempted to seize the Sinn Féin flags they were carrying, but were prevented from doing so. The principal speakers at the meeting were to be Seán Milroy, P. J. Ward and Maud Gonne MacBride, who was the target of an arrest warrant issued some time earlier.

The local Volunteer intelligence officer, Joseph Murray, organised a decoy party comprising Harry Kelly, proprietor of the Marine hotel, a visiting priest from Manchester and an English lady who bore a striking resemblance to Maud Gonne MacBride. Arrangements had already been made to hold the meeting at the West End, Bundoran. Murray told the committee that it was his intention to travel through the town, with the decoy party, in the direction of the East End and hoped to draw the British military in that direction. Accordingly, the four set out and people began to follow in groups. When they reached the outskirts of the town the party broke up and took a short route to the strand and climbed to the top of 'Rogey' rock, from where they could see military and police follow at the double in the direction of the East End. Immediately the official meeting got into full swing at the West End, with the voices of the speakers and the cheers of the crowd resounding clearly across the bay. A warrant had been issued for the arrest of Maud Gonne MacBride and she decided not to attend the meeting.

Realising that they had been hoaxed, the British returned as quickly as possible, only to find that the meeting had almost concluded. Although suddenly surrounded by a ring of British bayonets, the speakers continued to address the meeting. At the conclusion the military were ordered to fix bayonets as the surging crowd advanced down the street. The Manchester priest addressed the people from a window in the Marine hotel and asked them to disperse quietly and not give the British forces an opportunity of repeating the occurrence at Bachelor's Walk, Dublin in 1914.[45] The reference to Bachelor's Walk related to an incident following the landing of weapons at Howth, when large numbers of Volunteers marched back to Dublin with the guns. They were met by the RIC and British military who attempted unsuccessfully to seize the weapons. Later, as the military returned to their barracks they were attacked with stones at Bachelor's Walk, with some soldiers opening fire on the hostile crowd. Four people were killed and over thirty injured.

The following day Monday 2 December witnessed a large gathering at a meeting in Dungloe in support of the west Donegal Sinn Féin candidate. It was reported to be the largest gathering seen there since the days of the Land League. Later that evening Dan McMenamin, the Irish Party candidate, held a meeting in the parochial hall, which was filled to overflowing. As soon as McMenamin stood up to speak, shouts of 'Up Sinn Féin' and 'Four hundred pounds' were heard. Finally a Sinn Féin member asked the audience to give the speaker a hearing on condition that at the end of his speech he would answer questions. McMenamin agreed and he was allowed to proceed. He had not, however, gone far when he declared that the Sinn Féiners were receiving British gold. An uproarious scene followed and from all parts of the hall came cries of 'It used to be German gold' and 'Pull him down.' Order was restored only after the intervention of members of the Sinn Féin executive. Seaghan MacMenamin then put a question to the speaker: 'Is it the fact that the Irish Party, having failed to prevent conscription in the House of Commons, had no other recourse left them than to come over to Ireland to ask for a Novena to Our Lady of Lourdes? Now I put it to the brave men and women of West Donegal, are they going to tolerate this scoff, this outrage, upon their most cherished instincts. Or will they make a ring of steel against such unholy invasion?' Finally, the meeting, which was intended to be in support of the Irish Party, broke up with cheers for Sweeney, who was then carried out on the shoulders of the crowd.[46]

As part of the preparation for the campaign, the Sinn Féin canvassers of South Donegal were educated on related matters, including election law. P. J. Ward's election agent for South Donegal, P. H. Gallagher, solicitor, Donegal town, held classes for all election workers at which he spoke on various topics and held question and answer sessions on what he had covered at his previous lecture. In this way all the election workers were very well versed in election law and practices.

The South Donegal campaign was also continuing apace with meetings at Malinbeg, Malinmore, Glencolmcille and Teelin on Tuesday 10 December with the Sinn Féin candidate, P. J. Ward, addressing each meeting. At Teelin the meeting was held at 8 p.m. and the attendance was very large with the scene along the way being described as 'not only picturesque but unique'. Candles were lit in the windows of numerous houses, which, added to the flare of the many torches carried through the street, made up a picture never before witnessed in this pretty village. The candidate was greeted by loud and prolonged cheering, and in an exhaustive speech he ably dealt with the policy of Sinn Féin, outlining the immense advantages that an independent Ireland would enjoy compared with an Ireland tied for ever to the apron strings of England.

A number of election meetings were also held in the Inishowen area in support of the North Donegal candidate. On market day, Monday 9 December, large crowds from Culdaff, Malin, Clonmany and Carndonagh assembled in Carndonagh in support of Joseph O'Doherty.

On Thursday 12 December another meeting was held in Buncrana. Addressing the meeting, Fr Philip O'Doherty informed the people that they were involved in a life and death struggle and concluded with an urgent appeal to the Sinn Féin voters to come out early on polling day and before voting to go for instruction at the Sinn Féin clubrooms.[47]

On the same day the two parties availed of another fair day, this time in Glenties, for a final debate. The Irish Party meeting, which attracted a large gathering, was presided over by Fr Cunningham, PP, Glenties, who made a strong appeal on behalf of the party candidate, Dan McMenamin, who also addressed the gathering. Dr J. P. McGinley subjected McMenamin to a severe cross-examination regarding the oath of allegiance. McMenamin replied that Parnell had taken the oath and as they left the platform there was uproarious laughter from the crowd. As the Sinn Féin delegation made their way to Dungloe a number of speakers addressed an impromptu gathering at Doochary. They then proceeded to Meenbanad where another meeting was addressed by representatives from Sinn Féin.

The date for polling was Saturday 14 December and early indications suggested an overwhelming victory for Sinn Féin. In the North Donegal constituency reports suggested there would be an overwhelming majority for Joseph O'Doherty. The Irish Party candidate was poorly supported and very few unionist votes were cast. Nowhere in Ireland had the electoral battle been fought with such thoroughness and vigour as in West Donegal. The distribution of literature on both sides was widespread and an extremely large number of meetings were held.

In East Donegal Sinn Féin and Irish Party supporters worked enthusiastically to secure the triumph of E. J. Kelly, to whom, under arrangement with Sinn Féin, the seat was allocated. It was expected that he would be returned with a large majority.

There was an exhaustive poll in the South Donegal constituency and the early indications were that P. J. Ward was likely to be elected with a considerable majority.[48]

The Letterkenny Volunteers were called to Churchill to protect the ballot boxes as the AOH endeavoured to take complete control of the Churchill polling station, even attempting to prevent Sinn Féin supporters from registering to vote. Members of the Volunteers and Sinn Féin were obliged to turn out on election day to ensure that Sinn Féin supporters could attend at polling stations and record their votes without hindrance.[49] There were no polling stations in the Bundoran area, which created problems for Sinn Féin, as the nearest polling station was at Ballyshannon. The scarcity of polling stations and the long distances that some voters had to travel was a particular handicap to the young Sinn Féin organisation. The AOH had the funds to commandeer all means of transport for voters travelling to the polling stations.[50]

The Donegal election results were published in the local press on Monday 30 December:

Area:	Total Vote	Candidate	Party	Votes	Majority
North Donegal	17,538	Joseph O'Doherty	Sinn Féin	7,003	3,928
		Philip O'Doherty	Irish Party	3,075	
West Donegal	19,296	Joseph Sweeney	Sinn Féin	6,712	2,596
		D. McMenamin	Irish Party	4,116	
South Donegal	16,804	P. J. Ward	Sinn Féin	5,797	1,045
		John T. Donovan	Irish Party	4,752	

East Donegal	16,015	E. J. Kelly	Irish Party	7,596	2,799
		Major R. L. Moore	Unionist	4,797	
		Sam O'Flaherty	Sinn Féin	40	

The main feature of the 1918 election was the success of Sinn Féin throughout the country; the greater number of the elected Sinn Féin candidates were in jail in Ireland and England. Nationally, Sinn Féin won seventy-three seats, unionists twenty-six seats and the Irish Party six seats.[51]

The news that Joe Sweeney was elected for West Donegal by a considerable majority generated great celebration in the Rosses. On the night of Saturday 28 December bonfires blazed on every hill, but it was the following day that the people gave the most striking indication of their delight. Early in the afternoon the Annagry, Mullaghduff and Ranafast bands marched to St Mary's chapel, Annagry, followed by huge numbers of men, women and children. The weather was unfavourable, but even that failed to dampen the spirits of the crowd moving triumphantly along the slushy road towards Crolly. Fife and drum bands preceded the large crowd the tricolour fluttering over their heads, and on their arrival at Crolly Bridge a band from Gweedore and a large crowd awaited them. The gathering was addressed by Patrick Gallagher of Crolly, president of the Annagry Sinn Féin cumann. He gave them a hearty welcome and congratulated the electors of Gweedore and the Rosses on the great victory.[52]

On learning the result of the election and the huge majority of Joe Sweeney, the people of Glenties celebrated by lighting bonfires all over the area; several barrels burned, while the people converged on the streets cheering for the new TD. A large crowd gathered outside Molloy's hotel and inspiring addresses were delivered in support of Joe Sweeney, after which the people dispersed quietly.

When the result of the North Donegal poll became known in

Clonmany, torchlights and tar barrels were lit in a number of areas. People travelled from other parts of Inishowen to Clonmany and the numbers soon swelled to over 3,000. The crowd was addressed by Fr Maguire, who said that Sinn Féin had a necessarily virile policy, had behind it the best brains of Ireland and under wise counsel was the only means of gaining freedom for our native land. He encouraged anyone who was still outside Sinn Féin in the parish to throw in their lot with the policy of the parish – the policy of Ireland.

At the close of his address the large gathering reformed into processional order and the people were returning to their homes when they were met by a number of youths bearing a coffin with the inscription 'Irish Party and Conscription' which was then burned on a tar barrel to great cheers and applause. There were similar scenes in every parish, village and town throughout the county, with the successful candidates later touring their respective constituencies. It was reported in late December that the Sinn Féin prisoners interned earlier in the year were to be released from English prisons. Count Plunkett, one of the Sinn Féin TDs returned unopposed, reached Dublin on Tuesday 31 December having been unconditionally released.[53]

After the elections the Volunteers returned to drilling and training throughout the county. The Volunteer companies set about collecting all arms in their area from anyone known to possess weapons; in the majority of cases the arms were handed over willingly.[54]

The December edition of *An t-Óglach* confirmed that all Volunteers were directed to leave the politics to the politicians; instead their focus should be on the impending military struggle with the forces of the crown:

> The energies of Irish Republicans have for the past fortnight been occupied chiefly by political work. Now that the General Election is over, the road is clear for Volunteers to resume to the full their military activities.

They should apply themselves to their duties with a renewed order, conscious that the efficient organising and arming of the army of Ireland is not less essential to the establishment of an Irish Republic than any other work, however important. In fact the creation of a strong, armed and efficient army is the one essential element in the work to secure our independence.[55]

9

1919 - GOVERNMENT AND WAR

THE IRISH PEOPLE delivered a resounding message to the British government through the overwhelming endorsement of Sinn Féin in the December 1918 election. This was also an endorsement for the Irish Volunteers to resist the British military and police by force of arms. In preparation for this the General Headquarters (GHQ) of the Irish Volunteers directed all divisions to ensure all brigades were properly organised and sufficiently armed. The next phase of conflict with the British establishment would be different from the methods employed in 1916. Then the policy was to commit an entire army with the hope of inflicting enough damage in the initial strike. The new policy would be based on ambush, hit and run tactics – guerrilla warfare. This would have the effect of frustrating the RIC and military, who would be unprepared for the ambush tactics, coupled with the fact that there would be no visible target to pursue.

In late 1918 Ernie O'Malley met with Michael Collins in the 'dugout', a room in the basement of St Enda's, the first school founded by Pádraig Pearse. The two men studied a map of Donegal as Collins intended to send O'Malley to the county to reorganise and train the Volunteers. Collins said to O'Malley cheerfully: 'You will freeze to death up there.'

O'Malley wasn't overly impressed by the response he received from the Donegal Volunteers and described some of the officers as slack, considering them to be great talkers, but unwilling to do anything when they had to. However, at the time of O'Malley's visit many of the Volunteers were preoccupied with preparations for the elections. O'Malley remained in Donegal for several months and helped establish a number of companies and carried out military training classes.[1] The general attitude changed with the successful election results.

In early January 1919 a meeting was held in Inver for all Irish Volunteer officers in the South Donegal area. The South Donegal brigade area was to take in portions of Leitrim and Sligo. The meeting, which was presided over by Ernie O'Malley, appointed the newly elected Teachta Dála (TD) P. J. Ward as Officer Commanding (O/C), Seamus Ward, Ballyshannon as vice-O/C, Liam O'Duffy, Donegal town as adjutant, Michael Dawson, Mountcharles as quartermaster and Charlie Keeney, Meenabrock, Dunkineely as intelligence officer.[2]

The Bundoran Volunteers were reorganised and became the South Donegal No. 1 battalion. Ernie O'Malley presided at the election of the battalion staff, with the following officers being selected and their appointments later confirmed by GHQ: battalion O/C Thomas McShea, vice-O/C Patrick Doherty, adjutant Patrick Gilvarry, quartermaster Joe Meehan and intelligence officer Joseph Murray.

The battalion was made up of the Bundoran, Ballyshannon, Kinlough, Cliffony, Tullaghan and Pettigo companies. Joseph Murray made valuable contacts as intelligence officer through the various hotels in Bundoran which were often frequented by British military officers from Finner camp and also established friendships with hotel proprietors, stationmasters and justices of the peace. The latter were always in close contact with senior police officers and Murray procured useful information from this source. Ernie O'Malley visited

1919 – GOVERNMENT AND WAR

many other areas as part of the restructuring campaign, moving from the old parish company structure into one of battalions and brigades, and establishing new companies where possible.[3]

In early 1919 the Volunteers focused on training, raiding for arms, and general disruption by cutting roads, railway lines and telegraph wires. Most of the raids for arms were carried out in the Lagan area of east Donegal, which was predominately unionist. Many of these unionists were members of the Ulster Volunteer Force and quantities of weapons, ammunition and equipment were obtained in that area. About the same time two Volunteers were detailed to watch a drill hall used by the Ulster Volunteers, which was located on the Boyd Yard near the Boyd's Estate (Ballymacool Woods), Letterkenny. On one occasion while watching the hall James McMonagle was discovered. He made an attempt to get away, but was captured and held prisoner for twenty-four hours, during which time he was closely questioned as to what he was doing in the vicinity of the hall. No action was taken against him, however, and he was released.[4]

The RIC began to show signs of aggression and in Dungloe they acquired a black Ford van, open at the back with seats along each side, in which they patrolled the outlying areas of the district. However, the force was not as formidable as in previous years and was about to experience a sudden climate change. The Volunteers were drilled, trained and now prepared for physical force resistance.

The RIC lost many members to the war in Europe and the British imposed a moratorium on recruitment to prevent competition between it and the British army. The force's national strength in 1910 was 10,222 and this figure was at least 1,000 below the strength in eviction and coercion days. The national strength in 1919 was 9,229 or 993 below the 1910 figures and very probably 2,000 less than in the force's heyday in the nineteenth century.[5] In December 1918, the RIC in Dungloe began to hassle the Volunteers, but rather than have a showdown at that time, Volunteers were warned not to carry arms or to have documents on their person unless instructed. The Volunteers in the west of the county responded to the harassment and decided to make things difficult for the police by trenching roads. One of the first trenches was near Loughanure, located in a dip in the road into which water was drained from the surrounding bogs. This had the effect of looking like a water splash. The police drove into it at speed and the two front wheels were torn off, injuring the occupants and putting an end to the van patrols. This was the first application in the country of instruction in road-trenching issued by GHQ.[6]

The police mounted a vigorous search for the West Donegal director of elections, Seaghan MacMenamin of Kingarrow, who had been on the run for some time. He was subsequently arrested in the early hours of Saturday 4 January when six armed policemen raided his father's home. MacMenamin was also the president of the West Donegal Executive of Sinn Féin and it was surmised that his role in the election was the reason why he was so vigorously sought by the authorities.

At a meeting in Donegal town on Sunday 5 January a demand was made for the release of the Irish political prisoners. A torchlight procession preceded the large crowd through the town before the meeting, headed by a large banner reading 'Release the Prisoners'. P. M. Gallagher, who presided over the meeting, said: 'There was a power growing up in this country that would make England render an account of the treatment she meted out to Ireland.'

The successful South Donegal candidate, P. J. Ward, addressing the meeting said: 'It was plain these men were kept in prison because they loved their country ... Was it not ridiculous to imprison men for singing "The Felons of Our Land" and for reading a simple statement demanding the application to Ireland of those principles for which they were told the war was fought ... if in response to this appeal the prisoners were not released other means would be taken to have them released.'

On the same day there was a meeting of the Willie Pearse Sinn Féin cumann in the parochial hall, Tamney and also of Rosnakill Cumann na mBan, Fanad. At both meetings resolutions were unanimously passed condemning the action of the British government in keeping the Irish prisoners so long interned without charge or trial and demanding their immediate release.

The following day at the Letterkenny Urban Council meeting a resolution was moved by Jim Gibbons for the release of the prisoners. The resolution, which was seconded by John Gallagher, was passed unanimously. Over 3,000 people attended a meeting held at Gortahork, which was specially convened for demanding the immediate release of the Irish prisoners.[7]

THE FIRST DÁIL AND FIRST BLOOD

AT A MEETING of Donegal County Council on Tuesday 7 January the following resolution from Kerry County Council was read:

> Ireland is a nation one and indivisible, is entitled to the rights and status of full and complete nationhood; the people of Ireland have never at any time even for a single moment renounced their just claim to their rights and status of full and complete nationhood; the Irish people have always protested, are now protesting, and will continue to protest, against the usurpation of their rights to nationhood by the British parliament. The Irish people demand as a right, not as a privilege ... Ireland must be made safe for the Irish people. If the Wilsonian dictum – consent of the governed – is to prevail, Ireland must have the right of self-determination; if a people must not be forced to be under a sovereignty they abhor Ireland must get her freedom; the realisation of this ideal is the be all and end all of our existence.

There was some laughter during the reading of the resolution. Council secretary: 'I suppose we may adopt it.'

The council chairman replied: 'It is a matter of indifference.' Councillor Anthony Lowry said: 'Some people think it is as important to make democracy safe for the world as the world safe for democracy.' And when William Kelly, solicitor, suggested they 'start with the road contractors first and make the roads safer for traffic', laughter ensued. The subject was dropped.[8]

On the same day in Dublin the first meeting of the newly elected Sinn Féin members was held in the Mansion House; thirty members were present. Count Plunkett was elected chairman for the day and all the members subscribed their names to the republican pledge. It was decided to draw up a protest statement against the imprisonment of the fellow members, and the following statement was issued:

> We, the members present at this meeting of the Irish Republican Party, freely elected by the people to voice the demand of the nation for independence, being assembled together in the Mansion House, Dublin, for the purpose of convening a Dáil or constituent assembly of Irish elected representatives hereby call the attention of free peoples of the World to the fact that thirty-seven of our members are at present imprisoned in English jails in Ireland and England or exiled from their country by England and thereby debarred from exercising their duties as the elected representatives of the Irish people. Thirty of our members have been kept in prison in England for eight months without charge or trial, four others are imprisoned in Ireland by sentences of English court-martials and the remaining three are exiled from Ireland for their activities in the cause of Irish freedom. On behalf of the people of Ireland who have selected them and ourselves as their representatives by overwhelming majorities, we demand their release.

The Glenties Sinn Féin cumann held a meeting on Sunday 12 January at which a resolution was passed calling on the British government to release all political prisoners. It read:

> While all the belligerent powers have released their political prisoners on the signing of the armistice, Britain, the hypocritical champion of justice and liberty, keeps the intellect of Ireland behind prison bars, whose only offence is that they love their country.

Similar meetings were held in Termon and Raphoe with similar resolutions being passed calling for the release of the prisoners. Numerous Sinn Féin cumainn around the county passed resolutions condemning the attitude of the Donegal County Council in its response to the Kerry resolution. Some considered the council's attitude as 'disrespectful and unpatriotic' and reassured these men that when the election came in June they would get a long rest from their 'sneering at the noble aspirations of their fellow countrymen for freedom and nationhood'.

Alice Cashel, Cumann na mBan organiser, was in the county visiting centres in east and west Donegal. On Friday 9 January she met with a hearty reception from the members of the Letterkenny branch to whom she delivered an instructive practical lecture on the duties and responsibilities of membership. She spoke of the fine work done by the cumann, particularly its success in raising funds for the cause. The following Wednesday, accompanied by two of the Letterkenny committee members, Miss Cashel attended a meeting of the district council at Raphoe, at which were present delegates of the several cumainn entitled to representation.[9]

A meeting was convened of the Central Branch of Sinn Féin in Dublin, on Monday 13 January, to discuss the road ahead; Alderman Thomas Kelly, TD, gave the main address. He said he hoped the new Irish Parliamentary Party would not develop the bad habit of speechmaking, but would devote itself to work for the country. The difficulties ahead of the party, who had taken the republican pledge inside and outside of jail, were immense. The de-Anglicisation of Ireland, he continued, was a work of tremendous difficulty. They had to break down the outposts and inposts, which the Britons and west Britons had captured for the purpose of their movement. That work was of tremendous greatness, but he believed most of them were equal to it and that the establishment of an Irish Republic, which was the high ideal set before the Irish people, might be brought about in one of two ways – physical force or moral persuasion.[10]

The constituent assembly called by Sinn Féin gathered in the Round Room of the Mansion House at 3.30 p.m. on Tuesday 21 January 1919 and was constituted as Dáil Éireann. The constitution of Dáil Éireann was drawn up, containing five short articles. Cathal Brugha was elected as chairman, having been proposed by Count Plunkett and seconded by P. Ó Máille. The Dáil session was conducted entirely in Irish; the only English spoken was when the chairman said: 'We desire there should be no cheering.' When the chairman called on Sir Edward Carson to answer to his name there was an outburst of laughter, as it was obvious he would not be there. Amidst a tense silence the Declaration of Independence was read out in Irish by Cathal Brugha, with all the members present standing throughout. A Dublin solicitor, Mr Duggan, then read an English translation, which was followed by the reading of the Democratic Programmes of the First Dáil.[11] A disappointing feature of the new parliament was the adoption of the practices and procedures of Westminster. This was a missed opportunity to create a truly independent form of government.

On the very same day there were reports of an attack on an RIC patrol at Soloheadbeg, County Tipperary. Two policemen were escorting a cart of gelignite when ambushed by Volunteers. Shots were fired and the two RIC men were killed. Dan Breen and Seán Hogan jumped onto the cart and drove off, while the others took the rifles and ammunition from the bodies of the dead policemen.

1919 – Government and War

This was the 3rd Tipperary brigade, led by Seamus Robinson, and included Dan Breen, Seán Hogan, Tadhg Crowe, Paddy McCormack and Paddy Dwyer.[12]

The War of Independence was now officially launched and to some extent interrupted the political campaign as war was waged against the British throughout the country. Following the Soloheadbeg ambush there was general confusion as to what was the official policy, and condemnations from senior political Irish figures only added to the uncertainty. Seamus Robinson, the O/C of the South Tipperary brigade and officer in charge of the Soloheadbeg ambush, was summoned to Dublin shortly afterwards to meet with Michael Collins.

The other members of the ambush party, Seán Treacy, Dan Breen and Seán Hogan, were also summoned to attend, but were given a wide berth by many as they were considered 'hot property', with the possibility of the police and military being in pursuit of them. They were met by Michael Collins on the street, with Collins scanning every person that passed. The conversation went as follows:

> Collins: 'Well, everything is fixed up; be ready to go in a day or two.'
> Robinson: 'To go where?'
> Collins: 'To the States.'
> Robinson: 'Why?'
> Collins: 'Well isn't it the usual thing to do after …'
> Robinson: 'We don't want to go to the States or anywhere else.'
> Collins: 'Well a great many people seem to think it is the only thing to do.'

Robinson feared that GHQ was being influenced by the Sinn Féin pacifists and said to Collins: 'Look here, to kill a couple of policemen for the country's sake and leave it at that by running away would be so wanton as to approximate too closely to murder.'

Collins asked: 'Then what do you propose to do?'

101

'Fight it out of course,' Robinson replied. Collins, walking off with the faintest smile on his lips but with a big laugh in his eyes, said: 'That's all right with me.'

Neither the Dáil nor GHQ could or would declare war, but it was considered unnecessary as the Dáil declared that the war was still on from 1170, when Strongbow, Richard FitzGilbert, Earl of Pembroke, led the Norman invasion of Ireland.[13]

This was the first indication that the policy of Sinn Féin was at variance with that of the Volunteers, something that resurfaced again and again, creating friction between them. Some Sinn Féin leaders considered the shooting of policemen as a mistake and preferred a different approach to the impending conflict. The military campaign against the police was as much about viewing that force as antagonists through their suppression of the population under the shadow of a gun, even in times of peace, and as an organ of the British establishment with whom Ireland was once again at war. The campaign to turn the people against the RIC and convince the public that the police were enemies of Ireland took some time. Before the outbreak of hostilities, the general public considered the RIC to be honest and decent men with discipline and self-respect. Yet the election campaign and other events in 1918 showed that it was in fact the enforcer of the British law that suppressed the political and cultural organisations endorsed by the people.[14]

At the beginning of 1919 the Donegal Volunteers were very active, cutting off roads and disrupting the rail service, with the Letterkenny Company cutting off the only railway line to west Donegal. At the request of the west Donegal Volunteers the traders in Dungloe boycotted the British military and police by refusing to supply them with food. The British forces found it very difficult to procure sufficient supplies of food locally and were forced to bring in supplies by rail from Derry.

In the 3rd battalion area of No. 1 brigade West Donegal the instructions were well adhered to, but there were a few exceptions. In one case at Creeslough a man supplying turf to the RIC in the village refused to stop when instructed to do so by the local Volunteers. He was later arrested and had the shafts from his cart sawn off, leaving him without any transport. In another case the Volunteers burned the lorry of a trader in Dunfanaghy who, although having been warned, continued to convey goods to the police. It was later discovered that he was also delivering mail to the RIC.[15]

The Volunteers in Letterkenny received information that a passenger train from Derry had two wagonloads of supplies for the British stationed in Dungloe and that a small party of military in civilian clothing would be on the train as an escort. The escort consisted of one non-commissioned officer and four soldiers all armed with revolvers. A party of ten Volunteers led by James McMonagle was hurriedly mobilised in Letterkenny and set out in two cars to the railway station at Churchill. Arriving in good time, they took up positions around the station. When the train pulled in the Volunteers immediately boarded and disarmed the military escort. The food was unloaded onto the railway line and as there was inadequate transport to remove the items the Volunteers set them on fire.[16]

The Letterkenny Volunteers were forced to concentrate on activities outside the town due to the presence of RIC barracks at both ends of the town, which would prove to be thorns in the side of the local Volunteers. One of the barracks was situated beside the courthouse and the other at Lower Main Street, with a garrison of British military occupying a section of the county asylum (St Conal's hospital). At any one time there were over a hundred personnel between the two barracks and many referred to Letterkenny as a garrison town. Open warfare was ruled out, as the local Volunteers feared reprisals would be severe due to the large number of troops and police stationed in the town.

The annual meeting of the Sinn Féin South Donegal Executive was held in the Richard Bonner Sinn Féin clubrooms, Donegal town on Saturday 25 January. Delegates from the following cumainn attended: Ballyshannon, Bundoran, Pettigo, Ballintra, Cashelard, Lahey Bar, Donegal town, Tawnawully, Frosses, Mountcharles, Drimarone, Ardaghey, Killaghtee, Killybegs, Ardara, Kilcar, Carrick and Glencolmcille.

The newly elected member for South Donegal, P. J. Ward, addressed the meeting and dealt at length with the work done by Dáil Éireann and what the future held. He assured all that the leaders whom they trusted most would soon be with them. On his own election, he said that the credit was due to the members of Sinn Féin and not himself.[17]

On the same night the Volunteers of Creeslough Company received information that the local justice of the peace, Andrew Wilkinson, held weapons in his house. Believing it would be a simple operation, the Volunteers approached Wilkinson's house and knocked on the door, stating their objective. He refused to open it, however, and could be heard running up the stairs. Company captain, James McNulty, was assuring him that there was no cause for alarm when Wilkinson fired a revolver from an upstairs window. McNulty was struck in the shoulder and fell to the ground. A number of Volunteers immediately burst open the front door and made their way up the stairs where they disarmed the occupant. They searched the entire house and recovered several weapons and a large amount of ammunition. McNulty was then conveyed to Carrigart in a waiting car and examined by Dr McClusky, who advised that he should be taken to the Mater Hospital in Dublin to have the bullet removed. Joseph Sweeney was then contacted and the arrangements were made to have McNulty brought to Dublin and admitted to the Mater Hospital.

On the same night that McNulty was wounded, a party of Volunteers from Gweedore arrived at Creeslough railway station in a commandeered car. The plan was to seize the mailbag, censor the mail and then return the normal mail for delivery. Bernard McGinley of the Creeslough Company met the Gweedore Volunteers at the station and informed them of the presence of an RIC patrol who were there to protect the mail. They received further information that similar patrols were posted at the stations in Falcarragh and Dunfanaghy. The Volunteers boarded the train at Creeslough and forced the driver, at gunpoint, to drive past Falcarragh and Dunfanaghy stations.

They continued for a distance to a quiet part of the line where they removed all the mail destined for the RIC and military. The ordinary mail was then taken back to the nearest station by horse and cart.[18]

In early February the National Teachers Board requested a number of schoolteachers in Donegal suspected of being associated with Sinn Féin to relinquish their connection with the organisation. Refusal to comply with the order would lead to instant dismissal. The majority of teachers in the north-west complied.[19]

Also in February the military and police began executing warrants under the 'Dangerous Associations' provision for people reported to be associated with Sinn Féin. The first such arrest was in Carndonagh on Monday 10 February when Patrick J. Cole, merchant, Bridge Street, Carndonagh, was arrested by a party of military and police. The raiding party arrived in the town early that morning. Cole was taken into custody and transported to Ebrington barracks, Derry, but fell ill and was removed to hospital for treatment.[20] Despite the arrest of Cole and the 'Dangerous Associations' provision, the local Sinn Féin members continued to conduct their business and the annual meeting of the East Donegal Comhairle Ceantair was held at the Sinn Féin clubrooms in Raphoe on Saturday 15 February. Dr McGinley presided over the meeting, which was attended by delegates from Letterkenny, Raphoe, Castlefinn, Glenswilly, Drumoghill, Murlogh, Gleneely, Killygordon and Clady. The county council and district council elections were discussed; it was unanimously decided to contest every seat possible and instructions were issued regarding funds for the support of Dáil Éireann. It was also decided at the meeting that arrangements were to be made in the constituency to have Irish taught as a living language, not as a dead language as it was in many areas at that time.[21]

The raids by military and police continued. In the early hours of Monday 17 February raids were carried out in the Killygordon area and Mathew McGranaghan, a prominent member of Sinn Féin, was arrested. On the same day news was received that Sam O'Flaherty had been released from prison in England.[22]

On Monday 24 March Westminster tabled the Local Government (Ireland) Bill, which was to introduce proportional representation for all future elections in Ireland. Colonel W. Guinness, supporting the bill, stated it would damage the rising support of Sinn Féin.[23]

At a special court in Raphoe on Saturday 29 March, Mathew McGranaghan was prosecuted on three charges of unlawful assembly – at Castlederg on 28 December 1918, Ballybofey on 5 January and Killygordon on 19 January 1919. McGranaghan contended that he was charged before a court that denied him justice and fair play. The court set bail at a personal surety of £50 for the next two years and two sureties of £25 each, default of which would result in six months' imprisonment. McGranaghan chose prison and demanded to be treated as a political prisoner. There was applause in the court and McGranaghan sang the 'Soldier's Song' as he was led away, followed by a crowd of supporters.

Raiding for arms and ammunition continued with a party of Volunteers from the Inishowen area taking advantage of a dance held in Buncrana on Wednesday 9 April. This was a weekly dance and the British military stationed at Ned's Point were frequent visitors, leaving their base exposed. The local Volunteers easily overpowered the small party of men on sentry duty, successfully removing all weapons, ammunition and other useful items.[24]

The following day in the Dáil a decree was passed – an official declaration that the general population were to boycott the RIC. This had been unofficially exercised throughout Donegal for some time, but as official policy the public would face sanctions from the Volunteers if they were observed associating with the police.[25]

The Creeslough Sinn Féin cumann held a public meeting on Sunday 15 June, which attracted a large crowd made up of bands, Volunteers and Cumann na mBan. Many areas were represented, including Rosses, Gweedore, Cloghaneely, Doe, Termon, Carrigart, Fanad, Kilmacrenan and Letterkenny. Pádraig Mac Phaidín presided and asked all present to continue their efforts until Ireland was placed in her rightful position among the nations of the world. The guest speaker, Seasamh MacGuibhal, referred to the historic meeting held there some twelve years earlier at which Michael Davitt assured the crowd that the eyes of the world were fixed on Ireland. He had said: 'The ears of the world were listening to her cry and her case, while the "champion of small nations" stood exposed as the greatest hypocrite on earth.'

Dr McGinley also addressed the gathering and referred to the 'boys in blue' as the meanest creatures on God's earth. 'America, Australia and all liberty-loving lands demand Ireland's independence and God willing we will have it,' he said.[26]

The Sinn Féin meeting at Carrick two weeks later attracted approximately 3,000 people from surrounding areas including Ardara, Killybegs, Kilcar, Teelin and Glencolmcille. P. C. O'Mahony was introduced as being as well known to the people of Carrick as he was to the warders of the jails in Derry, Belfast and Reading, where he had spent time as a political prisoner. In his address he eloquently traced the rise of republican ideas all over the world and maintained that Ulster was really the cradle of republicanism. It was, he said, 'men – brave men – banished from Ulster by oppressive English laws that fomented the little disturbance in North America that ended in the establishment of the greatest and most powerful Republic in the world – the United States'. He continued:

> The stalwart Presbyterians of Ulster – such men as Tone, Russell, McCracken and Orr – endeavoured to establish the republican form of government in Ireland and sacrificed their

lives for its attainment ... Now that Sinn Féin has reached such a strong position in the fight of world politics, it is necessary for us to review and study our surroundings to safeguard our nation, and in doing so to peep back at the hard road we have travelled, every inch of which is dyed with the blood and with the sacrifices of the noblest and best that our land could produce. Republicanism is old and has an honoured place among our hills and along our valleys and deep in the hearts of our faithful people.[27]

Shortly after eleven o'clock mass on Sunday 31 August, in Donegal town, two companies of the Irish Volunteers marched in military formation in the direction of Killybegs as a decoy to attract military attention away from the town. The decoy worked and a meeting was held on the roadside at Brackey; the meeting was conducted entirely in Irish, but was eventually dispersed by the military and police. Meanwhile, Seán Milroy and P. J. Ward, TD, arrived in the town and made their way to the Diamond, where within a short time the principal meeting of the day was in full swing. Milroy, who had escaped from Lincoln jail in February along with Éamon de Valera and Seán McGarry, delivered a spirited address in Irish and also spoke in English:

> In a few moments you will have an actual demonstration of British rule in Ireland – the rule of the sword and bayonet, the rule of brute force. Last December you elected by a splendid majority a representative who was pledged, not to misrepresent you at Westminster, but to represent you in Ireland's National Assembly and today your representative is denied the right of addressing his own constituents. (A voice from the crowd shouted: 'That's John Bull's interpretation of the freedom of small nationalities.')

Seán Milroy continued talking as the military approached, saying to the crowd: 'They should be careful not to throw themselves upon their bayonets and thus give their enemies the opportunity they were seeking.' The military took up position in front of the speakers and the local head constable ordered Milroy to desist.

Milroy: 'By what authority?'

District Inspector (DI) Moore then instructed the head constable to read the proclamation, at the conclusion of which the district inspector ordered the speakers to leave at once.

Milroy: 'Did Hackett Pain [Brigadier-General Hackett Pain, former chief of staff to Carson's army] get this authority from Carson's Provisional Government or from the British government?'

DI Moore: 'I suppose from the British government.'

P. J. Ward: 'Do you mean to say that it was fear of grave disorder that caused the proclamation of this meeting?'

DI Moore: 'The proclamation has been issued under the Defence of the Realm Act.'

Another point was put to the DI by a man called Brennan: 'We are only accustomed to instructions from the government of the Irish Republic.'

DI Moore: 'I will hold the speakers responsible for any trouble that may arise in dispersing the meeting', to which a man called Keeney replied: 'We are not responsible for bringing the military here and any trouble that may ensue will be clearly attributable to military interference.'

A bayonet charge was then ordered. The car occupied by the speakers moved off slowly, with the soldiers prodding the back seat passengers with their bayonets as they passed. None of them were seriously injured and later joined in the singing of the 'Soldier's Song'. The captain of the local Volunteers received a bayonet wound to the right hand.[28]

On Friday 12 September, the Sinn Féin hall in Ballybofey was raided by local police assisted by men from barracks in the surrounding areas. The premises belonging to John Cassidy was also raided. He was out of town and the police smashed their way in, with some fifty military used as backup during the raids.[29]

On the same day the premises and apartments of Domhnall O'Boyle, manager, Meentagh Co-operative Society at Ballyliffin, John McCarron, Clonmany and Patrick Gallen, MacDonagh & Co., Clonmany, were searched by the police for seditious literature etc., but nothing of an incriminatory nature was found. The old hall, Carndonagh, part of which was used by Sinn Féin, was also searched, but nothing was found, as were the premises of Messrs Langan and the residence of James Doherty, Cashel.

Similar searches were carried out in Donegal town on the same day, beginning at 11 a.m. when the premises of Ambrose Kennedy, Hugh Britton and Patrick Gallagher, Main Street, were subjected to an exhaustive search for weapons and seditious material, but again nothing was found.

Raids continued throughout the day when the premises of Frosses Sinn Féin president, John Harley were raided. The residence of P. J. Ward-O'Byrne, auctioneer, and John Ward, Killybegs, were raided, but nothing was found. Later that night every room in the premises of Patrick Gallagher, Crolly Bridge, was searched.

An example of the ineffectiveness of this series of raids was when the residence of Hugh O'Duffy, Beltany, Gortahork, was raided at 10 a.m. on Friday. The police surrounded the house before forcing their way inside, to find Hugh O'Duffy's two children, aged fifteen and thirteen, and in the presence of the two terrified children the police began to ransack the house, but failed to find anything. In the early hours of Monday 22 September a combined force of police and military from Dungloe and Burtonport surrounded and searched the home of Bernard O'Boyle, Rutland Island, Burtonport. It was dark at the time, blowing a gale and raining furiously, and to cross in a boat to make an arrest in such conditions gave an indication of the seriousness of the operation. O'Boyle's mother, startled at the banging at the door, inquired who was there. The reply was: 'It's all right Mrs O'Boyle, it's only the police.' After some time Mrs O'Boyle opened the door and the district inspector told her they wanted to speak to Bernard. Mrs O'Boyle replied that it took a great number of police to speak to him. Bernard O'Boyle had heard of their arrival on the island and made a clever escape; the police returned to the mainland, not only duped, but famished and wet. It was not known what the nature of the charge was, but it was thought that it was in connection with a speech delivered at a meeting in Dungloe on 1 September. O'Boyle, a prominent member of Sinn Féin, was the Donegal superintendent for the Irish National Assurance Company Ltd.[30]

In late September Volunteers of the 1st battalion, 4th brigade, South-East Donegal received information that a number of rifles, the property of the UVF, were stored at Barnscourt, County Tyrone near Sion Mills. A raid was carried out but nothing was found. Further information was received that the rifles had been moved to Sir Robert Anderson's summer residence at Greencastle. Anderson was the mayor of Derry.

The No. 4 Brigade O/C, Sam O'Flaherty mobilised men from his area including Thomas McGlynn, Castlefinn, and four Volunteers from the Liscooley Company which included John Byrne, Edward Thomas Coyle, Michael Doherty and Michael Bogan. In preparation for the raid the telegraph wires were cut between Carndonagh-Moville and Moville-Derry. Ernie O'Malley, who had been in the county to oversee the reorganisation of the Volunteers, assisted in carrying out the raid. Some of the Volunteers were picked up by John McGroarty and Dr Kerrigan from Killygordon; they travelled via Raphoe to Bridge End, where they were joined by three other carloads of Volunteers, including Frank Aiken from Armagh. They arrived at Greencastle in the early hours of Thursday 2 October.

Ernie O'Malley went off to inspect the area, and on returning was told that the original plan was cancelled as a couple of cars from

Letterkenny had failed to arrive. O'Malley was disappointed but said that they would 'go on with the little game anyhow'. He ordered the men to form a line and directed each man to catch hold of the coat of the man in front so that no one would get lost in the dark. They broke into the house and conducted a thorough search, but all they retrieved were two old rifles and two antique swords. On the return journey they discovered Dr McGinley's car had mounted a fence, after his lights had failed. The convoy stopped to lend a hand and fix the lights on his car. Between Muff and Derry they came upon the other carload of Volunteers who had failed to turn up. The broken down car was towed to a garage at Pennyburn in Derry. In the confusion Ernie O'Malley and another Volunteer were left behind at the garage. They eventually reached Letterkenny aboard the early morning train from Derry.[31]

A large number of military arrived in Ballybofey on Friday 31 October in response to rumours that Sinn Féin was intending to hold a large public meeting there. The military received information that a meeting would be held in either Stranorlar, Ballybofey, Crossroads, Killygordon, Liscooley, Drumkeen or Welchtown. Prior to this there were no military in the town, but on this particular day soldiers from the Dorset Rfegiment arrived in three lorries. More troops and police arrived by train, all from bases in Derry, and Ballybofey had its first experience of the British military machine. The reason given for such a large force was that the meeting would 'give rise to grave disorder and would thereby cause undue demands upon the police'. It was therefore decided to prohibit any such meeting, assembly or procession in pursuance of the British policy to make the world 'safe for democracy' a place where right shall reign and might be vanquished.

By the following night reports from the outlying posts of Stranorlar, Killygordon, Liscooly, Crossroads, Drumkeen and Welchtown indicated that the 'utmost tranquillity prevailed' with the result that some troops left Ballybofey and returned to Derry.[32]

10

DONEGAL ENGAGES WITH THE ENEMY – DECEMBER 1919

ON THURSDAY 11 December Anthony McGinley and Charles McBride were arrested at Dungloe. The charge against McBride was for distributing handbills at Dungloe chapel in favour of the Dáil Éireann loan. Both men protested against being treated as ordinary prisoners and as a result spent the night in the kitchen of the police barracks. The local Volunteers decided not to affect an escape due to the lack of arms; instead they would target the escort on its return from the crimes court in Letterkenny. This was to be the first official engagement of the Dungloe Company and it was decided that all available members would play a part – to blood them if nothing else.

An unsuccessful attempt was made the following morning to arrest Joseph O'Doherty, TD for North Donegal. Shortly after 9 a.m. five policemen entered his home in Clarendon Street, Derry. O'Doherty was having breakfast in his bedroom at the time, and when he appeared at the top of the stairs one of the policemen read the warrant for his arrest. O'Doherty then had a conversation with a servant in Irish and she went to get his heavier clothes. The police waited downstairs in the belief that O'Doherty was finishing his breakfast and getting dressed. They then asked Mrs O'Doherty would her husband be long and she replied that he had gone out the back window; he had made his way across a number of roofs to safety. The police immediately made their way to the rear of the house only to see O'Doherty disappearing over a wall. It was stated he was wanted in connection with a speech he gave at Carndonagh in October. The meeting was also addressed by Patrick Porter, who was arrested by the RIC at his home in Buncrana earlier that morning. At a special court in Derry the following Friday afternoon, 12 December, Patrick Porter was charged with having, at Carndonagh on 19 October, 'solicited contributions for the purpose of the illegal association known as Dáil Éireann' and for taking part in an unlawful assembly at the same time and place. He was remanded in custody to attend again. In a further raid Dr J. P. McGinley was arrested at his home in Letterkenny on Friday morning and brought to the barracks at Lower Main Street. The 9 a.m. train from Derry arrived in Letterkenny with twenty-five soldiers of the Dorset Regiment on board; more military arrived by lorry and there was a large force of extra police drafted into the town for the day.

The 11.30 a.m. train arrived with Anthony McGinley and Charles McBride, both from Dungloe, and they were taken to the same barracks. While the prisoners were in custody there was considerable excitement in the town owing to the extreme popularity of Dr McGinley. He was subsequently charged with advocating the Sinn Féin loan during a speech at a meeting at Rosnakill, Fanad on 26 October. Anthony McGinley and Charles McBride, both from Dungloe were charged with distributing leaflets in connection with the loan outside Dungloe chapel on 2 November. All men refused to recognise the court. The resident magistrate granted an application that Dr McGinley be remanded to Burnfoot and that he would allow bail. McGinley said the suggestion that he should give bail was an insult and he wished to make it clear that he denied the right of that, or any other foreign court, to try him. Whatever excuse there might have been for agreeing their authority to try him before December had been nullified by the action of 75 per cent of the Irish people in the election of December 1918. If it was a crime to advocate a fund for the development of Ireland's resources, Archbishop Walsh was also a criminal if the courts followed matters to their logical conclusions. In such circumstances he was proud to be a criminal. At the conclusion of Dr McGinley's case the charges against the other prisoners were heard. They declined to take off their hats and these were removed by a policeman. The resident magistrate (RM) said he would accept bail and encouraged Charles McBride, an elderly man, to accept. The men were remanded in custody to Burnfoot on 19 December; they were removed to Derry via military lorry under heavy escort.[1]

A coded wire was sent to the Volunteers in Dungloe informing them that the escorts had started on the return journey. The Dungloe Volunteers began preparations for an ambush of the RIC party, but they had to cover four possible routes. The RIC could leave the train at Crolly station, Kincasslagh Road station, Dungloe Road station or the terminus at Burtonport, so scouts were sent out to cover the different stations. One Volunteer was instructed to drive to Crolly and Kincasslagh Road stations and another cycled to Dungloe Road station. The police eventually got off at Dungloe Road station at approximately 10 p.m. and the Volunteer cycled back in time to inform the others.

The escort party began walking to Dungloe, a distance of three miles. The road leading to the ambush positions was very dark and to ensure accurate identification of the targets a scout was instructed to walk in their direction and to whistle a certain tune when they passed him. The ambush party was mobilised at a place call the Fairhill, also known as the Rampart, an old school house approximately two miles outside Dungloe. They were divided into three sections: No. 1 section – Patrick Breslin, Bernie Sweeney and James McCole – was positioned behind the schoolhouse wall; No. 2 section – Joe Sweeney, Patrick (Kit) O'Donnell and Frank O'Donnell – was positioned twenty yards along the road in the direction of Dungloe and No. 3

115

section – Patrick McCole and John Molloy – was positioned twenty yards further on.

The plan was to allow the RIC party to walk into the ambush position before opening fire. Before long they heard the scout whistling his tune and could make out the silhouette of District Inspector Wallace, Sergeant Farrell and the two constables. In total the Volunteers only had a revolver, shotgun, the rifle rescued from the RIC in January 1918 and a grenade. Each section had a weapon and as the RIC reached the ambush James McCole fired his revolver, quickly followed by two shots from the shotgun held by Patrick McCole. McCole had never handled a self-ejecting shotgun before and when he opened the breach after firing, the two empty shells struck him in the face. Patrick Breslin was also firing the rifle, but the grenade was not used as John Molloy had let his cigarette die out and this was to be used to ignite the grenade. The RIC ran from No. 1 section into No. 2 and No. 3 sections, with the Volunteers firing as they ran.

The sergeant was hit in the leg, but managed to drag himself behind a rock for cover as the others returned fire. The Volunteers kept up the attack until they were forced to retreat due to lack of ammunition. As they retreated over the nearby fields they could hear the remaining RIC running over the bridge towards Dungloe. In the ambush one RIC man was seriously wounded while the others were peppered with shotgun pellets. As a precautionary measure the telegraph wires between Dungloe station and the town were cut.

The ambush had an amusing sequel and resulted in some of the ambush party being reprimanded by the local Sinn Féin officer board a few days later. The local Sinn Féin cumann had passed a resolution the previous week which stated that no member should attend or support any function sponsored by the local AOH branch. However, immediately after the ambush some of the Volunteers considered it necessary to establish alibis and decided to attend a dance organised by the AOH at a local hall. While there they heard that the RIC were looking for the local doctor and it was then the Volunteers realised that some of their shots had hit their targets. The following week the Volunteers who attended the dance were reprimanded, but were obliged to sit and listen as they could not give an explanation for their presence there. Later that month Sergeant Farrell and the two constables, Cunnane and McGinley, lodged claims amounting to £4,000 in respect of personal injuries received during the ambush.[2] Dr J. P. McGinley, now a prisoner at Derry jail, wrote to Seán Mac Loingsigh, Convoy and, referring to the Dungloe incident, stated: 'Donegal is awake in earnest now ...'[3]

On Sunday 14 December detachments of the Dorset Regiment arrived in Dungloe on the 8.30 a.m. train. Owing to the now hostile feeling towards the police in Dungloe they were unable to procure a car locally and one had to be hired in Letterkenny to convey the injured police to the county hospital in Lifford. In response to the ambush the RIC, supported by the Dorset Regiment, carried out a series of raids and searched a number of houses in the town and surrounding area, but no arrests were made and nothing incriminating discovered. At a sitting of Donegal County Council the following day a resolution was adopted from Tipperary County Council condemning the actions of the Volunteers in their attacks on the police.[4]

On Friday morning, 19 December, Dr J. P. McGinley, Letterkenny, Éamon McDermott, Derry, and Charles McBride and Anthony McGinley, Dungloe, were conveyed in military lorries from Derry jail to Burnfoot county court. Patrick Porter, Buncrana, was also present at the court for the hearing. He had previously been released on bail owing to ill health. All along the route there were armed police patrols and at Burnfoot there was a great demonstration of force, a large number of armed police supported by a detachment of soldiers. Seán Milroy, who had been arrested two weeks previously in connection with the Sinn Féin meeting at Bundoran in August and imprisoned in Galway, was brought before the same court. Milroy had been suffering from ill health and had been held in the prison hospital in Galway. All the prisoners were handcuffed and remained so for some time in the court. The court was presided over by Mr Hardy, RM, and Major Brett, RM. The first case was against Patrick Porter, who was charged in connection with a speech at a meeting in Carndonagh presided over by Fr Philip O'Doherty.

Sergeant Maguire gave evidence that the defendant spoke about paying dues to John Bull and appealed for subscriptions for the loan. Cross-examined by Mr Hugh O'Doherty, solicitor, Maguire said that he could not remember any of Fr O'Doherty's speech and they had no charge against the priest. Porter, on being ordered to enter into bail to keep the peace for two years, excitedly declared that it was such unfair sentences that made men extremists and that he was prepared to go to jail. There was loud cheering and applause in the court. Éamon McDermott, similarly charged in connection with a meeting near Culdaff on 5 October, refused to recognise the court. Dr McGinley then addressed the court: 'We know old Hardy well. His clique will not rule Ireland much longer', to which McDermott added: 'Up the Republic – we will not flinch, we are pledged to this old country and we will die in the cause if necessary.' The members of the public present in the court then started singing the 'Soldier's Song', which was taken up by the crowd outside.

Seán Milroy was next to be charged and on refusing to recognise the court quoted from Edward Carson: 'There are some crimes which are not illegalities, and some illegalities which are not crimes.' Milroy then asked the police sergeant if he agreed, to which he replied: 'I never heard that before.' Milroy advised the police to be careful what they said about Edward Carson, their boss. He added that the police witnesses were perjuring themselves, that he had refrained from any reference to the Dáil loan at any meetings and protested that he had been brought directly from Galway without being informed of the charge against him. The resident magistrate, Mr Hardy, said the three defendants had openly defied the law and apparently glorified in it. He sentenced the defendants to two months imprisonment and ordered that they enter into sureties to keep the peace for two years. If they failed to do so, they would be imprisoned for a further three months. Éamon McDermott then addressed the court: 'You have gone further than any other magistrates in similar cases. Three months has been the limit set down. That's British justice.'

In the case of Anthony McGinley and Charles McBride proceedings were adjourned and they were further held on remand, as the two police witnesses were in Lifford hospital suffering from gunshot wounds following the attack the previous week.[5] They were again brought before a special court on Friday 2 January, 1920, but the police witnesses were again unable to attend. The two men were remanded further and the magistrate said he would accept bail. Anthony McGinley replied that he did not ask for bail as he denied the right of the court to try him. Charles McBride was released on bail.[6]

11

1920 - THE GUERRILLA SOLDIERS AND THE DONEGAL GUN-RUNNER

THE BRITISH GOVERNMENT had been exploring various options of response to the intensified IRA campaign against the RIC, which forced many outlying barracks to be evacuated. There was also the general population's aversion towards the force and ignoring the RIC as the enforcers of law and order. In late 1919 the British government authorised a recruitment campaign for a subsidiary force to assist the RIC. The introduction of such a force was so ill-planned that there were insufficient supplies of uniforms and the new recruits were dressed in khaki trousers and the green tunics of the police, earning them the name 'Black and Tans'. Effectively an ill-trained unit of mercenaries drawn largely from the ample supply of ex-soldiers and unemployed workers in England sent to support the RIC, the Black and Tans had no regard for the usual code of warfare. Several thousand were eventually deployed in Ireland with the purpose of instilling terror among the populace in an attempt to force the Irish people to desist from cooperating with the Irish Volunteers. Over the next eighteen months they engaged in countless acts of rape, murder, burning, plundering, kidnapping and the wanton destruction of property. At first their arrival did not please many of the RIC as their tactics were considered forceful and disrespectful, but it wasn't long before the same RIC were happy to have the reinforced presence.[1]

The municipal elections of January 1920 represented the first real effort on the part of Sinn Féin and the Irish people to turn each of the municipal councils into a bulwark of the national and economic welfare of Ireland. The Proportional Representation Bureau compiled an estimate of the number of seats in local authorities nationally: approximately 1,500. For these seats Sinn Féin put forward 717 candidates and the Labour Party, with which a working alliance had been established in most parts of the country, put forward 595 candidates. Unionist candidates totalled 436, with 588 other candidates. The numbers in Ulster, fighting for 421 seats, were as follows: Sinn Féin (SF) and Labour, 250; unionist, 329; constitutional nationalists and independents, 192. Polling for the elections took place on Thursday 13 January; the results were known the next day. Those elected were:

> **North Area:** John Doherty (SF); Michael McGinley (SF); Patrick Porter (SF); Daniel Friel; John McLaughlin (SF); John Murphy (Nationalist).
> **South Area:** Michael McGrath (SF); Trew Colquhoun (Unionist); John O'Donnell (SF); John Porter (SF); William Doherty (SF); R. S. Parke (Unionist).
> **Letterkenny Urban Council:** Dr J. P. McGinley (SF); Charles Kelly (Rate Payers Association – RPA); Edmund McDaid (RPA); John Curran (SF); W. G. McKinney (RPA); William Boyle (SF); J. P. Speer (RPA); John Doherty (Labour); William Gallagher (RPA).[2]

The AGM of the Letterkenny Urban Council was held on Friday 30 January and a letter from Dr J. P. McGinley, who was serving a four month sentence in Derry jail was read to the council. John G. Larkin, town clerk, read the letter to the members present:

HM Prison
Derry
19 January 1920

Dr Mr Larkin,
It is only the other day that I heard of my election to the Urban Council of Letterkenny, which I appreciate very deeply indeed. As, of course, you are aware, my position as MOH [Medical Officer of Health] to the council precludes my accepting the honour conferred on me by the electors. I know it was meant as a protest against my arrest and imprisonment and shows to all whom it may concern the views by the majority of the town's people, and on this account I especially appreciate it. As I do not, of course, intend to sit on the council I am certain they will co-opt in my stead a man who holds the same ideas as myself. In this way only could the electorate by fairly represented and the spirit of proportional representation complied with, a fact which all will no doubt be broadminded enough to recognise. I am especially pleased that at the present time a certain party which I may not mention polled more votes than any other in Letterkenny.

As I cannot write to thank the electors I hope you will be good enough to convey to them my deep appreciation of their action. I also earnestly hope that the administration of the new council may be crowned with success and may open up a brighter outlook for Letterkenny and that their views on matters of national importance will conform to the will of the majority.

I am faithfully yours,
J. P. McGinley

When the letter was read to the council William Boyle moved and John Curran seconded a motion to co-opt Jim Gibbons, chairman of the old council. A document signed by a large number of electors was handed to the clerk by John Doherty and read to the council: 'That an election to the vacant seat on the council be held by ballot in the ordinary way or by a plebiscite as may be arranged by the candidates seeking such election … and we pledge ourselves to co-opt to the council the successful candidates at such ballot or plebiscite.' A heated debate followed and eventually Patrick O'Donnell was co-opted after a vote. William Boyle said the council had made a bad beginning and they had flouted the wishes of the electors, who had returned three Sinn Féiners.[3]

On Saturday 7 February Dr J. P. McGinley, Éamon McDermott and Patrick Shiels were transferred from Derry jail to Mountjoy jail. They were taken in a military lorry to the Great Northern Railway station under heavy escort and as they walked up the platform sang the 'Soldier's Song'.[4] On the same day a number of houses were raided by military and police along the shore of Lough Erne in search of Joseph O'Doherty, TD, who had been on the run since December. The houses searched were that of his father-in-law and their neighbours.[5] O'Doherty was arrested a short time later.

In early February, James Cunningham, a native of Carrick in south Donegal, formed a Volunteer company in Birmingham, England, with the principal duty of procuring arms and ammunition for shipping back to Ireland. Cunningham had joined the IRB while working in Glasgow in 1918. He, along with Patrick O'Neill from Armagh and James O'Brien from Limerick, were elected as officers of the Birmingham Company. In the beginning they were contributing to the arms fund from their own pockets and eventually they began raising funds through collections, dances, lotteries, etc. Their activities met with some success in the early stages and it wasn't long before the 3rd Dublin Battalion sent over its quartermaster, Captain Leo Duffy, to witness the methods used. It was decided that the arms would be sent to Ireland via parcels addressed to a number of established drapery stores, which acted unknowingly as receiving depots.[6]

Meanwhile, back in Donegal on the night of Tuesday 2 March the Derry to Burtonport train reached Kincasslagh Road station shortly after 10 p.m. Up to fifteen Volunteers marched onto the platform, bound the stationmaster and porter with ropes and locked them in the waiting room. Two Volunteers boarded the train, detained the driver and guard while other Volunteers conducted a thorough search of the train. The raid lasted for half an hour, but nothing was removed. Information that the train was conveying ammunition to the police proved to be inaccurate, and the train was allowed to proceed to its destination.[7]

British Prime Minister Lloyd George tabled the Partition Bill in the House of Commons on Friday 5 March and it was stated that a month would elapse before it would be taken up for consideration. The proposal was nothing more than a rehash of the 1914 charter, which had been repealed. The bill sought to establish a parliament for counties Tyrone, Fermanagh, Derry, Armagh, Antrim and Down, with a separate parliament for the remaining twenty-six counties. The proposals were restrictive in many fundamental areas and any decision of either parliament would be subject to the assent of the king at the discretion of a viceroy. The twenty-six counties would have a 'Southern House of Commons', which would consist of 128 members and the northern equivalent, would have fifty-two elected by proportional representation. It was also proposed that Ireland would send forty-eight MPs to Westminster, a number that could not be altered by either of the Irish parliaments.[8]

The Ulster Unionist Council held a meeting in response to the reading of Lloyd George's Partition Bill and declared that the Bill 'may make Irish history'. The decision resolved 'to slam, bar and bolt the door of the six counties against the other twenty-six'. The Unionist Council attached to the permanent isolation of the core of north-east Ulster an importance which had justified, in its eyes, a final breach of its Solemn League and Covenant. Those who had signed the Covenant had pledged to use 'all means which may be found necessary' to oppose the creation of a Home Rule parliament, but even this was preferable to being part of an Ireland ruled by a nationalist parliament in Dublin. According to the members of the council, the unionists of Donegal, Cavan and Monaghan were to be thrown 'into the outer darkness, unwilling victims to the perpetual segregation of the six-county area'.

The council was of the view that if the three excluded counties were to be included that at some future stage the nationalist vote might be large enough to enforce overtures to the southern executive, and that danger the Ulster Unionist Council had resolved to remove at any cost. The council's resolution revealed an insistence on permanent partition.[9]

At a special court in Derry on Monday 8 March, Anthony McGinley, who had been remanded thirteen times, was finally released from custody. The only witness in his case was a police sergeant who had spent over three months in hospital suffering from a leg wound received during the ambush near Dungloe on 12 December 1919. The sergeant subsequently had his leg amputated and was unable to attend court to give evidence. On McGinley's return to Dungloe he was accorded an enthusiastic welcome by the large crowd at Dungloe Road railway station.[10]

The gun-running operations of James Cunningham and the Birmingham Volunteers were attracting the attention of GHQ, and before long a message was received requesting a representative from the Birmingham Company to attend a meeting in Dublin. The purpose of the meeting was to discuss the possibility of developing the Birmingham operation on a larger scale. James Cunningham was introduced to Michael Collins, who questioned him on the possibility of establishing Birmingham as an arms' supply centre. Cunningham, who was given instructions by Collins to further develop the gun-running operation, immediately returned to England where he made contact with Paddy Daly in Liverpool informing him of the new arrangements. Liverpool was the port of departure for all arms and ammunition to Ireland.

On returning to Birmingham, Cunningham arranged to increase the procurement of weapons. He made a number of useful contacts, one being Dan O'Malley, an ex-British soldier of Irish extraction, and Tom Gilmore, a master gunsmith. They soon established a number of arms' dumps, one of which was in the cellar of an all-night restaurant frequented by policemen from the local station. The Volunteers used a back entrance to access the cellar and store weapons while the police drank coffee and talked in the restaurant above them. On one occasion as Dan O'Malley and James Cunningham were returning to the arms' dump with a consignment of weapons they met a policeman on the street. Both men were carrying a number of Lee Enfields concealed in long coats, a considerable weight to carry. Cunningham wanted to make a run for it, but O'Malley said he knew the policeman and told him to 'keep calm, say nothing and I will do the talking'. The policeman and O'Malley had a keen interest in horse racing and discussed that day's racing and tips for the following day, before departing. The Volunteers had to rest for a long time in the cellar that night to recover from the shock and the fatigue from carrying the heavy load.[11]

The RIC in south Donegal were vigorously pursuing the South Donegal TD, P. J. Ward and were raiding various places in the area. On Monday 22 March they raided the house of Ward's aunt, Mary Ferguson, who lived in Dunkineely with her two daughters. During the raid the police subjected them to a two-hour ordeal. Even the postman was searched on his way to the house and the mail addressed to Mrs Ferguson was opened and read.[12]

Over a week later in the early hours of Tuesday 30 March P. J. Ward was arrested at his lodgings in Donegal town, with up to twenty soldiers and a number of police taking part in the arrest operation. Prior to this, Ward's house was raided in Killybegs, during which the police searched every room, including a bedroom where one of Ward's sisters lay ill. This raid was led by a vicious RIC Head Constable named Duffy, who personally ransacked every press, cupboard, drawer and bed from the ground floor to the roof, even going so far as to roughly fling about the vestments of the late Fr Michael P. Ward, the TD's uncle.

Meanwhile at approximately 4 a.m. on the same morning two lorries carrying soldiers from Finner camp accompanied by a large number of police arrived in Dungloe to arrest Joseph Sweeney, TD for West Donegal, who was detained at his father's hotel along with Seamus Kavanagh.[13] The prisoners were first held at Derry jail and after a week transferred to Crumlin Road jail in Belfast. They were taken to the Belfast docks by lorry and in a deliberate act were removed from the lorry where they were attacked by an orange mob who threw nuts, bolts, lumps of coal an other missiles with some prisoners suffering serious injury. Eventually the prisoners were put on a boat to Wales; aboard they were presented with a document stating that they were being interned under the Defence of the Realm Act 1914 (DORA) and that they were suspected of acting or were about to act in a manner prejudicial to the safety of the state. From the time of their arrest the men refused food as a show of solidarity with the prisoners on hunger strike in Mountjoy, and this continued as they were imprisoned in Wormwood Scrubs prison in London.

On their first day at the prison the warders and doctors did not appreciate the seriousness of the situation and couldn't understand why men would refuse food. There was laughing and jeering from the prison staff, but on the second and third day the situation changed. From then on the prison officers became very aggressive towards all republican prisoners and many were mistreated. Due to their weakened state the prisoners were unable to move about and refused to get out of their beds when ordered. They were then aggressively removed from their cells and taken to other parts of the prison. When they were taken from their cells their property was stolen by non-political prisoners with the full knowledge and permission of the prison staff. The bad treatment continued, with the prison staff refusing to supply newspapers and cigarettes to those on hunger strike.

The British government were not prepared for such a large-scale protest and were reluctant to have large numbers of hunger strikers continuing to the death. They adopted the policy of releasing seriously ill prisoners on parole for the purpose of receiving necessary medical treatment under the Prisoners Temporary Release for Ill Health Act 1913. The men on hunger strike at Wormwood Scrubs became progressively weaker and were eventually taken to a hospital in London where they received essential fluids, at which point they called off the strike. However, the British policy was to rearrest the Volunteers as soon as they returned to full health. After more than a week in hospital their health began to improve and they were informed that they were going to be rearrested. At this point the prisoners voted to stage a walkout to prevent rearrest. The prisoners would need assistance from the outside and contact was made with the Self-determination League in London to secure safe houses. They also requested help from Irish people living in London and they arrived at the hospital pretending to visit relatives. On the day of the walkout the London-Irish arrived at the hospital and each prisoner was assigned a guest with whom they simply walked out. A week later funds were organised and all the prisoners made their way back to Ireland.[14]

The Volunteers in Donegal increased their efforts at turning the local population against the RIC, and as part of their campaign published the following proclamation:

> (1) Whereas the spies and traitors known as the Royal Irish Constabulary are holding this country for the enemy and whereas said spies and bloodhounds are conspiring with the enemy to bomb and bayonet and otherwise outrage a peaceful, law-abiding and liberty-loving Irish people.
>
> (2) Whereas we do hereby proclaim and suppress said spies and traitors and do hereby solemnly warn prospective recruits

that they join the RIC at their own peril. All nations are agreed as to the fate of traitors. It has the sanction of God and man.
By Order of GOC,
Irish Republican Army.[15]

At the same time general headquarters issued an order for a one-day strike as a protest against the British military authority's action in forcing Irish railwaymen to carry military personnel and war material for use against the Irish Republican Army. The Irish Labour Party took a leading role in the action. Thomas McShea, O/C of the 1st battalion, south Donegal, received instructions to sabotage trains. He consulted a man who worked at the railway terminus in Bundoran about the most effective way to immobilise the engine. The railway employee recommended the removal of the engine's fire box gates or bars. McShea with two other Volunteers, Owen Gallagher and Joe Meehan, went to the Bundoran terminus at 2 a.m. on the morning of the strike, accompanied by the railway employee. Two young men cleaning an engine in a shed were locked in a store, before the Volunteers removed the fire box from two engines and carried them for about a mile across fields, eventually dumping them in a river. In response to this the railway company closed the station at Bundoran for some time.[16]

The British took measures to strengthen outposts in the county and sent the cruiser *Heather* to Killybegs harbour on Friday 2 April. This was reported to be for the protection of the local coastguard station, which was then guarded by relays of her crew each night. In addition, the RIC began strengthening a number of police barracks throughout the county, using wire entanglements, sand bags and metal shutters on windows.

Some time between 11 and 12 noon on Friday 2 April, a party of Volunteers visited the residence of Mrs Patton, in Knather, less than a mile from Ballyshannon. One of her sons held the office of income tax collector. Two guns were seized and all official income tax material was taken away and thrown into the River Erne. The next day the military discovered the items floating in the river.[17]

In early March, Volunteers in the Donegal brigades were ordered to burn all unoccupied RIC barracks and carry out raids on excise offices; this action was later postponed until the night of Easter Saturday, 3 April, to coincide with the fourth anniversary of the 1916 Rising. That night 160 police barracks throughout the country were either burned or blown up, while about fifty income tax offices were raided and documents destroyed.

One operation involved a party of Volunteers, under Letterkenny battalion O/C Jim Dawson, who moved out to burn Glenswilly RIC barracks. Knowing that it was an all-Ireland operation that had been postponed for such a long period, the Volunteers were nervous, fearing that such a large-scale operation would almost certainly reach the ears of the enemy. However, the attack at Glenswilly was a success, and that night there were over 400 similar operations throughout the country. The British were taken completely by surprise.[18]

In a related incident a party of Volunteers from Derry crossed into Donegal having received information that the barracks in Carrigans was unmanned. A flying column made up of five Derry Volunteers – Joe Doherty, Hugh Morrison, William Mayne, John MacShane and Seamus McCann – travelled to Carrigans, where they cut telephone wires before proceeding to the barracks. The men entered by the back door, sprayed the stairs and the woodwork with paraffin oil and set it alight. Over that weekend barracks at Glencolmcille, Barnesmore, Gweedore, Breenagh, Brockagh, Killeter, County Tyrone, Convoy and Culdaff were burned. Telegraph wires had been cut and in some instances the telegraph poles were blown out of the ground.

The Churchill police sergeant's wife resided in the Breenagh police barracks and when the Volunteers arrived shortly before midnight they allowed sufficient time to remove all personal belongings before torching the building. In the early hours of Easter Sunday morning a party of Volunteers from the Dungloe, Lettermacward, Doochary and Meenacross companies destroyed the unoccupied barracks at Lettermacward and Doochary. The same night the barracks near Gweedore hotel was destroyed by a party of Volunteers of the 2nd battalion assisted by Volunteers from the 1st battalion, No. 1 brigade area of west Donegal.[19]

The barracks in the Glencolmcille area, which had been abandoned just a few days earlier, was also burned and all telegraph wires in the vicinity were cut. The excise office in Buncrana was also targeted, with a party of Volunteers entering the building and destroying all official documents.

The same night Volunteers carried out a raid on the custom and excise office in Donegal town. All records relating to customs and Inland Revenue were taken away and destroyed. Raids were also carried out on the collector of taxes, John Kennedy and on the office of the clerk of petty sessions, Anthony Dunleavy, with all records being removed from their offices.[20]

The disused police barracks at Culdaff was broken into in the early hours of Sunday 4 April by Volunteers and the interior smashed up, rendering it uninhabitable; the barracks at Barnesmore was burned to the ground the same morning.

On Friday night 16 April the vacated police barracks at Leamagowra, six miles from Ardara, was burned. A local farmer had a considerable quantity of oatmeal, turf and straw stored in the building, but these were removed by the Volunteers to an adjoining field and carefully covered with straw.

A party of military accompanied by police raided houses in Buncrana before daybreak the following morning, resulting in the arrests of Joseph McLaughlin and William Cavanagh. Later that night the Doaghbeg barracks, evacuated some time earlier, and Tamney courthouse, both in the Fanad peninsula, were completely destroyed by fire, while Volunteers from the other side of the county burned the Castlecaldwell police barracks situated in County Fermanagh the following night.[21]

Meanwhile the Birmingham gun-running operations were continuing apace with James Cunningham making contact with a man named Sweeney from Tipperary, who was a janitor at a local seminary. The seminary was attached to an officers' training corp (OTC) and Sweeney informed Cunningham that the OTC had an armoury with rifles and ammunition. An ex-British sergeant major kept the keys attached to a leather belt which seldom left his possession. After a while Sweeney noticed that the caretaker of the OTC took off the belt when he slept. When the opportunity arose Sweeney was able to get a wax impression of the key by using a small box of wax supplied by Cunningham; a key was then made from the mould. When the college declared a holiday, the Volunteers quickly arranged to complete the job. They entered the college through an unlocked back gate and removed twenty rifles and approximately 4,000 rounds of ammunition.

This was then safely transported to Dublin via Paddy Daly in Liverpool, to the delight of Michael Collins, who asked Daly to convey his appreciation to the men. On another occasion, with the help of a patriotic priest, Fr O'Connor, Cunningham was able to procure twenty Martini-Henry rifles from a drill hall in the Pottery district of Birmingham. The firing pins had been filed away, but Cunningham arranged to have them replaced by his gunsmith friend, Tom Gilmore.[22]

Back in Donegal the IRA Volunteers at Castlefinn received information that the RIC barracks in the village, which had been occupied at the time of the major operation on Easter Sunday, was to be evacuated on Sunday 18 April and they set about making plans to destroy it. It was situated near a new factory and the owners petitioned the parish priest to speak with the local IRA officers for the barracks to be spared, as its destruction would endanger the factory. An undertaking was given that the barracks would not be burned. The RIC became aware of the undertaking, and on the night of the evacuation some locals noticed a light flickering inside the barracks; this was immediately reported to the local Volunteers who, having forced their way in, found a candle burning under the stairs, which by that time had caught fire. The fire was extinguished and a patrol was then posted to protect the building from any further attempts to burn it. A few days later a large party of British military left Lifford and travelled by lorry to an area near Clady, from where they continued their journey on foot up the Finn Valley railway line to Castlefinn. A man noticed the advancing military and immediately warned the local Volunteers, who withdrew from the village. The military raided a number of houses in the area; they dragged men from their homes and ordered them to paint over anti-British slogans on the walls of the former RIC barracks. The irony was that the men forced to do this were loyalists and were supporters of British rule in Ireland.[23]

The military were now employing more aggressive tactics to arrest suspected members of the IRA. A large convoy of lorries arrived in the Finn Valley and Raphoe areas on Saturday morning, 24 April and a large number of raids were carried out. They arrested John O'Flaherty at his home in Castlefinn and Patrick Kelly was arrested in Killygordon, where several houses were also raided and smashed up. The raids in the Raphoe area failed to produce any arrests.

Over the same weekend Dr J. P. McGinley, Seán Milroy and Éamon McDermott were released from Mountjoy jail. Dr McGinley arrived back in Letterkenny on Tuesday 27 April to be greeted by over a thousand people at the Port Bridge; these included members of the Fianna boy scouts, Volunteers, Cumann na mBan and the Jim Connolly Sinn Féin cumann. With lighted torches the crowd marched towards the town and through the streets to Dr McGinley's residence at Asylum Road (High Road). Addressing the gathering, McGinley dealt with the national question and referred in a touching manner to the treatment meted out to republican prisoners in Mountjoy and Wormwood Scrubs.

Joseph O'Doherty, TD, was released from Derry jail on Saturday 30 April having spent a month on remand. By the beginning of May there were 180 republican prisoners on hunger strike in Wormwood

Scrubs. Of the ten prisoners on hunger strike in Mountjoy, nine were released under the Prisoners Temporary Release for Ill Health Act.[24]

THE REPUBLICAN JUSTICE SYSTEM

AT THE BEGINNING of May instructions were conveyed to all Sinn Féin executives throughout the country to prepare for the establishment of republican arbitration courts in each parish and district to operate independently of the British justice system. A clerk and three justices were to be appointed for each parish and it was decided that all British courts would be prevented from functioning. Magistrates and petty session clerks of the British courts listed within each area were notified of the decision; magistrates were warned not to hold courts and litigants were told not to attend at petty sessions or county courts. All British justices of the peace were called on to resign and Volunteer companies were detailed to employ whatever methods necessary to prevent the attendance of magistrates and litigants at court sessions.

The republican courts comprised a supreme court, district courts and parish courts, with parish courts being presided over by a man or a woman elected by the local Sinn Féin cumann. The republican or Sinn Féin courts were established by decree of Dáil Éireann in June 1920 in an attempt to administer justice fairly and impartially, providing a prompt and inexpensive method of settling disputes. Justices of the Sinn Féin courts were directed to apply the law as it existed on the first sitting of Dáil Éireann on 21 January 1919. They were to apply Brehon, Roman, French and other laws identified as suitable, but not English law.

Brehon Law was the ancient legal code of Ireland and was developed from customs, which had been passed on orally from one generation to another; the legal code was first written down in the seventh century. Most offences and disputes were settled by way of a fine with the most severe punishment being exile or deportation. The penalty of a fine was not solely confined to the status of the offence and related also to the status of the perpetrator. Brehon Law did not contain any reference to capital punishment and was considered progressive, with the recognition of divorce and equal rights between men and women.

It was envisaged that the RIC and British military would actively endeavour to suppress the new institutions, and so republican courts could be held at any place and on an ad hoc basis to deal with individual cases where it was considered unsafe to hold a regular sitting. The raids and arrests of republican justices and registrars necessitated each command area to establish a list of suitable people to form a panel of replacements as this would ensure regular sittings.[25]

With the establishment of the Sinn Féin courts in early June each area had to prepare facilities to hold prisoners and in Donegal the provision of a prison came about sooner than expected. Shortly after the courts were established Dr J. P. McGinley arrived in west Donegal looking for accommodation for a prisoner. Phil Boyle, captain of C company, Meenacross, was asked to provide a temporary prison and the local herring curing station was selected. Known locally as Magherameena prison, the prisoners were held there under armed guard, including some British military captured by the Volunteers. It was never discovered by the British and was used up until 1922.

A British officer, Lieutenant William Lindsay Loutelle, was held at this prison for over six months in 1921. He had arrived in Dungloe in January of that year and was arrested on suspicion of espionage. He was eventually released in July 1921 shortly after the Truce. Lindsay Loutelle returned to the area many years later as a civilian; he was said to have had no complaints about the treatment he received and held the IRA officers and Volunteers in high esteem.[26]

Sir N. Macready was appointed GOC of the British forces in Ireland in January 1920 and by early May the *Daily Herald* in London reported: 'General Macready's plans in Ireland are much on the lines of a re-conquest of the country. Hundreds of block-houses are to be established and strongly garrisoned by troops.'[27]

The pronouncements made by the local councils in the aftermath of the 1916 Rising generally condemned the actions of the leaders. However, with the changes in the political landscape in the succeeding years many of the statements were now being retracted by the new councils, many of which by now had a Sinn Féin majority. At a meeting of the Inishowen District Council on Monday 9 May Councillor McCarron proposed the following: 'That the resolution adopted by the Inishowen Rural District Council at their meeting on 8 May, 1916, as follows – "That we deeply deplore and strongly condemn the action of the Sinn Féin leaders in causing wanton destruction to life and property in Dublin and elsewhere" – be rescinded.' McCarron then addressed the council, stressing how the previous council had condemned the leaders of the Rising as he put it: 'the men who were placed against the walls and shot like dogs. I move the rescinding of the resolution. It was a disgrace to pass it.'[28]

On Wednesday 12 May, Volunteers from the Dungloe Company carried out a raid on the Dungloe excise office, located about 150 yards from the RIC barracks, which was then occupied by about fifteen members. A number of Volunteers were posted to cover the barracks to prevent interference by the RIC, and Denis Houston, Anthony McGinley and Frank O'Donnell entered the office to remove all documents. During the raid Frank O'Donnell found a book written by James Connolly and, despite the urgency of the situation, proceeded to read aloud extracts from the book to his comrades.[29]

On Wednesday 26 May one of the Donegal TDs imprisoned as part of the 'German Plot', Joseph Sweeney, arrived home from England to a rousing welcome. Up to a thousand people gathered from all over west Donegal to greet the TD. On the road between Dungloe and Burtonport he was met by Volunteers, headed by bands and accompanied by members of Cumann na mBan. A public meeting was held at which J. C. Boyle presided. Joseph Sweeney addressed the assembled gathering at Burtonport in a stirring speech, during which he referred to the hardships of the Irish political prisoners whose courage he said, neither cruelty nor prison rigours could subdue.[30]

Another opportunity to further frustrate the British administration in Ireland came with the elections for county councils and rural district councils. The elections for Donegal County Council took place on Wednesday 26 May in the four contested areas, the first time that proportional representation was used. The election was remarkable for the apathy and indifference of the electorate, with less than 50 per cent going to the poll. This was the general experience in Buncrana, Letterkenny and Milford, where there was an exceedingly poor turnout. At one station in Rathmullan only three votes were recorded during the day out of a possible 140, while in another station in the same area the total was six. Keener interest was shown in the Donegal town area, but the total number of invalid votes for the county was 9,193.

The counting of votes started on Thursday and was completed on Saturday with the following results:

> **Buncrana area:** P. H. Doherty (SF); Frank J. Langan (SF); Michael Bonner (SF); James McNally (SF).
> **Letterkenny area:** John O'Flaherty (SF); James McCool (SF); James McFadden (SF); James Clarke (Unionist).
> **Letterkenny Rural area:** N. Kelly (SF); Robert Roulstone (Unionist); J. E. Sweeney (Nationalist); John Mullan (SF); Patrick McGrenra (SF).
> **Milford area:** Thomas McElhinney (SF); Neil Murray (SF); M. A. McCreadie (Nationalist); J. B. O'Donnell (Nationalist); William McGarvey (SF); E. Friel (Nationalist); Christy Lavey (Nationalist).
> **Rathmullan area:** Edward Deeney (Nationalist); James Green (Nationalist); Patrick Loughrey (Nationalist).

Dunkineely area: Patrick Barry (SF); A. F. Gallagher (SF); Charlie Keeny (SF); Thomas McShane (Nationalist).

Donegal town area: James McGahern (SF); John McDermott (SF); John Stevenson (Unionist); Edward Melly (Nationalist); Michael Dunnion (Nationalist).

Mountcharles area: Bernard Friel (SF); Charles McDaid (SF); Paddy Gallagher (SF); James Boyle (SF).

Laghey area: Hugh Gallagher (SF); Daniel Gallagher (SF); James Harron (Unionist); Jacob Gorman (Nationalist); William John Shaw (Unionist).

Dunfanaghy area: Hugh Duffy (SF); C. McLaughlin (SF); Shane McNulty (SF); John McNulty (Nationalist).

The existing members of the councils in the Gweedore/Gortahork, Rosnakill and Fanad areas were returned unopposed.[31] Sinn Féin secured majorities in twenty-nine of the thirty-three county councils and 172 out of 206 rural district councils, with the majority gradually declaring allegiances to Dáil Éireann. The fact that many councillors were also Volunteers and attending regular meetings posed a risk of arrest, delayed the Sinn Féin-led councils from declaring this allegiance. With the people's endorsement of the Dáil as the legitimate government of Ireland and now the local councils, the British administration's response was to withhold revenue generated by local taxes and rates. Dáil Éireann countered by establishing the Dáil loan, which operated in Ireland and America, and to a lesser extent in Britain and France.[32]

The success of the Sinn Féin candidates in the recent local elections brought about a change of policy from local and county councils. Prior to this, British administration through local government was managed by Local Government Boards. A declaration of support was observed at the first sitting of the newly elected Donegal County Council on Friday 18 June. A resolution was passed declaring support for Dáil Éireann, stating:

> That this council as the elected representatives of the County Donegal at a duly convened meeting, hereby acknowledge the authority of Dáil Éireann as the duly elected government of the Irish people and undertakes to give effect to all decrees duly promulgated by the said Dáil Éireann in so far as same affects this council; that copies of this resolution be forwarded to the republican minister for foreign affairs for transmission to the governments of Europe and to the president and chairmen of the Senate and House of Representatives of the USA.[33]

In the days immediately following the elections the Inishowen area council was one of the first to disassociate with the British administration. Trustees were appointed to control and administer the funds and all documents relating to the affairs of the council were carefully hidden. P. H. Doherty was elected on the first count and had sufficient surplus to secure the election of two more Sinn Féin candidates. Doherty was later elected chairman of the district council, but was only able to attend a few meetings as he was forced to go 'on the run'. The British often turned up at council meetings in the hopes of apprehending him there.[34]

On 30 May Volunteers from the Bundoran Company travelled to Ballyshannon to carry out a raid on the customs office in the town. Small parties of Volunteers were posted at strategic points to protect the men carrying out the raid. Staff members were held up and all documents removed without any difficulty. Local loyalists witnessed the raid and immediately contacted the military stationed at Finner camp; before long a large party of soldiers were on their way to the town, where they immediately set up a cordon, with a number of soldiers positioned on the bridge, the only exit by road to Bundoran. A rope was tied across the road which was used to line up members of the public for search and questioning.

Thomas McShea, a member of the raiding party, was anxious about being identified. He walked over to one of the soldiers on the bridge and, acting like a simpleton, said: 'I'll bet I jump that rope.' The soldiers thought they would have a bit of fun with this buffoon; at first they held the rope too high for him, but eventually lowered it to a height he was able to jump. When McShea jumped over the rope, he said: 'Now, am I not a great fellow.' The soldiers admitted that he was, and let him go without question.[35]

On the night of Tuesday 1 June, Volunteers from the Dungloe area arrested two youths on suspicion of theft. They were conveyed to a house several miles away where a parish court was convened. The two were charged with theft of money and goods from various traders in Burtonport. Three Volunteer officers acted as judges while two others as prosecutor and defence. Both accused admitted their guilt and were ordered to make restitution before a certain date; both agreed and were subsequently discharged with a warning that any repeated behaviour would result in a long jail term.[36]

As part of the campaign to undermine British authority in the county a general order was circulated to burn documents in all income tax offices around the county. Some of the Carndonagh Company made preparations to break into the local office, which was situated in a room on the second floor of a house adjacent to the RIC barracks. It was impossible to enter the house from the rear as this meant entry by the barracks yard. The Volunteers noticed that the front window was slightly raised at the bottom and this was selected as the point of entry. Leo Lafferty, the company captain who had been sent to Carndonagh by Michael Collins in early May to organise the area,[37] James Diver, Charlie McLaughlin, Barney Fitzsimons and P. H. Doherty were to carry out the operation. McLaughlin and Fitzsimons were employed in McDonaghs' hardware store and were instructed to bring suitable levers for opening the drawers where the documents were stored. A ladder was procured and when all the RIC had returned to barracks it was considered safe to proceed, as the occupants of the barracks could only see directly in front of the building. When McLaughlin and Fitzsimons arrived they informed the company captain that they had forgotten to bring any lever. Lafferty immediately called off the operation. If Lafferty's plans were upset in the slightest way he was not prepared to alter them and would cancel operations.

As part of the functions of Dáil Éireann IRA Volunteers were instructed to establish a republican police force and to carry out duties in their respective area to contend with the various breaches of the law. On Tuesday night 24 June Volunteers in the Cloghaneely area received information that some people were trying to introduce poitín at a dance in the Irish college. Members of the local company made their way to the college and put sentries at the front door. The O/C stopped the musicians and then addressed the crowd, stating that certain persons who were not from the area intended to distribute poitín during the dance. The Volunteers were directed to the hiding place and surprised the culprits; some escaped, but the leader of the gang and his poitín cache were captured. As this was a first offence the perpetrator was told that he would only suffer confiscation of the poitín, but was warned that any repeat would be treated by court-martial and severely dealt with.[38]

On the same day at a sitting of the Donegal Guardians and District Council a resolution passed in the aftermath of the 1916 Rising was burned. The resolution was similar to many passed at the time condemning the actions of the Volunteers and Citizen Army. The council then passed its own resolution in support of the Sinn Féin courts and Dáil Éireann, which read: 'That where any disputes arise between the board and officials same will be left to the courts recognised by Dáil Éireann.'[39]

In early June the Carrick battalion in the 3rd brigade area south Donegal received information that reinforcements were being sent to strengthen the garrison at the Malinmore signal station, situated at Rossan Point, a headland on the coast. The Volunteers of the Carrick battalion were finalising plans for a raid on the signal station to procure weapons, ammunition and any useful military items before destroying the building. The Carrick battalion set the date of the raid for 27 June and had requested the assistance of neighbouring companies. However, late on the night of Tuesday 8 June, a member of the local battalion informed Éamon O'Boyle, vice-O/C, that a boat was to land at Teelin the following day with reinforcements. O'Boyle was faced with a dilemma; he had only a small number of men and weapons at his disposal, but nonetheless a decision was made to carry out the raid that night. Due to the short notice, Éamon O'Boyle could only gather four Volunteers to carry out the mission. The five men approached the station that night armed with a shotgun, an ancient revolver and a bundle of hay. However, the Volunteer with the hay could not acquire any paraffin to ignite it, but was assured that the British government would provide that. As they approached the signal station they heard one of the coastguards walking along the path and were forced to take cover and wait for him to pass. One Volunteer was sent back down the path to keep an eye out for his return. The others continued; one Volunteer stayed at the gate, armed with a shotgun, to cover the other three Volunteers' retreat. The door of the station was closed and the windows protected with heavy shutters. The building looked uninhabited but for a light from a window facing seaward. Éamon O'Boyle knocked on the door with a claw hammer and called on those inside to surrender in the name of the Republic. He received no reply and again hit the door with the hammer and shouted that the place was surrounded. There was a sudden crash from inside as one of the coastguards fell over a bucket.

One of the occupants opened the door and, on being told that the place was surrounded by eighty men, replied: 'All right. Are you Sinn Féiners? We have no ill-will towards Sinn Féiners.' The garrison of three were then marched out and ordered out to the gate where they were covered by the Volunteer on duty there. The other Volunteers then removed a large supply of rifles, revolvers and ammunition and found a two-gallon tin of paraffin. The hay, and other items, were stacked, doused in paraffin and set alight. The prisoners were released and told to go to the coastguard station with a password should they meet any of the imaginary eighty men on the road. The local telephone wires were then cut and the raiding party withdrew from the area as the blazing building lit up the night sky.[40]

Meanwhile members of the No. 4 brigade laid plans to destroy the unoccupied RIC barracks at Pettigo as at that time Pettigo was a strong pro-British town. The local loyalists had declared that if any attempt was made to interfere with the barracks there, they would employ armed resistance. On Tuesday 1 July the officers of No. 4 brigade decided to call the loyalists' bluff and ordered that the barracks be destroyed. The family of the former sergeant in charge, Sergeant Andrews, was living in the building at the time. Volunteers of the South Donegal brigade travelled to Pettigo and on arrival could hear the local Orange band playing, but did not see where they were located. Arriving at the barracks they found the sergeant's wife and family, who they moved to Brennans' hotel. They then removed anything of value belonging to the family and set the building on fire. The local butcher shop, located next door to the barracks, was also damaged by the fire and the smell of roast beef gave out an appetising aroma.

Sergeant Andrews later applied to the county court at Ballyshannon for a claim under the Malicious Injuries Code and was awarded compensation. In his evidence he alleged that his family had been ill-treated by the Volunteers. This was perjury in the eyes of the brigade adjutant, Liam O'Duffy, and he decided to clarify the issue by writing a letter to the local paper, the *Donegal Vindicator*. Within days of the letter being published the military authorities in the area seized the newspaper offices and removed the metal type.[41]

The destruction of Mullaghmore Castle was the next operation of the South Donegal brigade. Willie Gilmartin, O/C Cliffoney Company, called a meeting with members of the Bundoran Company in Peter Finlay's house, known as 'The Rock' just outside

Bundoran. Gilmartin had information that Mullaghmore Castle was to be occupied by a company of British military. The meeting was not long in session when a sentry rushed in to say that two lorryloads of British troops were approaching. The Volunteers separated and escaped, with the exception of James Brennan, the Bundoran Company intelligence officer. This worried the Volunteers and the plan to destroy Mullaghmore Castle was dropped. The raid was unexpected and naturally the Volunteers believed someone had informed the British, but subsequent enquiries failed to uncover any information.

It was decided that the coastguard station at Mullaghmore would be targeted as an alternative. The station was occupied by one coastguard and on the night of the operation he refused to open the door when ordered to do so. The Volunteers eventually forced their way into the building and set it alight. However, this attempt was not successful as only part of the building was destroyed, so the Volunteers decided to return to Mullaghmore the following day to complete the task. On arrival they found a police guard and also a large crowd of sightseers surveying the damage. Thomas McShea approached the policeman and engaged him in conversation, condemning the action of the people who had set fire to the station. At that time there was a strict boycott of the police and anyone seen talking to them was liable to be punished. While McShea was conversing with the policeman the other Volunteers removed cans of petrol from nearby parked cars. They then set fire to the building before driving away. This time the building was completely destroyed.[42]

The seizure of post destined for the military and RIC proved to be very useful to the local brigade areas and documents captured in one of the raids in west Donegal contained details of the British plans to put a garrison into the old Rutland barracks situated between Dungloe and Burtonport in the townland of Meenmore. The building was then a summer residence of the Maudes, a landlord family living in Clondalkin, County Dublin. The occupation of the building by British military would have created problems and interfered greatly with the work of the local Volunteers, so the building was subsequently destroyed on the night of Monday, 5 July.

To counter the development of IRA Volunteers policing their command areas a directive was issued by Dublin Castle on Tuesday 6 July ordering all RIC divisions to arrest any members of the IRA found to be operating as a police force.

The campaign of suppressing British administration was in the most part adhered to by the general public, with the result that the local Volunteers were called upon to carry out various tasks in addition to their usual military duties. These ranged from community work and civic policing to executing the findings of the republican courts. In early June Volunteers from Dungloe and Letterkenny were called upon to convey patients to the psychiatric hospital in Letterkenny, then called the County Asylum. Volunteers in the Glenswilly area received a report that a man there was constantly under the influence of alcohol, and was very abusive to his wife and family, causing damage to their home. He was subsequently arrested, brought before the republican court and found guilty of the charges. The Volunteers later conveyed him to an unknown destination to undergo a period of imprisonment with hard labour. This usually meant being put to work on a farm or other jobs in the local community. The man was also given a warning by the court that if he did not amend his lifestyle and provide for his family he would be served with a deportation order.[43]

The second sitting of Dungloe Sinn Féin court was held in the parochial hall on Thursday 8 July. The hall was filled with litigants and spectators. There were twelve cases listed, all of which were satisfactorily disposed of within a space of three hours.[44]

The British military and police continued to raid for Volunteers, and in the early hours of Friday 9 July, in Killybegs, a party of twenty British soldiers were drafted in from Finner Camp and nine of the local police raided the premises of Sarah Brady, Killybegs in search of her son Hugh, who not at home. A thorough search of the house was carried out, but nothing of a seditious nature was found.

The Volunteers were not the only targets of the RIC. Three American tourists had been visiting relatives in the Dungloe area since early July. They were walking through Dungloe village one evening and were stopped by the notorious RIC sergeant John Mooney, who was well known for his reputation as a thug and was always abusive to the locals. He struck one of the American tourists with the butt of his rifle, causing serious injury to his jaw. The incident was reported to the local IRA and Volunteers were instructed to deal with the troublesome sergeant. The Volunteers decided to ambush Mooney on his return from the post office on Saturday 10 July. The sergeant was accompanied by a constable and they were returning to the barracks with the mail when two Volunteers, concealed in an unoccupied house, opened fire.

The sergeant was hit and fell to the ground while the constable ran for the nearest open door. Mooney received serious injuries and was removed to the county hospital at Lifford where he was confined for a long time. The news of Mooney's plight was met with delight by the local population.[45]

The following week, on Wednesday morning 14 July, a detachment of military arrived in Dungloe and commandeered the parochial hall, the location of the Irish Summer College. The summer college was due to commence at 11 a.m. that morning, forcing the organisers to secure another venue.

At 12.30 that afternoon the mail car travelling from Fintown to Dungloe, was held up by four Volunteers and the driver was ordered to retreat a certain distance, at which point the mailbags were searched. All correspondence relating to the RIC were removed and the mailbags returned. When the driver reached Dungloe the incident was reported and a party of military was despatched to the scene, but no trace of the Volunteers could be found.[46]

Also on Wednesday 14 July, Joseph O'Doherty, TD for North Donegal, was brought before a special court in Derry, having been arrested again on 21 June and charged with having on 18 October 1919 solicited subscriptions for the Dáil Éireann loan. O'Doherty's father, brother and sister were present in the court. The three men would not remove their hats and ignored a request by the magistrate to do so. A policeman was ordered to remove their hats, but the case was unable to proceed as one of the witnesses failed to attend due to illness. A request was made to have O'Doherty remanded to the petty sessions at Buncrana, where he was asked by the magistrate if he had any questions. O'Doherty replied: 'No, I don't recognise your authority at all.' He was remanded to return to Buncrana court on Thursday 22 July.[47] The Volunteers in Buncrana were informed that O'Doherty was to be tried at Buncrana court and the building was subsequently burned. In anticipation of the case being heard at the Burnfoot courthouse, this was also destroyed.

On the evening of Thursday 15 July, the goods train from Derry to Burtonport was held up at Crolly Bridge by a party of up to twenty Volunteers. The driver and fireman were ordered off the train and the Volunteers conducted a thorough search of the carriages for supplies destined for troops stationed at Dungloe. The train was held for an hour and all supplies were thrown into a nearby field. A mixed party of police and military had travelled to Dungloe station to collect the supplies and as they returned empty-handed found the road blocked. A barricade had been erected with the remains of their supplies which were smashed and strewn all over the road. On the same day four Volunteers seized the mailbags at Burtonport and all correspondence relating to the RIC was removed, with the ordinary mail being later returned.

On Friday morning the engine men and guard of the 11.45 a.m. train refused to allow a party of military to travel from Carndonagh to Derry, and stopped the train at Clonmany. The military alighted and the train proceeded, only to be boarded again by military at

Buncrana. Military personnel then boarded the 4 p.m. mail train at Clonmany and this time the train was held for an hour and a half. During this time locals brought tea and food to the guard and engine men. When this train arrived at Buncrana the 11.45 a.m. service was still held up there with the military occupying the seats.[48]

The Sinn Féin arbitration courts were by now well established and were functioning on a regular basis. Orders were given to destroy courthouses to prevent British courts being held in the county. There was little difficulty in persuading litigants to take their cases before the Sinn Féin courts and in the majority of cases the parties were satisfied with the outcome. In one case, however, an old man decided to take his case to the county court in Letterkenny. Volunteers from the Inishowen area decided kidnap him, to prevent him appearing at Letterkenny. On arrival at his home they found an old man looking extremely frail and so decided to make him swear, on his knees, that he would not attend the court. Frail as the old man looked, he attended at the court in Letterkenny the following day and told the judge the story about the raid and the threats. The Volunteers decided to be less soft-hearted in the future.[49]

To help the men who resigned from the RIC, Sinn Féin instructed all local areas to select a deputation to approach such people and assist them and their families in any way possible. The directive stated:

> Every effort should be made to get employment for RIC men who have already resigned. In cases where emigration is unavoidable, Irish organisations in the United States have already expressed their desire to help ex-policemen from Ireland and to secure them employment as soon as they land in America. Sinn Féin is also in favour of local government bodies passing resolutions commending the policemen who had resigned.[50]

The British were aware of the situation concerning the RIC and had even considered dissolving the force following reports of a complete erosion of morale in southern and eastern counties. The authorities considered a number of options to suppress the advancing actions of the Volunteers and the continued demoralisation of the RIC.

The introduction of a new force was considered in early May and by late July the Auxiliary division of the RIC was deployed in Ireland. This new force took on a role quite similar to that of the Black and Tans, with little regard for discipline or the code of war. It acted independently of the RIC or military, creating some disquiet among those ranks.[51]

The policy of destroying all court houses in the county continued. The Carndonagh courthouse was the next target and was destroyed by fire in the early hours of Tuesday morning 20 July. The Carndonagh Company were acting on information that the trial of Joseph O'Doherty was to take place there later in the week. O'Doherty, who was TD for North Donegal, had been charged with soliciting subscriptions for the Dáil Éireann loan and had been arrested on 21 June at Enniskillen after many fruitless attempts to arrest him by the military.

The campaign of suppressing the British legal system continued with the courthouse at Malin being burned to the ground in the early hours of Thursday 22 July. Later that day at a special court in Derry Joseph O'Doherty, TD, was again remanded. Since his arrest four courthouses in Inishowen had been burned to prevent the holding of crimes courts in the area. The magistrate informed O'Doherty that the burning of the Buncrana courthouse was the reason for his further remand. He asked O'Doherty if he had anything to say, to which the TD replied: 'I don't recognise your authority. I look upon this as an unlawful assembly and I have no intention of taking part in it.'[52] While the old legal system was experiencing problems, the development of the new Irish legal system continued with the third sitting of the republican court at

Dungloe on the same day. Two cases of assault were heard and fines of 10*s* were handed down to each of the defendants. There was also an equity suit, which was adjourned for six months pending the attendance of an essential witness who resided in Scotland, while a right of way case at Glasbeggan was also dealt with. The republican justice system was having the desired effect; the monthly petty sessions of the English court was due to be held in Dungloe on the same day but was quickly adjourned as there were no cases scheduled to be heard before it.[53]

A General Headquarters directive called for an increase in raids for mail travelling by road or rail. The mail destined for the local police, military, magistrates and loyalists would be removed as it usually yielded valuable information.[54] An example of the valuable information was a document with instructions to the military on the subject of overcoming road cuttings and how to get vehicles through the damaged sections with the use of iron girders. This allowed the Volunteers to improve their methods of road cuttings and the different ways of disguising the trenched portions of the road. On Tuesday 20 July, the early morning train to Donegal town was stopped at Barnesmore railway station by a party of Volunteers. The guard was held at the side of the track while the mailbags were removed.

Later that evening the 5 p.m. Derry to Burtonport train was raided at Churchill station by eight Volunteers from the Letterkenny Company. The engine driver, fireman, guard, stationmaster and other officials were taken to the waiting room and held under armed guard. Supplies destined for the military at Dungloe were either thrown away or destroyed. The petrol supplies were placed on a waiting car and driven away.[55]

On the morning of Monday 26 July, the train from Strabane to Letterkenny was held up for two hours owing to the presence of armed police in one of the carriages. Four members of staff were dismissed for refusing to obey orders. Later that evening a party of

Volunteers took part in an ambush on an RIC patrol between Kilcar and Killybegs. The RIC were returning from the fair at Kilcar when the ambush party, consisting of up to twenty Volunteers, opened fire on them; a sergeant was seriously wounded and a number of constables received minor injuries. The following night the courthouse at Churchill was broken into and all law books and legal documents burned. The building was preserved as the upper storey had been used as a National school.[56]

In late July it was announced that the Derry to Letterkenny train service was to be suspended at the end of the month due to passengers refusing to travel or staff refusing to work on trains conveying armed forces of the crown. Local members of the National Union of Railways (NUR) held a meeting on Tuesday 27 July and passed the following resolution:

> That we, the representatives of the majority of the employees of the Lough Swilly railway, at this specially convened meeting, wish it to be clearly understood that under no circumstances will we convey or assist in the conveyance of armed military or police to be utilised for the destruction of our fellow countrymen. We absolutely and emphatically refuse to be parties to the creation of a second Amritzar, and we pledge ourselves to support by every means in our power our colleagues who have already been suspended for advocating this principle.[57]

Traders and merchants in west Donegal joined in the boycott of unionist wholesalers in support of the campaign against mistreatment of Catholics in Lisburn, Banbridge, Belfast and other towns in the six counties. Sales representatives of these firms had been previously warned off in response to the plight of Catholics living in areas of Banbridge, Lisburn and Belfast. The violence escalated following the assassinations of two senior RIC officers, one of whom had been implicated in the murder of Tomás MacCurtain in Cork.

As a consequence of the Belfast Boycott, initiated in January 1920 in accordance with a decree of the Dáil, a Belfast commercial salesman was handed a document while doing business in Ballyshannon on Friday 30 July and told to pass it on to other salesmen:

> To representatives of Belfast unionist firms – you are hereby ordered to leave this area within twenty-four hours and no return by you or members of your firm will be permitted until the unionist population of Belfast learns that fair play and tolerance which have always characterised the people of the county of Donegal are also necessary virtues to that city.
> By Order – Competent Military Authority.

Subsequently the salesman was given two hours to leave town. An order was also issued to boycott Belfast unionist firms until the nationalists recently sacked from the shipyards were reinstated. Protestant shopkeepers in Ballyshannon were asked to sign a petition condemning the action of unionists against the Catholic population in Belfast. On their refusal pickets were placed outside their premises and Catholics were prevented from shopping at their businesses.

The general population continued to ignore the authority of the British administration, instead recognising the authority of Dáil Éireann. An example of this was an application submitted to the Sinn Féin court in Letterkenny by J. Wilkinson, hackney driver, to the commandant of the Letterkenny Volunteers. The request, which was granted, was for a permit to drive a resident magistrate to petty sessions courts in the district. The Volunteers knew the hackney driver would be getting paid for pleasure drives as few cases were being heard due to the increased support of the Sinn Féin courts. Another application was made by a Belfast man who travelled to the county on an annual basis for the purposes of shooting duck. He was granted permission to carry guns for that purpose by the Letterkenny Volunteer Authority.[58]

1920 - The Guerrilla Soldiers and the Donegal Gun-runner

The British government, seeing that every aspect of its authority in Ireland was being undermined, believed that the staunchly Catholic population would only respond to a denounciation of the republican cause from the Pope himself. Consequently the British foreign secretary, Balfour, was sent to Rome on Sunday 1 August to put two questions to the Pope:

(1) Would the pope denounce all incitements to disturbance in Ireland?
(2) Would he personally appoint to vacant bishoprics instead of leaving the choice to the diocesan clergy?

The reply from the Vatican the following day was 'no' on both counts. Negotiations on the matter were subsequently dropped, with the British stating: 'That the pope should remain neutral is the best that can be hoped.'[59]

Meanwhile in Donegal the Volunteers were kept busy with incidents of civil disorder, and the Buncrana Company was called upon to deal with alcohol-related disorderly behaviour in the town. On Monday 2 August Volunteers arrested an intoxicated man who was smashing the windows of a public house. They detained him until the affects of alcohol had passed. The Volunteers took no further action having learned that the publican had served the man alcohol the entire day and then ejected him when he was heavily intoxicated. Later that day four young Derry men were arrested by the Volunteers for behaving in a disorderly manner and smashing the windows of another public house. They were tried at a republican court, fined 50*s* and ordered to leave Buncrana and not return for at least six months. Later that night the recently burned courthouses at Buncrana and Burnfoot were decorated with some humorous graffiti, including 'RIC Café', 'Ruins of the British Empire', 'No Magistrates Wanted Here' and 'Work of the IRA'.

The following day two young Buncrana men, William Doherty

153

and Patrick Fletcher, were shot at as they walked through the grounds of the Castle estate near the town. Both received pellet wounds to the face and were greatly shaken by the incident, which they reported to the local IRA. Volunteers carried out an investigation and arrested the estate caretaker, Berkely Crowe, an ex-British soldier, as he walked through the town. Crowe was driven to a house outside the town where a republican court was quickly convened. Berkely Crowe gave evidence that in the previous two weeks a number of poachers had been operating in the grounds of the estate and when he came across the two young men walking through the grounds he had mistaken them for the poachers. Based on this evidence, Crowe was acquitted of all charges; he thanked the republican justices and Volunteers for their kindness and fairness.

The Glenties republican court was formally opened on Wednesday 4 August; its president, Daniel Mulhern, set out in detail the objectives of the court, declaring that under the English administration, which had now ceased to exist in Ireland, law was an expensive luxury. He said all the people had the right to demand, and would be given, at no cost, the protection of the republican courts against evildoers so long as they remained loyal citizens of the Republic. As there was no business before the court at its first sitting the president called on anyone who had claims or disputes to lodge them with the registrar before the second sitting.

The Killygordon republican court was also held on Wednesday 4 August and Patrick McGlinchey was fined 7s 6d for assaulting John McCullough, a Protestant farmer from Gleneely. The defendant pleaded guilty and said he was drunk on that occasion. He was cautioned by the court and told to be careful in future as he faced the threat of two months' imprisonment.

Following a stabbing incident at Ardaghey in the same week two young men were arrested by the IRA and brought before a republican court. Two others suspected of involvement evaded arrest by leaving the area and it was reported that they had left the country. The two accused were remanded on bail to appear at the next sitting of the court.

A young man was brought before the republican court in Bundoran charged with being under the influence of alcohol and causing trouble while on a visit to the town. He was fined £1 and told to leave the town immediately. Another visitor was also brought before the same court and ordered to leave within the next hour after he refused to drive the local priest on a sick call.[60]

In the same week magistrates living in the Buncrana area received letters purporting to come from 'GOC IRA – North West District' requesting them to resign their commissions immediately, adding that in the event of ignoring the request they would have to suffer the consequences. The Volunteers were informed about the letters and following a thorough investigation identified the author, an individual living outside the county. In an unrelated incident a number of magistrates refused to attend the petty sessions at Carndonagh and Milford, preventing the courts from sitting.

The RIC, acting on information from an informant, raided the house of Miss Byrne, Navenny Street, Ballybofey, early on Thursday 5 August. They carried out an extensive search and ransacked the house. They had been informed that the house was to have been used as the base for an attack on an RIC patrol the previous evening, but the patrol failed to pass the house, so the attack had not happened.

That evening a party of Volunteers from Ballintra ordered all residents not to use lights in their houses when darkness fell. The Volunteers arrived back in the village after dark and made their way to the recently abandoned police barracks, which was being used as a store by a local merchant. The Volunteers removed all the bran, flour, meal, etc. to a safe place before burning the building to the ground.

The raiding for mail on the Donegal railways certainly proved to be very beneficial to the activities, and for the safety, of the Volunteers. The mail raids presented the Volunteers with valuable information on those targeted for arrest and the intended movements and plans of the British military in the county. Some of the information captured was in code and all coded communications were sent to GHQ in Dublin to be deciphered by the spies in Dublin Castle.

One example of this was when a despatch arrived from GHQ stating that Eamon Donnelly, a Volunteer from County Tyrone and serving with a Donegal brigade, was being targeted for arrest. The timely warning gave Donnelly an opportunity to move to another area of the county and evade arrest. Another example was observed when the Carrick Company received information from GHQ in Dublin that a vacant hotel in that area was to be taken over by a detachment of military. The hotel in question was under the ownership of the local landlord and had often been frequented by English people visiting the area for fishing trips. On Thursday night the Carrick Volunteers moved all furniture and other valuables to a nearby store before setting the building on fire, and as a precaution the local police barracks was also burned to the ground.[61]

The following day attention switched to west Donegal when Frank O'Donnell received information that an RIC cycle patrol from Falcarragh was expected in the Gortahork area to patrol the village during the fair that day. Captain Frank O'Donnell immediately organised an ambush party which consisted of Dan Sweeney, Dan Walsh, Jeff O'Donnell, Willie Sharkey, James McGee, John McCole, Michael Walsh and a Volunteer from County Tyrone called Ray McSorley.

A number of the Volunteers were issued with shotguns and detailed to take up positions at some of the stalls while the remainder armed with revolvers were instructed to walk around the town. The RIC cycled into the village at approximately 11.30 a.m. and began walking up the street. The company captain, Frank O'Donnell, gave a pre-arranged signal by pulling his handkerchief out and blowing his nose. With that the Volunteers moved into action. One of the RIC noticed the Volunteers with the shotguns and drew his revolver. Volunteer McSorley immediately fired, hitting the policeman on the wrist. The other members of the patrol immediately surrendered without resisting and were relieved of their caps, tunics, belts, weapons, ammunition and bicycles. They were then ordered to walk back to Falcarragh.

Frank O'Donnell had developed a good reputation for disarming the police and had held up and disarmed Sergeant Cafferty on three separate occasions. On the fourth occasion Cafferty was unarmed. When O'Donnell asked why he was unarmed the sergeant said that his superior officer refused to issue him with a weapon following the last seizure, so the Volunteers decided to relieve him of his bicycle instead.[62]

The campaign against the administration of British justice continued with the courthouse at Donegal town being burned in the early hours of Saturday morning 7 August. The Volunteers gained access by knocking on the door, which was opened by the caretaker. They first ensured that the caretaker, his wife and children were safely removed and were placed in a house nearby. The Volunteers then removed the caretaker's furniture and personal belongings before burning the building. The RIC barracks were situated close by and was covered by two Volunteers, but during the operation the police remained in their quarters.[63]

On Sunday night 8 August a general raid for arms was carried out in the No. 1 brigade area. Frank O'Donnell and Patrick Breslin with a number of other Volunteers visited all the houses in the townland of Toberkeen and collected a large quantity of shotguns, revolvers, rifles and ammunition. A few days later Captain Frank O'Donnell led another party of Volunteers in an ambush on an RIC patrol; the police were held up on the outskirts of Burtonport but had enough time to turn their bicycles and escape. Willie Sharkey, then only seventeen years old, hopped on his own bicycle and pursued the two RIC, shooting at them until his ammunition ran out. Three days later another RIC cycle patrol was ambushed by the same party of Volunteers led by Frank O'Donnell, this time at Falcarragh. During this incident a shot was fired, wounding one of the RIC, and they were then relieved of their weapons, ammunition and bicycles.[64]

The Inishowen Volunteers were kept busy with policing duties and carried out a raid on a party of poitín stillers a few miles outside Carndonagh on the night of Saturday 14 August. The still was in full working order at the time of the raid and approximately five gallons had been run through. Having destroyed a quantity of wash, the Volunteers brought the still head and worm to Carndonagh, where it was exhibited outside the grounds of the chapel the following day as a deterrent to others.

Also on Saturday an elderly man was assaulted and robbed of £4 19s 6d on his way home from the fair in Letterkenny. The RIC were notified, but no effort was made to investigate the incident, and on hearing of the assault and robbery the local Volunteers conducted an investigation resulting in an arrest of an ex-soldier the following day. He was taken away by car and brought before a republican court in the Churchill area on Sunday evening. The elderly man identified the prisoner as the person who assaulted and robbed him but declined to give sworn testimony and so the prisoner was discharged. The prisoner expressed his gratitude for the treatment he received while in custody.

The following night the Mountcharles Company carried out an attack on the local RIC barracks, which was garrisoned by a sergeant and five constables. The barracks was part of a terrace of houses and the Volunteers occupied positions at the front and rear of the building. This attack was intended as a supporting operation to a major offensive against the barracks in Donegal town. The Mountcharles Volunteers opened fire on the barracks and after the first volley called on the police to surrender, but the RIC responded with a volley of shots. A battle ensued for a short time before the Volunteers called off the attack. The plan to attack the barracks at Donegal town, which was to be a large-scale operation, was abandoned as many of the Volunteers failed to show up at the appointed time.

Further support for the Sinn Féin courts was observed later that week when four Donegal magistrates – Michael O'Callaghan, Letterkenny, James Campbell, Anthony McElwee and Patrick McGettigan, Milford – resigned as commissioners of the peace.[65]

The Volunteers of the 3rd battalion at Ardara in the No. 3 brigade area ambushed an RIC patrol early on Tuesday 17 August. All four members of the patrol were injured, two seriously. That night the post office in Dunfanaghy was raided by Volunteers, who removed telegraph, telephone and wireless instruments.

Meanwhile on the same night members of the 1st, 2nd and 3rd battalions of the No. 1 brigade prepared for a similar raid on the village of Falcarragh to remove the wireless telegraph equipment from the local post office. They gathered in Dungloe at 9.30 p.m. that night and paraded through the town, before setting off for Falcarragh, a distance of over twenty miles, arriving at midnight. Patrick Breslin was in charge of the section detailed to cover the RIC barracks and these positions were maintained for about two hours until the operation at the post office was complete. The raiding party succeeded in removing all equipment and returned safely to Dungloe.[66] The equipment was used to set up a communications network to improve communications between the different areas. The Volunteers were also able to tap police phone wires with this equipment.

The Volunteers from the 3rd battalion at Ardara remained active and carried out another ambush on a party of four RIC in Ardara on Wednesday 18 August. The RIC patrol was passing the chapel when Volunteers opened fire with shotguns; two RIC officers were injured. On the same day Frank O'Donnell's unit continued to procure arms and ambushed a party of three RIC and a Black and Tan member at the Rampart, Dungloe. Two more RIC men were disarmed near Burtonport later that day, all without a shot being fired.

Another justice of the peace resigned his commission in support of the Sinn Féin courts. John Gallen, Donegal town, in his resignation to the lord chancellor, said:

In view of the fact that your government by its actions and declarations of responsible ministers has declared war upon the Irish nation and at the present time is engaged in a campaign of savage oppression and sabotage against my countrymen, I can no longer be associated even in the smallest way with such a regime of terror and I hereby resign my commission as a justice of the peace.

On Thursday morning, 19 August, Volunteers from Falcarragh seized mailbags from a man conveying them through the town on a horse and cart. Later that day in Buncrana soldiers passing through the Main Street were held up by a number of Volunteers and relieved of their weapons and ammunition. There were a number of people on the street at the time, but such was the speed and efficiency of the Volunteers that the task was completed before they realised what was happening. The Thursday morning train from Derry arrived at Buncrana about eight o'clock and five mailbags were transferred to the post office cart, destined for the naval authorities and military at Buncrana. As the two men were taking the mail back to the post office three Volunteers jumped out of a car and pointed their revolvers at the two men. They immediately transferred four of the mailbags from the handcart to the car and made off in the direction of the Derry road. When the train from which the mail had been taken passed Drumfries station, five miles further along the line, it was held up by eighteen Volunteers. They seized the rest of the mail, took possession of a number of letters destined for the RIC, and left the scene.

On the same day two RIC men were disarmed at Milltown near Inver in south Donegal. The Volunteers of south Donegal also had to contend with a case of theft. A bicycle belonging to a young man in Donegal town was stolen and the matter was reported to the Volunteers. An arrest was made and a man was brought before a republican court where he pleaded guilty and was ordered to pay 25*s*.

The accused acknowledged the justice and impartiality of the court and the bicycle was returned to its owner later that day.[67]

A very interesting letter appeared in the *Derry Sentinal*, a predominantly unionist newspaper, praising the efforts and good work of Volunteers in the quelling of poitín production in the Inishowen area. The letter, later published in the *Derry Journal*, stated: 'I am a unionist but have no hesitation in declaring that Sinn Féin has done more in the past three months to stop the deadly industry than the police have been able to do in the last twenty years.'[68]

FIRST DAYLIGHT ARMS RAID

IN MID-AUGUST SAMUEL O'Flaherty, No. 4 brigade O/C, summoned a meeting of the brigade staff at Castlefinn and informed them that a constable named Johnston, who he described as honest and friendly, had approached him with information while home on leave in Killygordon. He informed O'Flaherty that the RIC garrison in Drumquinn, County Tyrone, were heavy drinkers and the barracks would be easily captured. He said there were two sergeants and eight constables manning the barracks and most of them could usually be picked up in licensed premises in the town. While discussing the plan for the attack, Dr J. P. McGinley suggested a daylight raid. The reasons for this were the unfavourable location of the barracks, less chance of confusion among the Volunteers, and a better opportunity of rushing the barracks. After some discussion it was agreed that it would be carried out in daylight and the date was set for 26 August, a fair day, which would ensure the Volunteers could move freely through the town without arousing too much attention. The raiding party was to be made up of officers and men from companies in Letterkenny, Castlefinn, Clady and Ballybofey companies.[69]

In the early hours of the morning of Thursday 26 August, the planned attack on Drumquinn barracks was set in motion, with

161

the Letterkenny Volunteers commandeering four cars in the town and surrounding areas to convey the raiding party to Drumquinn. They had painted Monaghan number plates and placed them over the original plates before setting off from Letterkenny. They picked up Volunteers at different points along the road, with a fifth car joining them at Castlefinn, and before long there were twenty-five Volunteers in total, with five in each car. The raiding party were instructed to travel to a point near Drumquinn where final instructions would be issued. The five cars reached the designated point without incident and discussed the outline of the plan before entering the town. The Volunteer instructions were:

- Move into the town under the pretext of buying cattle and scout the town for RIC men.
- Work in pairs to keep in close contact with each other.
- The main attacking party was to work its way to a point beside the barracks, so as to be in a position to rush it on a given signal.
- Some men were detailed to cut the telephone wires.
- Another party was detailed to move through the town in pairs to locate, hold and disarm any RIC they encountered.

On arrival Hugh McGrath cut the telephone wires while Anthony Dawson and Michael Doherty scouted the town to ascertain the location of the RIC men. Having found some of them in licensed premises the two Volunteers immediately reported to the rest of the party. The RIC men were then disarmed and taken to a secure area and were held there by two Volunteers. The Drumquinn RIC barracks was a two storey building located on the main street of the village. The next part of the plan was to collect a drove of cattle and drive them in the direction of the barracks. Other Volunteers were waiting in the vicinity of the barracks under the pretext of buying the cattle, so they could get all Volunteers right up to the required positions. Two Volunteers, James Curran from East Tyrone and James McMonagle from Letterkenny, were detailed to take up a position at a garden seat located beside the barracks door. When the remainder of the Volunteers were in position it was decided that the two Volunteers would knock at the barracks door and ask for the address of a local cattle buyer; when the door was opened the other Volunteers would then rush the guard.

This plan was never put to the test, however. The commotion caused by the Volunteers with a large herd of cattle pretending to make a bargain was apparently responsible for bringing an armed constable to the front door to investigate. On seeing this, brigade O/C Sam O'Flaherty give the signal, which was lowering his newspaper and placing it in his pocket; James McMonagle immediately drew his revolver and called on the constable to put up his hands. He first complied with the order, but in an instant dropped his hands and reached for his revolver. He was in the act of drawing his revolver when McMonagle fired a shot, hitting him in the forehead; he slumped down across the doorway and died almost instantly. The Volunteers leaped over him and dashed into the day-room as Dr McGinley knelt over the RIC man at the door to administer first aid. At the same time James McMonagle saw an RIC sergeant at the top of the stairs aiming his rifle at Dr McGinley's back and he fired two shots at the sergeant, who tumbled down the stairs. The Volunteers rushed the stairs and found three constables in a room. One of them apparently made an effort to escape through a skylight, but got stuck and the Volunteers left him there. They then collected all the arms and ammunition, which comprised twelve revolvers, twelve Lee Enfield rifles and a quantity of ammunition. They had no time to burn the building because of all the commotion and fearing that reinforcements would soon arrive from Omagh. As the convoy of cars made their way through Drumquinn a police constable threw a bomb from an upstairs window and the Volunteers immediately open fire on him to prevent him throwing any more until they were a safe distance from the barrack.

On the return journey the Volunteers were ordered to keep their revolvers at the ready, but not to use them unless necessary. The lead car pulled up to enquire if a Volunteer was in the second car, as he had travelled with them to Drumquinn. When it was discovered Patrick McMonagle was missing the entire party was anxious to return to get him. His brother James refused, however, as he felt it could risk the lives of all the men. The man in question had been on the other side of the town scouting for RIC men when the others departed the scene. He had been questioned by the RIC but bluffed his way out of it, eventually making his way back to Letterkenny.

The raiding party had to pass two RIC barracks, one at Castlederg and the other at Castlefinn; they had just passed the latter when the police were preparing to block the road. Information must have been wired to Castlefinn to be on the look out for a convoy of cars, as the Volunteers were then followed by a party of RIC. Along the road the RIC pulled up and asked a young boy if he had seen any cars passing that way. The young boy told them that the cars had passed a short time before and had turned right at the next crossroads. This put the RIC off their trail as the Volunteers had gone straight ahead. The entire party made a safe return.

Some of the arms captured in the raid were placed in the care of Anthony Dawson at the Letterkenny arms dumps, which were located in the heating chamber under Letterkenny cathedral and another dump at Langans' barn in the Glencar area.[70] The remainder of the weapons were taken in one of the cars to Killygordon by Sam O'Flaherty, Henry McGowan and John McGroarty. On arriving at a point near Killygordon O'Flaherty and McGowan left the car and made their way to McGroarty's house through the fields, while McGroarty drove home and put the car into his garage. The other two had only just arrived at the house when John McGroarty's sister came out to tell them that the local RIC sergeant was making his way to the house. It transpired that the sergeant was going to call to the house to pay for the hire of McGroarty's car on a previous occasion. John McGroarty later visited the RIC barracks to collect his money and the sergeant told him about the Drumquinn raid. He also told him that he had instructions to check on all cars in his command area, but told McGroarty that his task was easy as his was the only car in the area and that he had seen it in the garage the previous evening.[71] The Volunteers who took part in this operation were: Sam O'Flaherty, John McGroarty, Michael Doherty, James Curran, Henry McGowan, Patrick McGlinchey, Dr J. P. McGinley, Jim Dawson, Éamon Gallagher, Hugh McGraughan, Hugh Sweeney, William McLaughlin, Patrick McMonagle, James McMonagle, Anthony Dawson, Hugh McGrath, John McLaughlin, Edward McBrearty, J. J. Kelly, James McCarron, John Flaherty, Jim Hannigan, John Byrne, Edward Thomas Coyle and Michael Bogan.

The Volunteers of the Donegal Town Company planned to carry out raids for weapons and ammunition in their area in the early hours of following morning Friday 27 August. As part of this operation a decoy party was sent to fire shots at the local RIC barracks on Bridge Street. The decoy party only fired a few shots, but the police, thinking it was a full-scale attack, opened fire and continued for approximately two hours, causing major damage to the premises in the locality. Residents were lucky to escape death or serious injury such was the intensity of the firing from the police barracks.

While the RIC was preoccupied with shooting at ghosts and terrorising residents, the other Volunteers were carrying out raids in the town for weapons. This started with the commandeering of a number of vehicles from the garage of John Gallen. Three cars were secured to transport the Volunteers, who first visited the house of Rev. Montgomery, Methodist minister, where a gun was taken. The next house was that of William White, where another gun was secured. The Volunteers took three weapons at the house of James Crommer, while several other houses were also raided and further arms secured.

About the same time an attack was launched on Mountcharles RIC barracks; this was more prolonged, with Volunteers firing from front and rear for up to three hours. One policeman received minor injuries and a number of residents again were lucky to escape death or injury from police fire.

The following morning the 9 a.m. train from Letterkenny to Burtonport was held up at Cashelnagore station by a party of Volunteers who had boarded the train at Creeslough. They put the railway staff under armed guard and took the mailbags away in a waiting car. Later that morning the bags destined for Derrybeg and Bunbeg post office were seized by a party of ten Volunteers. They stopped the car conveying the mail at approximately 12 noon and the bags were taken into an adjoining field and sorted. All mail destined for the police and military was removed and the remaining mail was returned to the mail car.[72]

An order was received from GHQ in Dublin in late August stating that all arms in civilian hands were to be seized by the IRA. This order was carried out on an extensive scale in the Mountcharles area. All the houses of unionists who held arms were raided. The area covered was so large that the raiding operation had to be spread over two consecutive nights. At one house an exchange of shots took place, with a number of Volunteers being hit by shotgun pellets.[73]

In the follow-up operation a number of raids were carried out in the Gweedore area on Saturday 28 August and a large quantity of guns and ammunition secured. It was reported at the time that the Volunteers were most polite and assured the householders that their property would be returned to them when all the trouble had subsided. The next day witnessed much military activity in different areas, but no arrests were made. The local Volunteers kept up the pressure with the burning of the Annagry police barracks the following night. The building was evacuated the previous week and information was received through the mail raids that military were to be drafted into the area and stationed at the barracks.

During a raid on the train between Creeslough and Cashelnagore on Saturday, cash totalling £235 and over £70 worth of stamps were taken. This was contrary to volunteer regulation and the stamps were later returned to the postmaster in Letterkenny. On the same afternoon a party of Volunteers from Letterkenny visited a house in New Mills and took a rifle, revolver and ammunition. When they got what they wanted they departed and apologised for the annoyance they caused.

Volunteers continued to raid for arms on the outskirts of Letterkenny with raids in Glenswilly and Manorcunningham areas the following night. The houses visited were people with both unionist and nationalists aspirations. The Volunteers demanded the weapons in the name of the Irish Republic and some shotguns, revolvers and ammunition were handed over while other weapons were discovered following searches of houses and outhouses. The following night at about 11.30 p.m. a party of the West Surrey Regiment and two policemen raided the house of Patrick McDermott, Lower Main Street, Letterkenny. In response to a knock his sister opened the front door and the officer in charge told her that because of information received a search of the house would be made, however after searching the house for over an hour nothing was found.[74]

A large detachment of British troops from the Rifle Brigade arrived in Ballybofey and were billeted in the Butt Hall under the command of Captain McGregor. Henry McGowan had encountered McGregor, then a lieutenant, when he served in the British army from 1911 to 1914 and there was no love lost between the two. McGowan, then acting brigade O/C, thought that the place could be attacked and the weapons removed. He contacted an ex-soldier from the British army who lived in Ballybofey and had free access to the building as he often did odd jobs there.

McGowan acquired information on the defences around the hall and was also told that Wednesday was pay day and security more lax. McGowan decided to attack the hall on Wednesday 25 August

167

but was hugely disappointed to learn that the garrison had moved to Drumboe Castle, which had been commandeered a short time earlier. The Ballybofey Company considered a large-scale attack on the castle as high risk as there were sentries posted in various areas leading up to the building. They soon discovered that Ballybofey and Stranorlar had become heavily populated with British military and RIC, making it impossible to attack patrols or barracks.[75]

A few days after the Drumquinn raid the Letterkenny RIC district inspector, a man called Paddy Walsh, visited Dr McGinley at his surgery in the town. He produced a slip of paper and told the doctor he had the description of three men who took part in the Drumquinn raid – McGinley, Jim Dawson and James McMonagle. While the doctor was recovering from the shock, the DI told him that he was working for Michael Collins and would destroy the document.[76] He later gave alibis for the three men, informing his superiors that he had met them in the town at different times that day.

RAIDS ON FANAD COASTGUARD STATION AND BELLEEK RIC BARRACKS

THE POSSIBILITY OF raiding occupied RIC barracks in Donegal was very difficult because of the buildings being heavily protected with shutters and sandbags etc. early on in the campaign. Therefore the focus of the Volunteers turned to areas with less fortified barracks, usually located in areas with large unionist populations. In southeast Donegal the No. 4 brigade staff received a despatch from Frank Carney, O/C of the Fermanagh brigade, that a barracks in his area could be raided and would be a good source of arms and armaments. Carney requested the assistance of the South Donegal brigade for this operation. In preparation for this operation the South Donegal brigade deemed it necessary to test the response of the enemy garrison based at Finner camp.

The plan was to attack RIC barracks at Ballyshannon, Kinlough, Ardara and Bundoran simultaneously on Monday 30 August. The Bundoran and Ballyshannon attacks were to be nuisance attacks to test the reaction of the British troops at Finner camp and to give the impression of increased activity in the area, distracting attention from the major raid planned to take place in County Fermanagh. As part of the Bundoran attack, Volunteers were placed covering both the front and rear of the barracks. They opened fire using rifles, shotguns and revolvers, with the RIC immediately replying. It was not long before the military from Finner camp arrived and the Volunteers were forced to make a quick retreat. This attack led to a large concentration of military and police in the area followed by intensive raids. At the time of this attack Bundoran was full of holidaymakers, which prevented a large-scale attack. There was a general evacuation of all visitors, and anyone who did not leave immediately following the attack, did so the next day. The local tourist industry was greatly affected and the IRA became the focus of much condemnation from those with an interest in that sector. The nuisance attacks continued that night when an RIC patrol was ambushed at Mountcharles and shots were fired into Ballyshannon RIC barracks.[77]

The following day, Tuesday 31 August, attention switched to the Inishowen area when three lorries containing military from Derry arrived in Buncrana. They immediately began carrying out raids; four houses were searched but no arrests made. Later that day the Inishowen Volunteers carried out raids for weapons in Carndonagh, Clonmany, Malin and Culdaff and large quantities of shotguns, revolvers and rifles were captured. Other raids were carried out in Ardara, Dungloe and Ballyshannon in the early hours of Wednesday 1 September.

In Donegal town two guns were taken from the house of Alexander Montgomery, sheriff's bailiff, while nine rifles were seized from the homes of prominent Ulster Volunteer members in the area. The house of Captain J. S. Hamilton, JP, Ballintra, was visited and when the Volunteers knocked at the door the occupant opened fire. The Volunteers returned fire and the captain surrendered, was disarmed and all weapons in the house were taken.

Sometime during the summer months British forces including Black and Tans occupied the parochial hall at Dungloe and remained there for over three months. During the occupation they burned a house near the hall, evicting the lady occupant before setting the building on fire, claiming that the house could have been used by the IRA to launch an attack and that it obscured their view and line of fire in the event of such an attack.[78]

The September edition of *An t-Óglach* published an article stating that the British War Office had recently established Donegal and Derry as two main centres of military authority with a strong post at Lifford:

> This move of the English is an important milestone in our War of Independence because it has been done against their will and as a direct result of the success of our troops in Donegal. Hitherto the aim of the English has been to concentrate in the south of Ireland, hoping to be able to strip the north for that purpose. A divisional headquarters in Derry is a confession that they have failed in their aims. It makes a distinct strategic gain for our guerrilla warfare.[79]

The Inishowen Volunteers remained active in the procurement of weapons and carried out a large number of raids in the Buncrana and Fahan areas on Thursday night 2 September with a considerable number of rifles, shotguns and other weapons being captured. The Volunteers apologised to the inhabitants of the houses searched and it was reported that the police made no attempt to interfere with the raids. At approximately 8.30 the next morning a party of ten Volunteers entered Buncrana post office and ordered the staff to raise their hands and stand facing the wall. The Volunteers sifted through the mail for correspondence destined for the naval units based at Lough Swilly and the military HQ in Buncrana. The Derry train had been raided by eight Volunteers earlier that morning on its arrival at Ballymagen station and the mailbags were searched for military correspondence.[80]

In late August, Neil Blaney, O/C Fanad Company, informed Dr J. P. McGinley that soldiers stationed at the Fanad coastguard station were being deployed elsewhere due to the lack of Volunteer activity in the area. McGinley enquired when they were leaving, but Blaney didn't have that information. Dr McGinley then instructed Blaney to go to the station on the premise of selling insurance, as he was then an insurance agent.[81] Blaney went into the coastguard station the following day and asked if anyone would be interested in taking out an insurance policy. A soldier informed him that there was no point in buying insurance as they were leaving the area within the next few days.

This information was then conveyed to the Letterkenny battalion and the local Volunteers were summoned to a battalion conference where a plan was discussed to carry out the raid and the date was set for Saturday 4 September. The reason for the attacking party being drawn from the Letterkenny battalion was that they had more experience and more weapons. It was decided that the Fanad Company would act as scouts and backup for the raiding party.

On the evening of the raid ten Volunteers travelled in two cars from Letterkenny to within a few miles of the target. They were: Hugh and Frank McKay, Churchill, Dr J. P. McGinley, Hugh McGrath, Jim and Anthony Dawson, William McLaughlin, James, Frank and Packie McMonagle, all from Letterkenny. They made their way to Dan Callaghan's of Kindrum and were met by Jimmy Coll and Johnny Carr of the Fanad Company who were their guides across country to the coastguard station. The O/C of the Fanad Company, Blaney, failed to make an appearance for this operation. The back of the building faced the Atlantic with Mulroy Bay on one side and Lough Swilly on the other. There was little cover from the front or either side of the building, so the raiding party had little hope of gaining access to the building by a ruse. They took up positions along the exterior wall and began firing at the building for several minutes.

Dr McGinley, who was in charge of the Volunteers, then called on the garrison of eleven marines to surrender. 'We are members of the bulldog breed who don't surrender,' came the reply. Rapid fire was again opened on the station and after about half an hour the garrison called out: 'We will surrender if you spare our lives.' The Volunteers told them they had no intention of taking their lives and all they wanted was their weapons. The officer in charge was instructed to approach the wall with his hands up. The Volunteers moved into the building and disarmed the remainder of the garrison. They removed eleven revolvers, ammunition and a quantity of gelignite. Dr McGinley told the garrison that they were a flying column from County Fermanagh and he would appreciate some food for his hungry men. The garrison presented them with bully beef and, having eaten, the Volunteers left the area without further incident.[82]

Later that month during a hearing of a claim for damages to the building and personnel, the Volunteers learned that there was a British naval sloop anchored in Mulroy Bay, near the coastguard station. The sloop was there to salvage gold from the *Laurentic*, a Canadian ship that had been en route from Liverpool to Canada in early January 1917 with a large crew and a cargo that included 3,000 ingots of gold estimated to be worth £2.5 million. The ship had stopped at Buncrana to let a number of passengers off and the crew spent some time at the Lough Swilly hotel. After a few hours a telegram arrived ordering the crew to continue on their journey and they returned to the ship and set sail. While passing Fanad Head the *Laurentic* struck two mines, causing the ship to sink almost immediately.

When questioned by the judge as to why he did not go to the assistance of the garrison, the naval officer in charge of the salvage replied that a quantity of gold had been salvaged that day and was placed on the opposite shore. He went on to say that he thought the raid was a ruse to occupy his attention while an attempt was made to steal the gold, and he ordered the sloop to be moved across the bay to protect the haul of gold.[83]

The next big daylight arms raid was set for Sunday 5 September, to be carried out by the Volunteers of the No. 4 brigade, South-East Donegal, which included portions of County Tyrone and County Fermanagh. The target was the RIC barracks at Belleek village and the operation was under the command of Frank Carney, O/C of the Fermanagh brigade. Carney had planned the operation and had gathered his own intelligence about the personnel, the barracks and the general area. It was decided to launch the attack on a Sunday morning because the majority of the police at Belleek barracks were Catholic and attended mass on Sunday mornings, leaving one policeman on duty. Carney had requested the assistance of the Bundoran Company, No. 4 brigade for the operation. The success of the raid depended on securing the use of an ambulance, the property of the British army and easily recognised as such. The ambulance had been handed over by the British to the Ballyshannon Board of Guardians and was in the charge of the Sheeran family of Ballyshannon. John Sheeran was a Volunteer and he was instructed by Carney to be ready to travel with the regular driver when the ambulance was called out. They made the call to Sheeran's saying that the ambulance was required at a house on the Belleek Road; Frank Carney and Patrick Johnston were waiting along the road dressed as British military officers. As the ambulance approached the two men stepped out onto the road and stopped the vehicle at gunpoint, removing the two occupants.

To cover Sheeran's part in the operation both men were tied to a nearby tree. The remainder of the raiding party were picked up further down the road and they continued on to Belleek. The arrival of the ambulance in the village was the signal for two of the Fermanagh Volunteers to cut the telephone and telegraph wires and then to proceed to the chapel and lock the doors. This was to ensure that the RIC men attending mass could not respond in the event of any shooting and it would also prevent the congregation from running out in a panic. The ambulance drove up to the barracks door and Carney got out with a large envelope held conspicuously in his hand. He knocked on the door and told the policeman who opened it that he had business with the sergeant in charge and requested admittance. Once inside he held a revolver to the policeman's head and led him to the barrack yard, where he handed him over to Frank Ward while the remaining Volunteers entered the building. It was as easy as that. The Volunteers proceeded to load all weapons, ammunition, uniforms, official documents and police logs into the ambulance, before setting the building on fire. The entire party arrived back to Bundoran without incident and the local company took possession of the captured items, which were then stored in the local national school. The ambulance was then abandoned on the Bundoran Road. The following Volunteers took part in the capture of the Belleek RIC barracks: Frank Carney, John Sheeran, Joe Meehan, Jim O'Carroll, Patrick Johnston, Patrick O'Doherty, Frank Ward, Joseph O'Gorman, Alo Carroll, Owen Gallagher, Thomas McShea, John O'Doherty.[84]

The following morning in west Donegal a party of ten Volunteers held up a train at Bridgetown station. The driver, fireman and guard were put into the waiting room under the guard of two Volunteers. Twenty-one mailbags were removed and searched for mail to the military and police. The Derry to Burtonport train was held up at Cashelnagore station and mailbags were again removed and all official documents removed. Mail cars in Milford, Carrigart and Dunfanaghy were also held up and official documents removed.

In response to the Belleek raid large numbers of British military and police swarmed into the Ballyshannon area on Tuesday morning and carried out a large-scale raid and search operation. This resulted in the arrests of Charles Reegan, Joseph Sheeran, John Sheeran,

Patrick Magee and Charles Gallagher, who were all conveyed under heavy escort to Derry jail the following morning.

On the night of Wednesday 8 September a party of Volunteers raided the premises of Patrick Coyle, Kilmacrenan and took what was described as 'a very valuable double-barrelled gun' and a large amount of ammunition. The RIC barracks at Mountcharles was evacuated on the same day and in the early hours of Thursday morning was burned to the ground. On the same day at Bundoran an RIC sergeant was disarmed and another revolver was seized from a police constable during a hold-up at Burtonport.

A police constable was ambushed at 10 p.m. on the same night as he walked along a Buncrana street. A number of Volunteers seized him, dragged him into a gateway and took his revolver, cape and whistle. They then tied his hands and put a sack over his head before pushing him onto the street. A number of unionist houses in the Carrigans area were raided by Volunteers later that night and large number of weapons seized.

Owing to the large number of raids on the Donegal railway, company directors declared that if further raids were carried out the line would be immediately closed. The threat of closure was also related to the many railway workers refusing to work on trains conveying British forces.[85] In a related incident Dr McGinley received intelligence that a party of British military had boarded a train at Strabane bound for Letterkenny. The train crew – George and Willie McFeeley and Paddy McElwee – had stepped off the engine and refused to take the train while the British soldiers were on board. However, after a short time another crew were located and agreed to drive the train. A meeting was quickly summoned of the Letterkenny Company and, believing the driver and fireman would remain overnight in Letterkenny, plans were made for their arrest and court-martial. Before the meeting had concluded a Volunteer rushed in to inform the officers that the two men concerned were having a meal at the railway station and were to return to Strabane afterwards. Dr McGinley instructed James McMonagle to get a shotgun and a few cartridges loaded with buckshot. The two men then set off in the direction of Glenmaquinn to attempt an ambush on the train as it returned to Strabane. Before they reached Glenmaquinn railway station they heard the engine whistle and James McMonagle jumped from the moving car and raced across a field towards the engine. He was soon followed by Dr McGinley and just as the two reached the embankment the engine was passing at speed. McMonagle immediately fired both barrels, hitting the engine plating a foot behind and in line with the driver's head, with the driver receiving a number of buckshot to the back of the neck.[86]

On Thursday 9 September Bernard Sweeney phoned Sweeneys' in Dungloe to inform them that one sergeant and four constables had left Burtonport and were walking in their direction. A party of Volunteers was quickly mobilised and set out to cover the two roads approaching Dungloe from Burtonport. Frank O'Donnell took charge of the men on the Lower Meenmore or Shore Road and John McCole with Dan Sweeney took charge of the men on the upper Meenmore Road. The police were held up at Milltown on the lower road and ordered to raise their hands. The sergeant did so, but one of the constables opened fire and the Volunteers were forced to make a hasty retreat.[87] That night the RIC barracks at Creeslough was evacuated and was subsequently burned by Volunteers of A company, Creeslough, in the early hours of Friday morning. The Volunteers spent some time at the barracks stripping it of any useful items before pouring paraffin oil in every room and setting bundles of hay on fire, resulting in the building being completely destroyed.

An indication that the boycott of the RIC was also being adhered to by the employees of the railway was observed when four armed policemen entered the midday train at Donegal railway station on Monday 13 September. The driver, James Quinn, fireman, James Grant and guard, John Sweeney refused to proceed with the train. The policemen eventually left the carriage and after a delay of about half an hour the train departed from the station. On the same day John Sweeney refused to take charge of the midday train from Donegal to Killybegs until four armed policemen got off. He was dismissed by his employers and a replacement guard sent for, arriving in Killybegs the next day. He was refused lodgings in the town and had to return as a passenger on the next train.

As part of the Belfast Boycott the business community and general population in Donegal town were served with the proclamation setting out the prohibition of all trade and business with Belfast and the suspension of all accounts with the Northern, Ulster and Belfast banks. 'Infringement of this order,' stated the proclamation 'will be severely dealt with'.[88]

The Volunteers in the No. 3 brigade burned the Dunkineely RIC barracks in the early hours of Tuesday morning 14 September. The barracks had been evacuated the previous week. Later that day the home of James Connolly, captain of the Kinlough Company, was raided by members of the RIC and Black and Tans in reprisal. After thoroughly searching the premises and failing to find their intended target or anything seditious, members of the Tans began beating Connolly's father, who they then placed against an outhouse and shot him execution style, leaving his body riddled with bullets. These were the preferred methods of the Black and Tans as they ignored the usual code of warfare. These methods were repeated all over the country.[89]

The Letterkenny branch of Cumann na mBan held a very successful concert in the Literary Institute that night with all proceeds going to the Munitions of War Fund. The programme included Irish songs, recitations, and Irish step dances performed by the Fianna boys and girls, Anthony Dawson, Johnnie Doherty, James Gallagher, Maisie Bradley, Aggie Collins and Rose McManus.

Raids for arms continued all over the county with Volunteers in south Donegal seizing three revolvers and three rifles from two houses in Dooran. They met with some resistance at Gortward when

Francis Scot said he would rather be shot than give up the arms. The Volunteers put him up against a wall, but his brother intervened and handed over a rifle and a revolver. Up to ten other houses in the area were visited and a large number of weapons seized, and at the home of Francis Kennedy, Ardaghey nine weapons were discovered. It was clear that the most fruitful raids were those of unionist households as the weapons belonging to the Ulster Volunteer Force were still being stored in the county.

The continuous raids were putting the British under pressure and in an effort to recover some of the arms seized the military themselves increased the number of raids on known republican houses and premises. On Thursday 16 September, a large number of military and police surrounded the premises of the Inver Creamery and Co-operative store and the residence of Patrick Barry, manager. They made an exhaustive search of all the buildings, but failed to find anything. Patrick Barry was the chairman of the Donegal Board of Guardians, a Sinn Féin councillor on the district council and a member of Donegal County Council.

At a meeting of the Letterkenny Guardians the impartiality of the republican justice system was seen in a case concerning a wage increase. The issue had been raised with the Local Government Board for a decision, but this recommendation was not accepted by all councillors. Sinn Féin councillor, John Mullan raised two objections, one being opposed to all increases of salary and the other to any sanctions being imposed by the Local Government Board. The question, he said, should be referred to an arbitration board authorised by Dáil Éireann; this motion was passed and the issue was successfully concluded in this way.

Since the burning of Buncrana courthouse in July there were no cases entered in the petty sessions books. Republican courts took over the functions of the British law court and it was reported that IRA Volunteers regularly patrolled the towns of Inishowen and conducted the business of law and order.

1920 - The Guerrilla Soldiers and the Donegal Gun-runner

A large party of military and police made two arrests in Mountcharles on Saturday morning 18 September; two Volunteers – Hugh Lanaghan and Andrew Higginbottom, Mountcharles – were arrested in connection with arms raids in the area, but were later released.[90]

During the following week raiding for arms was intensified in the No. 2 brigade area, north-east Donegal, with a general raid for arms being carried out in all sections of the brigade. A number of unionist houses were targeted in the Letterkenny and Termon areas and large numbers of weapons and ammunition secured. A number of houses between Letterkenny and Ramelton were also raided but no weapons were found. Some residents produced RIC receipts for surrendered weapons. Other raids were carried out in the west of the county at Dungloe, Burtonport, Bunbeg and Derrybeg.

A two-man RIC cycle patrol had a very lucky escape as they cycled through the Doochary area in the No. 1 brigade area, on the evening of Wednesday 22 September. A party of Volunteers opened fire on them from a hill overlooking the road as they cycled past, but neither of the two suffered any injury.[91]

Volunteers were again raiding for arms in the Letterkenny area and on the night of Thursday 23 September a considerable number of shotguns and revolvers were seized. The police boycott was being rigidly maintained; military and police were forced to commandeer food and fuel from local businesses, creating further tensions. Two RIC men arrived by train in Donegal town on Thursday, but were unable to procure a car to transfer their luggage and had to commandeer a horse and cart to get their cargo to the police barracks.

Raids were carried out by military and police over a large area in Doorin, Frosses and Inver in south-west Donegal on Friday 24 September. In response to the intensified raiding by the Volunteers the police responded by collecting weapons in various areas from people with gun permits. RIC assisted by military collected weapons in Mountcharles, Ballintra, Donegal town and surrounding areas.

This was also the situation in other parts of the county, with the police handing over recovered weapons to the West Surreys stationed at Letterkenny courthouse. On Saturday 25 September a police lorry arrived in Letterkenny from west Donegal conveying eighty weapons of all types from permit holders.[92]

In the early hours of Tuesday 28 September, Volunteers from the Ardara battalion set out to blow up the courthouse and police barracks in the village. The two buildings were situated beside each other and as the Volunteers were in the process of setting the explosives they were disturbed by a policeman who had heard a noise outside. The police opened fire and the Volunteers were forced to make a hasty retreat. Their mission was to destroy the courthouse and the barracks and several tins of petrol that were to be used for this purpose were later recovered by the police.[93]

Early the following morning two Volunteers entered the home of Patrick Boyle, rate collector, Donegal town and demanded the weekly collections; approximately £420 was handed over.[94] Also that day raids were carried out by the police and military in the Gweedore area where a revolver and ammunition were found in a turf stack situated at the side of a house. A young man living in the house was severely beaten before being arrested and taken away. A thorough and aggressive search was then made of the house, with a police sergeant even emptying a basin of milk onto the bedroom floor. After two hours of searching and ransacking the house, they left. Later that night a party of military raided Breslins hotel, Bunbeg, but nothing was found.[95]

By October 1920 the increased war campaign saw more RIC barracks being evacuated; all those in west Donegal were evacuated with the exception of Dunfanaghy and Falcarragh. Once the police had left, the local IRA company would move in and destroy the building, or where the building was under local ownership it would be rendered uninhabitable by removing stairs, doors, windows, etc.

Shortly after 8 a.m. on Saturday 2 October, the train from Derry to Carndonagh was raided by Volunteers at Inch Road station and all correspondence destined for the naval base, military and police throughout Inishowen was removed.[96]

The Volunteers of west Donegal received reports of a vicious assault on a man at Derrybeg and following enquiries two young men were arrested at their homes in Middletown on Saturday night by a party of Volunteers. They were tried before a hastily convened republican court-martial and charged with having unmercifully and brutally beaten a man on the night of the last Derrybeg fair. Promising to pay the fines imposed, the two men were left on a lonely road about six miles from their homes in the early hours of Sunday morning and the fines were subsequently paid to the person authorised by the tribunal.

The Black and Tans, who had been gradually making their presence known since their arrival in the county, began to respond to the increased activities of the Volunteers in the Donegal town area. A notice signed 'Black Hand' was posted around the town, stating: 'Sinn Féiners, Beware! Any injury done to any loyalist or his or her property in this district, a swift and terrible reprisal will follow on all Sinn Féiners known in the district.' A publican in Donegal town, who was not a member of any political organisation, also received a copy in the post. The envelope displayed the Finner camp post-mark. This warning was in response to the intensified campaign by the Volunteers in the procurement of arms in that area and the fact that raids on loyalist households produced the greatest amount of arms and ammunition.

Volunteers in the north Inishowen area broke into the Kinnegoe coastguard station, near Moville on the night of Monday 4 October and set the building on fire. However, the fire only partly destroyed the interior of the building and the Volunteers had to return a few nights later to complete the task.

The following day a large number of military and police carried out a series of raids in the Fanad area. The raiding party arrived at 10 a.m. and remained for several hours in the area. They broke into the Kindrum hall, causing extensive damage to the interior, and then proceeded to raid the licensed premises of Dan Callaghan and the residences of Bernard Hannigan and Neil Blaney, Rosnakill, which were also ransacked during the operation. Prior to the raids the British military held up and searched the mail car twice as it travelled through the area, while other cars travelling through the locality were also held up and searched. The military smashed open the front door of the parochial hall, which was also searched and windows smashed.

On Wednesday 6 October the military and police raided the Sinn Féin hall and the houses of Sinn Féin members in the Ballintra area. A local farmer, Charles McGroarty, and his son John were arrested and taken to Finner camp where they were subjected to a vicious interrogation over two days.

A party of fully armed troops boarded the midday Carndonagh train at Buncrana on Thursday 7 October, but with the guard and fireman refusing to work the train had to be cancelled. The two men were suspended and the railway company announced that the service would also be cancelled if the actions of the employees continued.

Later that afternoon in Buncrana two soldiers were passing the post office when a Volunteer sneaked up behind them and snatched a rifle from one of their shoulders. They were then confronted by two other Volunteers, who ordered the armed soldier to put up his hands or they would 'blow his head off'. The incident brought a strong response from the military in the town and that afternoon a number of houses were searched. People were held up on the street and a number of business premises were also entered, with four men being arrested: Patrick Fletcher, William Harkin, Charles McLaughlin and William Doherty. Doherty was in Harkins' barber shop at the time of his arrest and it was discovered after the raid that a number of items were missing, including razors. The raids were carried out be a party of twenty-five soldiers including Black and Tans, who were most likely the thieves.[97]

The IRA in the No. 3 brigade, south-west Donegal area planned to attack the barracks in Ardara again in early October. The local RIC had been reinforced by personnel from outlying barracks that had been recently abandoned. A detachment of the British Rifle Brigade was also posted in the town, occupying the Market House. The Ardara Volunteers did not have sufficient weapons so brigade officer Liam O'Duffy made contact with Jim Dawson in Letterkenny, then commandant of the East Donegal brigade. Jim Dawson, Dr J. P. McGinley and Dr John Gormley from Castlefinn travelled to a pre-arranged spot near Barnesmore Gap with fourteen Martini-Henry rifles, ammunition and a few Mills bombs. They were met by Liam O'Duffy, Michael Gallagher, Patrick Gallagher and Phil Timony and the weapons were transferred to Ardara, via Altadoo, near Donegal town, and handed over to Patrick McHugh, battalion O/C. These munitions were used in the attack on the Ardara barracks on Thursday 7 October, but due to the large numbers of RIC and military the attacking party was easily beaten off.[98]

The military continued to keep up the pressure. There were raids on different areas of the county almost on a daily basis and on 9 October a cordon was drawn around Buncrana and a number of houses searched. The arrest targets were not found and no one was arrested, but the practice of wrecking houses and beating the occupants continued. The following morning five houses were raided in the Milford area by a detachment of military from Letterkenny.

The following morning raids and searches continued, this time in Killybegs and the surrounding areas. St Columba's industrial school and the residences of Patrick O'Byrne, John Ward, John Gatins, Francis McDwyre, Charles Sweeney, Barney Callaghan and Mrs F. Cunningham were searched but nothing was found. Young men were also stopped and searched; one received serious facial injuries when assaulted by a soldier.

On Tuesday morning, 12 October, the military and police raided the offices of P. J. Ward, TD for South Donegal, and the home of his manager, Liam O'Duffy. Some documents and correspondence were removed, but neither man was arrested. The military returned to Ward's office the next day and carried out another search, but again nothing was found. Later that day they raided the home of Patrick Barry, Inver, chairman of the Donegal Board of Guardians and District Council, but he was not at home. The house of Neil McGready in Frosses was also visited in search of his son who the police were eager to question, but he was not at home. During the raid his younger brother was pulled out of his bed and threatened with arrest unless he revealed the whereabouts of the 'wanted' man, but he was not taken into custody.[99]

At the same time while the military and police concentrated on the south of the county, the Volunteers in west Donegal continued harassing the rail service and held up the 7.30 a.m. Derry to Burtonport train at Crolly Bridge station on Tuesday morning. When the train pulled up to the station several Volunteers boarded, one taking control of the engine and another taking over the guard's van. The driver was then ordered to proceed until they reached an isolated area, where the mailbags were removed and searched. The mailbags were then returned to the train, which continued on its journey. The mail seizure provoked a quick response from the military and police, with large-scale activity in the Crolly area later that day. A number of cars were seized and people going about their business were stopped, questioned and searched.

Further operations were carried out by the military in Buncrana on Tuesday night; a number of houses were raided but no arrests were made. Checkpoints were set up along Main Street and military personnel were busy stopping and searching everyone that passed. A detachment of 300 soldiers arrived in Buncrana on Wednesday and were stationed at the naval barracks. The Black and Tans also arrived in the town, which was patrolled daily by Tans and police. The Inishowen Volunteers decided to send out a welcoming party to the notorious mercenaries and a three-man patrol was ambushed while returning to their barracks that night. All three were seriously wounded in the attack and spent some time at the county hospital in Lifford.

The effects of the general boycott were also felt on the islands off Donegal, frustrating the administration of British justice. A solicitor at Lifford quarter sessions on Thursday 14 October informed the court that a process server could not acquire a boat to serve a woman living on Inishbofin Island. An attempt to serve her had then been made by registered letter, but this also proved futile.

The Black and Tans began to make their presence felt in other parts of the county and a notice was posted at Falcarragh on Sunday 17 October stating: 'If the boycott of police is not removed within forty-eight hours, or any injury done to any member of the police, the Sinn Féin leaders of Falcarragh and Gortahork may look out for themselves. In addition their houses will be completely destroyed. Sinn Féin leaders are well known. Remember Balbriggan.'[100]

The reference to Balbriggan related to the Black and Tans' reprisal for the death of one of their comrades when they stormed the small town of Balbriggan in County Dublin, burning twenty-five houses and a small factory, throwing grenades indiscriminately and killing two of the town's residents with bayonets.

A mixed party of Tans, military and police descended on Donegal town on the night of Friday 22 October and carried out a series of raids. The premises of Mrs E. O'Neill, publican, the Diamond, Donegal town was searched, but the son the police were looking for was not at home. They then visited the home of Patrick Gallagher, Main Street, forcing open the front door before wrecking the interior of the house and smashing windows. Next was a house also on Main Street that was the venue for the republican court in the area. A thorough search was carried out and the house ransacked, but nothing was found, as the local court registrar, Liam O'Duffy had carefully concealed documents behind a wall in a bedroom. The raiding party then turned its attention to the people on the street, adopting the usual harassment tactics of searching and questioning.

Meanwhile the police in west Donegal began making way for the arrival of detachments of Black and Tans by evacuating the barracks at Dungloe and Burtonport on Friday 22 October. In the early hours of Sunday 24 October the Black and Tans fired into a number of premises as they passed through Donegal town. Their main target was McFadden's hotel. The proprietor and his daughter had a narrow escape as bullets screamed through every room at the front of the building. McFadden had been threatened some days earlier – if he did not stop the boycott of members of the RIC his hotel would be bombed.

Black and Tan activity was also stepped up in the Buncrana area with a series of raids. Accompanied by the military and police, many houses were searched and several gardens dug up in search of weapons. On Tuesday morning locals in Buncrana awoke to find the wall along the road from the railway station daubed with slogans such as 'Lift the Boycott', 'Up Queens', 'Up the RIC' and 'God Save the King'. This was the work of the Black and Tans as there was also a slogan painted on the wall of the burned courthouse which read: 'Gone, but not Forgotten'.[101]

On Monday 25 October, Terence MacSwiney, Lord Mayor of Cork, died in Brixton jail, following a long agonising hunger strike lasting seventy-four days. MacSwiney had been appointed lord mayor in February following the assassination of Tomás MacCurtain by a party of RIC earlier that month. He had been arrested on 13 August and immediately refused food in protest against British harassment of elected representatives. In response to the news of MacSwiney's death the Volunteers in Donegal approached all shopkeepers and asked them to close their shops on the day of MacSwiney's funeral. The efforts of the Volunteers were met with mixed reactions from the businesses visited. In Bundoran Thomas McShea and Patrick Johnston approached all business premises in the town where some agreed and some refused while others approached the RIC enquiring whether it was the orders of the IRA or the RIC that were to be obeyed.[102]

Following the announcement of Terence MacSwiney's death the intimidation campaign by the Black and Tans was stepped up. On Thursday 28 October the doors of houses belonging to Sinn Féin members in Buncrana were painted with numbers one to five. This was to let the inhabitants know that if anything happened to British forces they would return and attack the houses, and most likely kill the inhabitants. Walls and footpaths were also painted with the inscriptions 'Buncrana will follow Balbriggan' and 'Up the Black and Tans'. Notices were also posted in certain parts of the town:

> To all whom it may concern. Whereas it is stated that certain notices of a threatening nature have been posted on conspicuous parts of the town, take warning in good time; that if any harm whatever comes to any member of HM forces or to any person that chooses to associate with the above said, five of the prominent Sinn Féiners in this locality will be shot. Balbriggan and Trim will be sufficient warning to the sober mind. Buncrana – 29/10/1920.[103]

The killing of a member of the British forces would normally result in locals spending the night in fields and barns, so great was the fear of reprisals on the Balbriggan model. Similar atrocities were carried out at Trim, County Meath and Castleconnell, County Limerick.[104]

The Volunteers of Drimarone, Donegal town received a despatch from the divisional staff ordering the return of money taken from the home of Patrick Boyle, rate collector. It was taken in the mistaken belief that the money was the proceeds of rate collections, but in fact it was his personal savings. The despatch ordered that the money be handed over to Fr Kennedy, Frosses, Fr McAteer, Drimarone, P. J. Ward, TD, or George Dunnion. An agreement was reached between Boyle and the Volunteers that the money would be repaid in instalments.

The residence of Joseph McManus, Mountcharles was raided by police and military in the early hours of Tuesday 2 November. The house of Hugh McBrearty, who was employed by McManus, was also raided, but nothing of an incriminating nature was found in either house. Joseph McManus was a relative of Seamus MacManus the writer and on of the founder members of Sinn Féin, then exiled in America.

John Murphy, a barber, of West End, Bundoran was charged under the Defence of the Realm Act with having a revolver and six rounds of ammunition. He was tried before a court-martial in Ebrington barracks, Derry on Thursday 4 November. When asked to plead, Murphy said he declined to recognise the court and would answer no further questions.

The police evidence was that shortly after midnight on the 9 October 1920 the accused was halted in West End, Bundoran and ordered to put his hands up. A police sergeant searched him and found a fully loaded revolver. One of the bullets was flattened at the point and there was an incision made in it. The prosecutor said the offence was aggravated by the fact that Murphy was in possession of a bullet of this description and asked the court to impose the fullest penalty in its power. Murphy was subsequently sentenced to two years' hard labour.[105]

Three Buncrana Volunteers entered the house of the clerk of Buncrana Urban Council on the night of Friday 5 November and demanded the books belonging to the council, which was at that time deciding whether to disassociate itself from the Local Government Board.[106]

The committee of the Jim Connolly Sinn Féin cumann, Letterkenny forwarded the following letter to the *Derry Journal*, published on Wednesday 10 November:

> Re: a report that appeared in your recent issue of the court-martial of Joseph Vaughan, Letterkenny. The charge was that

he had in his possession Sinn Féin and Volunteer membership cards. He seems so as truly verified in the court-martial to have carried these cards for the purpose of giving himself and his employer's car a safe conduct through strong Sinn Féin areas. He was not a member of Sinn Féin cumainn and he never was a member of the Irish Volunteers. Cards are easily procurable and with a bit of erasing can be filled out in any person's name. This may clear up a misapprehension.

On the night of Thursday 11 November, parties of military and Black and Tans on their way through Mountcharles fired continuously at houses and shops. A number of people had a miraculous escape as bullets whizzed through the buildings.

Three days later John Francis Harley, a Volunteer, was stopped and searched at a military checkpoint at Quigley's Point. He was arrested having been being found with a receipt for 10s on notepaper headed 'Headquarters Inishowen brigade' and signed 'Philip O'Doherty, Commandant'.[107]

The Irish college at Cloghaneely and the cooperative stores adjoining were destroyed by fire early on Thursday 18 November. The previous morning a large number of military accompanied by Black and Tans broke into the college, broke the windows, piled chairs and tables in a heap and set them on fire. Locals had subsequently succeeded in extinguishing the flames on that occasion.

The military then made their way to Gortahork and raided a number of houses and McFadden's hotel, where they tore down a photograph of the late Terence MacSwiney, lord mayor of Cork. Before leaving a soldier remarked that they would be back again at midnight. Fearing that this threat would be carried out, many people from the area remained out of bed until daybreak, with some deciding to sleep in outhouses for safety. At 2 a.m. a lorryload of military stopped in the village for some time before making their way back to the college. Some time later locals observed that the college and cooperative stores were on fire, with a strong wind fanning the flames. By daybreak the two buildings were completely destroyed.[108]

Buncrana experienced further aggressive military activity later that day with raids on a number of houses in the town. The military presence was due to the visit of Darrell Figgis, a prominent figure in Sinn Féin. There was nothing seditious about the visit, which was to conduct inquiries regarding the fishing industry and to take evidence from those associated with it in the area. Figgis was in Donegal to examine the fishing industry in his capacity as secretary of the Commission of Inquiry into the Resources and Industries of Ireland established by Dáil Éireann. The authorities, however, thought the visit was in relation to the republican administration of justice. Figgis had been shadowed by Dublin Castle agents from the moment he left Dublin and for the duration of his visit to Donegal.

At Inver station, on the arrival of the 5 p.m. train from Donegal town on Friday 19 November, six Volunteers removed the guard from the train and made him promise he would not in future take charge of any train that carried armed soldiers or policemen. He was told that if he failed to keep his promise the full penalty would be exacted – he would be shot.[109]

In the early hours of Sunday 21 November, fourteen British intelligence agents were assassinated at various locations around Dublin. In reprisal, the Black and Tans drove into Croke Park later that day during the All-Ireland final between Tipperary and Dublin and shot indiscriminately into the crowd, killing twelve and injuring many more.

The following day, 22 November, a Donegal Volunteer Bernard O'Donnell, Ballylar, Fanad was charged before a court-martial in Derry under the Restoration of Order in Ireland Regulations (ROIR). He had been arrested on 10 November following a search of the co-operative store at Shanagh, Ballylar during which seventy-four rounds of .22 ammunition and two boxes containing seventy detonators were found.[110]

Later that evening a large party of Volunteers took up positions on the outskirts of Ardara and waited for a police patrol. At about midnight four policemen walked in the direction of the ambush point. The Volunteers opened fire and all four were wounded, with two receiving serious injuries.

Two days later, on Wednesday 24 November, the military and police raided the house of Fr Bernard Cunningham, Clar, but nothing was found. There was also a raid on the house and outhouses of Robert Lowry, Speertown, a Protestant farmer, and the home of Mrs Bonner, Summerhill, Donegal town. The military on this occasion were looking for her son, who was not at home, but a Sinn Féin membership card was found during the raid. The next day William Logue, Bomany, was arrested for being drunk and disorderly on the evening of the Letterkenny hiring fair. He was arrested for shouting 'Up Dublin' and 'Up Sinn Féin' and was fined 21*s* and costs. The following morning police and military searched the house of C. H. Ward, Barnesmore, but nothing was found.[111]

In late November the British military in Dublin enjoyed a significant victory in the intelligence war, which impinged on the 1st northern division command officers and Volunteers in Donegal. Richard Mulcahy, IRA chief of staff, was staying and working at a safe house at the time. He had just left the house and was cycling along the tramline when the forks of the bicycle broke, sending him face first into the ground. He was badly injured about the face and upper body and a number of passers-by picked him up and carried him back to the house. He was treated there and put to bed for the night, but at 3 a.m. a large party of military arrived. Mulcahy was woken by the sound of the lorries and quickly escaped through a skylight, but in his haste forgot to take his briefcase containing important documents, including lists of command areas, etc. Among the contents of the briefcase was a list containing the names of officers and commands in the 1st northern division area. A few days later a series of despatches were sent to inform officers in the various commands.[112]

Before notice of the captured documents was circulated, Denis Houston, lieutenant, Dungloe Company attended the Dungloe fair on Saturday 4 December. Dungloe had no RIC stationed in the village at that time and Houston considered it safe to visit. He had been on the run following the attack on the four-man RIC escort at the Rampart, Dungloe in 1919. Suddenly a large party of military arrived in the village from two different directions and rounded up everyone on the street. Houston was not unduly concerned as he was unarmed, had no documents on him and didn't think any of the soldiers would recognise him. To his astonishment a soldier searching him removed his Volunteer membership card from his wallet, something he had completely forgotten about. He considered making a run for it, but thought it would be too dangerous for the large crowd of people gathered on the street.[113]

The military also raided a number of business premises in the village, including one owned by two Volunteers, Patrick Breslin and Anthony McGinley. Breslin saw the military arriving and escaped out the back of the building; when he came back onto the street he saw Denis Houston being searched and arrested.[114] Houston was removed to the military post at Bunbeg and then transferred to Victoria RIC barracks, Derry city, for interrogation the next day before being lodged in Derry jail the following Monday.

The British were also active in Ballyshannon that night and a patrol of military, police and Tans approached a group of local men congregated in the town, one of whom was Thomas Rooney. As Rooney began to walk away a soldier pushed him into a doorway at the point of his bayonet. The soldier was then distracted and Rooney began running. The military immediately opened fire, hitting Rooney twice, who sadly died before medical assistance could be rendered.[115]

Roger Casement pictured (fourth from right) with locals on Tory Island 1912.
National Library of Ireland – Photographic Archives

Irish Volunteers pictured at Letterkenny 1913.   *McGinley Collection*

Dr Johnston, white waistcoat and white hair, standing beside his motorcar, IJ 88, shortly before its capture in March 1921. *McElhinney Collection*

Prisoners at Stafford jail, England 1916: Joseph Sweeney is far left in the back row. Eunan McGinley is also in the group and Michael Collins is marked with the x over his head. *Capuchin Archives*

A group of TDs at an early meeting of Dáil Éireann. Included are the three Donegal TDs: Joseph O'Doherty (far left, front row), Joseph Sweeney (standing directly behind O'Doherty) and P.J. Ward (third from right, second row). *Capuchin Archives*

British army base situated at the rear of the County Asylum (St Conal's Hospital). *McGinley Collection*

Liscooley/Killygordon IRA Company, No. 4 Brigade, 1st Northern Division.
McElhinney Collection

Ardara IRA Company, No. 3 Brigade, 1st Northern Division.
McElhinney Collection

Sinn Féin hall, Letterkenny 1918 (left to right): Dr J. P. McGinley, Nellie Grey, Willie McManus, Sam O'Flaherty, Jimmy Ó Dónaill.
McGinley Collection

Burned out RIC barracks (in the background) at Carrick shortly after its destruction in August 1920. *Cunningham Collection, Galway*

Drumquinn RIC barracks, County Tyrone. Scene of the first daylight arms raid carried out by IRA Volunteers from Donegal in August 1920.
Derry People and Donegal News Archives

The Donegal IRA No. 1 flying column, 1921. *McElhinney Collection*

Joseph Sweeney
Capuchin Archives

Peadar O'Donnell
O'Donnell Collection

Pat McGinley
Donegal Annual Archives

Joseph Murray
O'Carroll Collection

Seamus McCann
McCann Collection

Patrick 'Pappy' Johnston
O'Carroll Collection

Thomas McShea
O'Carroll Collection

James (Jim) Dawson
Dawson Collection

P. H. (Packie) Doherty
Doherty Collection

Denis (Donncha) McNelis
Donegal Annual Archives

James McMonagle
Dawson Collection

Group of prisoners, including five from Donegal, at Ballykinlar internment camp, hut no. 15, 'C' Company, 1920. **Top Row**: Joe Kelly, Tipperary; John McElhinney, Donegal; Jerry Killeen, Clare; Paddy Kelly, Donegal; Seamus Kavanagh, Derry. **2nd Row**: Jim McDonald, Dublin and Carlow; William Rooney, Dublin; Dan Montgomery, Clare; Leo Kerwin, Dublin; Peter Kerwin, Dublin; Joe Duffy, Louth; Edward Monaghan, Fermanagh. **3rd Row**: Denis Monaghan, Fermanagh; Jim McGlennon, Down; Hugh Deery, Donegal; Jim Dawson, Donegal; Con O'Leary, Cork; Jim McMonagle, Donegal; Peter McAleer, Tyrone. **Front Row**: Jim McClean, Liverpool; Bob Murphy, Dublin; William Bowles, Dublin; Joe Rooney, Dublin; Tom O'Connor, Dublin; Fred Jones, Dublin.
Dawson Collection

The result of Richard Mulcahy's documents being seized in Dublin was a large-scale search and arrest operation by military and RIC starting on Monday 6 December. The operation began at 9 a.m. when a convoy of lorries carrying military and police passed through Dungloe on their way to Burtonport. A series of raids was carried out in search of Joseph Sweeney, TD, Bernard Sweeney, James Maguire and Patrick Boyle. Failing to find any of the men they then carried out a raid on the house of William Gorman in search of his son John. Later that night the police raided a house in Glenties where John Gorman was staying. He was taken out and searched before being arrested. The Volunteers all over the county generally adhered to the order to stay away from their homes; however, some found it necessary to return home on occasion.

James McMonagle returned home on Sunday night 5 December and felt it safe to stay the night. The military and police carried out extensive raids in Letterkenny at 5 a.m. the following morning and McMonagle's home was targeted. He was arrested and brought to the No. 2 police barrack situated beside the courthouse. James McMonagle had known for some time that he was targeted for arrest by the RIC and his home at Castle Street was often raided. McMonagle would often hide out in the bell tower of St Eunan's cathedral as this overlooked the houses on Castle Street and he would often watch from the bell tower as the British and RIC raided his family home. On his arrival at the No. 2 barracks he found James Dawson, battalion commandant and a civilian named Hugh Deery already there. Hugh Deery was not a member of the IRA and was mistakenly arrested, but was commended for his silence and doing several months in internment as his arrest prevented the arrest of another Volunteer. The three men were transferred to Derry jail later that day and held there for a few days before being informed of their transfer to the newly opened Ballykinlar Internment Camp. The prisoners were conveyed to the railway station at Derry and entrained for Belfast where they were met by an angry loyalist mob. The prisoners were attacked and verbally abused as they stepped off the train. The angry mob shouted, 'You bastards, you are not behind a stone wall in Donegal now.' The military escort was forced to clear the platform and put the prisoners into the station waiting room for safety until the next train arrived.[116]

The residence of Dr J. P. McGinley was also raided that morning, but the doctor was not at home. At the same time the military and police raided the home of P. M. Gallagher, a seventy-five-year-old solicitor from Donegal town. A prominent member of the Gaelic League, he was arrested during the raid and taken to Derry jail. He fell ill a couple of weeks later and was transferred to the prison hospital. In similar raids throughout south Donegal, Thady Higgins, Inver, Charles Cunningham, Killybegs, and John O'Hara, Kilcar, all Volunteers, were arrested and immediately transferred to the new internment camp at Ballykinlar, County Down.[117]

INTERNMENT CAMP

ONE OF THE British responses to the intense IRA campaign was the introduction of internment and the opening of the Ballykinlar internment camp in County Down and the Curragh camp in County Kildare. Volunteers from the Ulster counties were often arrested and interned in Ballykinlar. The very nature of internment meant that Volunteers could be arrested on insubstantial evidence and held indefinitely[118]

The camp at Ballykinlar was situated on the coast near Newcastle, on Dundrum Bay, County Down. Previously used as a training camp for some battalions of the British divisions in Ireland, it boasted a high level of security, being surrounded on three sides by water.[119] The use of internment camps was possibly an acknowledgement by the British of the situation in Ireland and a concession to the Volunteers' of the Irish Republican Army and their demand to be treated as prisoners of war or political prisoners.

Membership of the IRA was regarded as sufficient reason for internment without trial, and the introduction of internment, designed to smash the republican military organisation, meant that camps throughout the country filled up rapidly.

The capture of the Mulcahy documents was a major boost to the British; the papers contained the names of hundreds of men in the movement, who were rounded up all over the country. The internees at Ballykinlar were kept in huts in batches of thirty and had straw to use as bedding; this was often kept outside and open to the elements, with prisoners forced to sleep on the cold floors. The British said the Volunteers were being treated as political prisoners, but the food they were given was very poor and the internees depended on parcels of food and other items from families and friends to survive.

On one occasion two internees named Joseph Tormy and Patrick Sloane left their hut to meet some men from their area who had just arrived in the camp. They had only gone a short distance when a shot rang out. A number of men went out to investigate and found Tormy and Sloane mortally wounded at the back of the hut. A bullet had hit Tormy in the neck before ricocheting off him and killing Sloane. The prisoners knelt around the dead men and had begun to say the rosary when a sergeant and two soldiers arrived unexpectedly. Their attitude incensed the prisoners, who were about to attack them when one of the camp commandants, Joseph McGrath, stood up and said: 'Boys, there are enough men outside to avenge this; all we can do now is to pray for the souls of the deceased.'[120] Tadhg Barry from Cork was also shot and killed while interned in the camp. Several others also died during their incarceration from various ailments and mostly due to ill-treatment. They were: Patrick O'Toole, Carlow; Maurice Galvin, Waterford; John O'Sullivan, Kildare; Maurice Quinn, Cork, and Edward Healy from Waterford.[121]

The British army engineers were adamant that no tunnels could be constructed underground in Ballykinlar as the ground was only four feet above water level. The IRA engineers interned in the camp, however, discovered that one particular spot could be tunnelled without reaching water level. The tunnel, when complete, would lead past a spot very near the guard room and finally come to the surface outside the boundary of the camp. Only a small number of men were selected to construct the tunnel, with a particular hut being selected where the floorboards were lifted and altered so they could be replaced at any time in a matter of seconds. The next problem was disposing of the sand removed as the digging progressed. Some prisoners decided to construct a ball alley a short distance away with a sand surface, and this was used for dumping the sand. Bed boards were then used as props and when missed during inspection the prisoners said they used them as firewood and they were always replaced. The engineers instructed the diggers to push up a marker to the surface at selected places, thus ensuring no errors in direction. The tunnel was eventually completed and contact was made with the outside for guides and other assistance. The prisoners sought permission to hold a concert on the designated night, as there would be no roll call and the escapees would not be missed until the next day.

Unfortunately a similar plan in progress at the Curragh camp was discovered only a few days before the Ballykinlar escape. A number of men, who were not IRA members, discovered the plan and alerted the soldiers in the camp. The following day the camp staff at Ballykinlar was alerted and instructed to conduct a thorough search of the camp for any tunnels. They began digging a deep trench between the outer and inner barbed wire and soon reached the roof of the tunnel, and the alarm was raised. After this the camp staff began taking extra precautions and subsequently reinforcing areas of the camp to prevent any further attempts to escape.[122]

The Donegal prisoners had been at Ballykinlar for approximately two months when, one day, James McMonagle was strolling around the camp. Standing a short distance from a wire barrier, he saw another prisoner being escorted by a British army sergeant.

The other prisoner was signalling to McMonagle to move away and he quickly did so. A few days later the other prisoner, Hubert Wilson from Longford, visited McMonagle's hut. Wilson informed McMonagle that he was signalling because the sergeant escorting him had recognised McMonagle as the man in charge of a raid on British military at Churchill railway station in January 1919. Wilson said the sergeant told him he intended reporting to his superiors that McMonagle was in the camp. However, Wilson had a long conversation with the sergeant on the Irish situation and eventually talked him out of reporting McMonagle to his superiors. The sergeant had been conscripted into the army and was nearing the end of his service. The camp commandant was informed of the incident and as a precaution instructed McMonagle to shave his head, change his name with another prisoner and move to another hut. This was the usual process for hiding a man in the camp.[123]

On Friday 3 December, Éamon de Valera, speaking from the US, responded to Lloyd George's recent announcement in the House of Commons that documents connected with the 'German Plot' discovered on de Valera's person when he was arrested in May 1918 were to be made public. De Valera said:

> There were no documents found in my possession that implicated me or anyone else in any conspiracy. There was no such conspiracy. If there were such documents why did not Lloyd George bring them to trial? With his mock tribunal he would not have needed very much evidence to obtain a conviction.[124]

Meanwhile back in the north-west on Wednesday 8 December the court-martials of Volunteers continued in Derry. Charles McLaughlin from Carndonagh was sentenced to two years' imprisonment for having documents relating to the affairs of the IRA, including a note from Derry HQ addressed to 'Phil, a Chara'.

He was also charged with acting as the recipient of messages on behalf of the IRA.

The military and police were actively pursuing Volunteers and officers named on the captured documents. At approximately 10 p.m. on Wednesday 8 December, two lorryloads of military returned to Burtonport where they surrounded Sweeneys' hotel and the residence of James Maguire. A dance was in progress and the military entered, ordering all young men to stand against the wall. They were searched and asked numerous questions about Joseph Sweeney and Bernard Sweeney. One of the soldiers asked one or two of the young men if they would shoot a British officer in cold blood, while another remarked that it was strange that the young men who attended the dance were not all Volunteers. Having expressed the intention several times of staying all night, the military eventually left after 1 a.m.[125]

The following evening the train from Derry to Buncrana reached Inch Road station and was boarded by a party of Volunteers, who seized the mailbags and removed any correspondence intended for the military and police.[126] Also on Thursday police and military raids in south Donegal resulted in the arrests of John Molloy, Belvin and Charles Haughey, Loughmult, Dunkineely. The houses of Hugh Boyle, Castlegrey, James Cassidy, Drimfin and Denis Tolan, Keelogs, Inver were raided on the same day but nothing was found.[127] Similar raids were carried out in the west of the county; John O'Gorman had been billeting in a house outside Dungloe when he heard voices outside. He immediately gathered his equipment and just escaped through the back as the police burst open the front door. O'Gorman escaped cross-country.

Frank O'Donnell led an ambush on an RIC patrol in Dungloe on the evening of Saturday 11 December and disarmed a police sergeant and constable on patrol in the village. O'Donnell had perfected this type of operation and had successfully procured weapons, ammunition and other items on several other occasions, securing much needed armaments for the No. 1 brigade area. Three days later the police barracks at Burnfoot, which had been recently vacated, was burned by a party of local Volunteers.[128]

Liam O'Duffy, acting O/C No. 4 brigade, South-East Donegal was arrested at the Diamond, Donegal town, on the morning of Wednesday 21 December, by a party of RIC. In a follow-up raid at his lodgings in the town the military discovered documents relating to the Sinn Féin courts. He was first taken to the local RIC barracks but, fearing a rescue attempt, the police transferred him to the local workhouse, then the headquarters of the Rifle Brigade. He was held there for a night before being taken to Derry jail under a heavy military escort the following morning. O'Duffy was also registrar for the district's republican court and had been present during a raid by the Rifle Brigade in October. Nothing was found or seized that day and no arrests were made at the time.

On Christmas night a party of drunken Black and Tans and military broke windows of Catholic-owned houses in the Stranorlar area. It was also stated that the military refused to issue motor permits to Catholic car owners in Donegal over the festive season. The British military command later stated that the actions of the soldiers was a reprisal for the assault of an unarmed soldier earlier that night with the result that there were further fights between civilians and unarmed soldiers in the course of which windows were broken.[129]

Neil Plunkett O'Boyle from Lackenagh, Dungloe, was arrested in Scotland that December for possession of weapons he was preparing to send back to Ireland. He was later imprisoned in Peterhead jail. O'Boyle had been forced to emigrate to Scotland in 1919 because of continued harassment from the RIC in Dungloe. He first gained employment in the mines and also became an active member of the IRA when he joined B company, 2nd battalion Scottish brigade IRA. He immediately began procuring weapons and ammunition to send back to Ireland and was very active up until his capture.[130]

Meanwhile, back in Donegal the Volunteers of the 3rd battalion carried out an ambush on a two-man RIC patrol at Ardara on Tuesday 28 December. The two constables were injured, with one receiving up to 100 pellets in the leg, knee and head while the other was struck by a bullet in the hand. Over the next two days military and police mounted large raids in the Donegal town area where seven young men were arrested on the evening of Wednesday 29 December: John Mullin, Castle Street, Thomas Gallinagh of Ballydevitt, Patrick Gallagher, a publican, Connell Byrne, Castle Street, Denis O'Neill, the Diamond, Charles Harvey, Main Street and John McDaid, Waterloo Place. All were arrested by a mixed party of Black and Tans and RIC and were later transferred to Derry jail.

Also on the Wednesday evening a large party of military and police arrived at the home of Hugh Doherty, Quay Street, Donegal town, to arrest his son, Michael. The son was not at home, however, and the raiding party failed to get any information from the Doherty family about his whereabouts. Evidently under the impression that he would return between their visit and the next morning, the lieutenant in charge of the raiding party placed a soldier at the house. He remained there until 6 a.m., but Michael Doherty did not appear. The military were evidently acting on information contained in the Mulcahy documents, and as a result many men were forced to go on the run on a permanent basis.[131]

12

1921 - THE DONEGAL FLYING COLUMN

THE VOLUNTEERS IN Donegal had rendered a good account of themselves since the war began in earnest in 1919. This was despite having to contend with a number of problems including the remoteness of the county itself and the loss on an annual basis of young and old to seasonal migration. Many families depended on the much needed money made in the fields of English and Scottish farms. These factors provide a ready explanation for the limited involvement of the county in the early part of the conflict.[1]

The beginning of 1921 brought a new and welcome addition to the Donegal IRA in the form of flying columns or full-time active service units. The principle of the flying column was to increase attacks on enemy forces by way of ambush based on hit and run tactics. They were also to bolster Volunteer battalions in major actions on police and military. Each column was to be made up of men drawn from each battalion consisting mainly of officers, usually experienced ones, with a recommended strength of eighteen men, two squad commanders and one unit commander. This would include men who were on the run, men who possessed technical knowledge and those with considerable fighting experience. The brigade area assumed responsibility for supplying the necessary arms, ammunition and equipment, and the duty of protecting each column moving from one locality to another, when going into action. Retiring from action was also the responsibility of the brigade command.[2]

The issue of forming a flying column to operate in Donegal was addressed by the newly appointed divisional O/C at a meeting in the Bogside, Derry in late December 1920. Local Volunteers were informed that Frank Carney was taking command of the 1st northern division, and at the meeting he asked for available men to join battalions in Donegal and also for Volunteers to form a flying column for full-time active service. The following night nine Volunteers attended a meeting in the Shamrock Hall, Bogside, Derry, and it was at this meeting that they first met Donegal man, Peadar O'Donnell, who was charged with forming a flying column to operate in County Donegal to increase the war effort. The names of those who volunteered for service in the column, under the command of Peadar O'Donnell, Dungloe, were: Alfie McCallion, Derry; William Cullen, Derry; James Tyler, Derry; Seamus McCann, Derry; James 'Ginger' McKee, County Armagh; Con Connally, County Monaghan; William Doheny, County Tipperary, and Jim Walsh and Tom Sullivan, both from County Cork.

Men were detailed to go to the dump to get arms and ammunition ready for the flying column. The dump was in an old cowshed and the arms were taken there after the June loyalist riots in Derry city – twelve rifles, two bolt machine guns and ammunition. Alfie McCallion had arranged with Peadar O'Donnell to get the rifles through the cordon of British military patrols that were blocking all roads around the city. The column met at the Shamrock Hall on the night of Saturday 31 December 1920, New Year's Eve, and decided to march into west Donegal under Peadar O'Donnell. The military were very active and were stopping and searching people on the streets. The column could not get through on the Saturday night but O'Donnell declared: 'We will fight our way through on Sunday night.'

On Saturday night, 1 January 1921, the No. 1 flying column

got through the cordon and met at the arranged place at the top of Bligh's Lane about a mile outside Derry city. Every member of the column was by then armed with a service rifle and 200 rounds of ammunition. They then started their march into Donegal and during the night, somewhere between Derry and Newtowncunningham, James McKee, Tom Sullivan and Seamus McCann became separated from the main body of men, losing their way. As they walked through Newtowncunningham they met two RIC men on patrol and both parties exchanged greetings with the policemen bidding the men good night. The rest of the column arrived in Letterkenny and were met by Volunteers from the local company who transported them to Duddys of Fox Hall, about four miles outside the town. A billet had been arranged for them at an old farmhouse with straw spread on the floor for them to sleep on. When the column arrived at Fox Hall they discovered that the three men were missing. At daybreak the missing Volunteers reached the outskirts of Letterkenny and discovered an old coal shed near the Port Bridge where they decided to rest for a short while. They discussed their situation and it was decided that Seamus McCann should go into Letterkenny and get in touch with some of their friends there. He walked into town and contacted John Curran, a Volunteer, who had been out with a party looking for them the previous night. Curran soon arranged for Dr McGinley to pick them up in his old Ford car. Seamus McCann returned to the shed and a short time later Dr McGinley arrived and drove them to Duddys of Fox Hall where the remainder of the column was waiting.

On arrival the missing men received a big cheer, as the others believed they had been arrested. The weary men then bedded down and fell asleep on the straw. That night they heard their first order from Peadar O'Donnell, an order they would hear very often over the coming months: 'Boys, put on your boots.'

Two Ford cars, belonging to Willie McKay and Dr McGinley, arrived to drive the flying column to the broken bridge at the top of

Glendowan. From there they marched in a downpour of rain to the top of the Glendowan mountains, where they rested. The rifles they were carrying were old and required cleaning, so they loaded up and fired a volley of shots into the mountain to clean them out. The column then marched past Lough Barra and into Doochary, by which time every man was soaked to the bone. Peadar O'Donnell called a halt at the village of Doochary and went into Pat O'Donnell's where he got dry underwear for the men. The next stop was at Derryhenney, where they slept on the floor beside good spring beds as they considered themselves too wet to get into the clean beds with their clothes on. That night the column met Frank O'Donnell for the first time when he arrived to take them to Dungloe by car.[3]

Meanwhile the Volunteers of A company, Dungloe and B company, Burtonport decided to get back to work after the numerous military raids following the seizure of Mulcahy's papers, and attacks were planned at the remnants of the RIC in the area. On the evening of Monday 3 January any useful items were removed from the unoccupied RIC barracks at Dungloe before the building was destroyed by fire. In the early hours of the following morning the coastguard station at Burtonport was also destroyed by fire. Both of these operations were carried out under the command of Joe Sweeney, and based on information yielded by the many mail raids that both buildings were to be reoccupied by military and Black and Tans.

The Burtonport RIC barracks was also targeted for destruction, but the local doctor asked that it be left untouched as he had recently purchased it and would render it uninhabitable in the hope of preventing any attempt of reoccupation by the British. The local Volunteers agreed but the doctor only pulled down the stairs and the military were able to occupy the building for a number of days.[4]

On Tuesday 4 January, the flying column received information that the Black and Tans were on their way to Dungloe from Glenties.

The flying column came on to the streets of Dungloe and this was the first time the public came into contact with a company of fully armed Volunteers wearing trenchcoats with gun belts and bandoliers strapped around them. The arrival of the flying column lifted the spirits of the local Volunteers. It was a fair day in Dungloe and the flying column walked through the streets calling on the people to remain indoors. During the night the ambush party were very well looked after by Cissy Doherty and Mary McBride of Cumann na mBan who carried hot tea and bread to all posts. The Black and Tans failed to make an appearance that night and the column was ordered back to their billet. They then received information that the Tans were travelling from Dunfanaghy and set off to take up ambush positions on the road leading from Dungloe to Crolly Bridge, but again the Black and Tans failed to show.

After that the No. 1 flying column decided to move to Meenmore, where a shack had been made ready for them. As they walked over the mountains James 'Ginger' McKee, the quartermaster, who was carrying the bag of food, fell into a bog hole. When a few of his comrades pulled him out he was completely soaked. The first question asked was: 'Is the grub all right?'

En route Peadar O'Donnell took the column to his parents' home at Meenmore. His father had just arrived home from his job at the mill and the first man he welcomed was big James 'Ginger' McKee, the only man standing. James Seán Mór said to Ginger: 'Man, why don't you take a chair?' When Ginger gave no answer, James Seán Mór spoke again: 'Have sense man and take a seat by the fire.' Ginger answered: 'I am too wet to sit.' Old James murmured under his breath: 'It beats the wild west.' After that they made their way to the old shack.[5]

At that time some of the civilian population were very anxious to help the Volunteers and kept a keen eye for any suspicious activity or strangers arriving in the area. One example of this vigilance was when a local man informed Patrick Breslin that a stranger had arrived in Dungloe and was visiting a number of business premises. He had called at a few businesses asking for statements of accounts for goods supplied or commandeered by the British military. He was representing himself as a British civil servant, but raised suspicions when he called to a number of houses of suspected agents and informers. Breslin phoned the No. 1 brigade O/C, Joe Sweeney and was instructed to put surveillance on the stranger. Some time later that day, a young girl who worked at Sweeneys' drapery, located beside Sweeneys' hotel, walked into the hotel kitchen for her dinner and saw a trenchcoat hanging beside the fire. After dinner she returned to the shop and found Willie Sharkey there, enquiring about the movements of a stranger. The girl told Sharkey about the trenchcoat and he asked her to return to examine it. This she did and found the 'Dorset Regiment' stamped on the inside. She immediately returned to inform Sharkey, who told Joe Sweeney.

Sweeney ordered Willie Sharkey to instruct Peadar O'Donnell to have the man arrested and held for questioning. Frank O'Donnell and James 'Ginger' McKee found the stranger in the dining room of the hotel eating his lunch. The two Volunteers were wearing masks and as they approached him he attempted to draw his revolver, but was disarmed by O'Donnell. He was taken to the back of the building, bound and blindfolded before being bundled into a waiting car. They drove him to the column headquarters, an empty house at the rear of a place known locally as the 'Whitehouse'. The prisoner was a British lieutenant called Bracen of the Dorset Regiment based in Derry. Following a thorough interrogation by Peadar O'Donnell and others he admitted that he was a British officer, but denied he was connected to the intelligence section, insisting he was in Dungloe to investigate claims against the British occupation of the area.

That night as the interrogation continued a unionist commercial traveller arrived at Sweeneys' hotel looking for Joe Sweeney. He left a message for Sweeney – if the officer was not released the British would come to the area and wreck the village. The Volunteers did not want large numbers of military and Tans returning and wrecking houses and businesses and so released Bracen with an order to leave on the first morning train. They held him until an hour before the first train was leaving Dungloe.[6]

The Donegal County Council meeting scheduled for Tuesday 4 January had to be cancelled owing to the absence of a quorum. Many of the councillors were also Volunteers on the run and considered it too dangerous to attend regular meetings. This was an indication of how the war was inhibiting the political development in the county, a situation most likely mirrored throughout the country.

The trial of the No. 4 brigade acting O/C Liam O'Duffy was held at Ebrington barracks, Derry on Wednesday 5 January. He had been charged under the Restoration of Order Act, 1920 with 'doing an act with a view to promoting the objects of an unlawful association'. The charge related to a Sinn Féin arbitration court on Wednesday 20 October 1920 in Donegal town that was raided by the military while the court was in session. A large number of witnesses and litigants were also present, and all were searched and questioned before being released. During the raid no documents were seized, but following a raid on O'Duffy's lodgings documents were discovered dealing with some seventeen cases relating to possession of land, recovery of premises, breaches of warranty, seduction, compensation and payment of goods.[7]

A second flying column was organised at Dungloe with Daniel Sweeney as column commander. This was a small column composed entirely of men recruited from the 1st battalion, No. 1 brigade. Known as No. 2 column, its objective was to engage in nuisance attacks on military and police patrols, which would give the impression that the main flying column was operating in a particular area.

The No. 1 flying column moved to the townland of Crovehy and established its headquarters there. The members of the column considered this area one of the best they had ever stayed in and the people of the area kept an open door for all men on the run. The first house they went to on their arrival was James Doran's, who met each Volunteer with the same welcome: 'A hundred thousand welcomes and while there is a cow in Crovehy you will never want.' The Volunteers sat around a big turf fire and somebody called on Frank O'Donnell for a song. He sang 'Bodenstown Churchyard' and Alfie McCallion sang 'When I dream of old Ireland I am dreaming of you'. Then Peadar O'Donnell, with his back to the fire, recited 'Dangerous Dan McGrew'. An old house had been prepared for the column at the top of the glen by Jack Boyle and Anthony Gallagher.[8]

MEENBANAD AND CROLLY AMBUSHES

ON THE EVENING of Tuesday 11 January, two Volunteers who were employed on the railway informed Joe Sweeney of the possible arrival of British troops in the area. They told Sweeney that the stationmasters and crossing-keepers received instructions that a fish train would be leaving Derry at 1 a.m. the next morning and was scheduled to arrive at Burtonport at 7 a.m. The two Volunteers were immediately suspicious as there had been no fishing at Burtonport for some time. Sweeney's immediate suspicions were that the recent prisoner, Lieutenant Bracen, was an intelligence officer and that the impending troop arrival was a result of information passed on by him. Sweeney then contacted Patrick Breslin instructing him to mobilise every available Volunteer and the flying column. The men of the flying column were preparing for bed when they received the command: 'Boys, get your boots on.'

Peadar O'Donnell sent a despatch to Philip Boyle, captain of the Meenacross Company, to mobilise as many armed men as possible under his command and to meet at a location near Meenbanad railway station. About thirty-five Volunteers moved off from Dungloe and arrived at the spot approximately one mile from the station shortly after 5 a.m.

Philip Boyle received the despatch about 2 a.m. and had to raise his men from their beds, and before long the entire company made off to the meeting point. Due to the late hour they had to run the entire distance, arriving at the ambush position shortly after the main body. Some men went up to Meenbanad station and asked the telephonist to contact another station farther up the line to ascertain the cargo. However, the system had been earthed and nobody could be contacted which almost confirmed their suspicions. The Volunteers had to make a decision. They were now quite certain the train had troops on board, but were reluctant to lift the tracks for fear of causing injury to the railway employees, many of who were good friends of the Volunteers.

Joe Sweeney decided to block the tracks with boulders and position men on both embankments with all men firing down at the target. A Volunteer was sent up the line armed with a grenade and instructions to throw it into the train if he noticed troops on board. Not long after getting into position they heard a train approaching at speed, followed by a grenade exploding. As the train passed, the Volunteers opened fire on the carriages from both sides of the track. The boulders failed to derail the train, but did bring it to a stop a few yards away.

Joe Sweeney had positioned himself where the train came to a screeching halt and narrowly escaped from the bullets of a Lewis gun mounted and manned on the cab of the train. Next came two shots from the rear, followed by shouts in a thick Cork accent: 'Oh fuck – the fucking O/C.' It was Mutt Walsh who, because of a leg wound, was told to remain in Dungloe, but limped behind the main party, arriving at the scene just as the attack started. The firing continued and the British troops began organising, taking up positions and returning fire, but as it was still dark they could not locate the Volunteers positions. After some time the retreat whistle was sounded as the British continued to shoot into the dark. Patrick Breslin, Joe O'Donnell and Patrick (Kit) O'Donnell were still in position and were not sure if they heard the retreat whistle. Suddenly bullets were passing their position and they could see khaki-clad soldiers moving along the line and firing in their direction. Bernard Sweeney then ran passed their position and said the retreat whistle had been sounded. They immediately retreated for a distance, when Breslin remembered a bag containing approximately 100 round of .303 ammunition. Breslin and Bernard Sweeney returned to retrieve the bag and could hear the rattle of machine-gun fire. They hid the bag of ammunition at a moss cliff until the next day. British military strength on the train was 150 men and some reports suggested up to twelve killed and thirty injured. However; other reports put the number killed much higher possibly over fifty and it was said that blood was seen flowing out of the carriages. However, an account of the ambush in an official report from Dublin Castle stated that the train was riddled with bullet holes but reached its destination without casualties to the occupants.

At the conclusion of the ambush Anthony McGinley and a number of Volunteers took a wrong turn and ran into a party of British troops. They came under heavy fire while retreating, but eventually escaped, with the exception of one Volunteer. William Cullen noticed a British military patrol and quickly hid his rifle and ammunition before being arrested. The rifle and ammunition were later recovered by the IRA.

Some of the men who took part in the Meenbanad ambush included Joe Sweeney, Peadar O'Donnell, Joe O'Donnell, Frank O'Donnell, Con Boyle, Anthony McGinley, John O'Gorman, Patrick Breslin, Patrick (Kit) O'Donnell, Philip Boyle, Patrick McCole, Charles Ward, James Boyle, Willie Sharkey and John Sweeney, all from Donegal; James Tyler, Seamus McCann, Alfie McCallion and William Cullen, all from Derry; Jim Walsh and Tom O'Sullivan from Cork; Bill Doheny from County Tipperary; Con Connolly from County Monaghan and James McKee from Armagh, from No. 1 flying column, A company, B company and C company, 1st battalion No. 1 brigade.[9] The ambush received some plaudits from GHQ through *An t-Óglach*, where an article said that 'Some valuable hints can be gained from the train fight in Donegal ...' The article was based on Joe Sweeney's report to GHQ.[10]

The uninjured members of the British military marched to Burtonport later that morning and occupied the old RIC barracks, the building that had been saved from destruction by the request of a local businessman. The interior was not habitable and they only remained there for a few days. Joe Sweeney was proved correct about the cargo on the train and Lieutenant Bracen was one of the officers on board. Bracen and other officers commandeered a car and drove to Sweeneys' hotel where they reconstructed Bracen's kidnap. He allowed himself to be blindfolded and was driven along the road, stopping at the Whitehouse, which was by that time evacuated. The British officers conducted a thorough examination of the building and spent over an hour trying to find any trace of the column.

After the Meenbanad ambush the flying column left Crovehy and made its way to Lough Keel, to the McGee family home, a known resting place for men on the run. While there the column heard that the British military had brought another train to remove the first one. Plans were made to attack the second train and the column left Lough Keel to make its way to Crolly, taking positions just opposite the station. The No. 1 flying column, under Peadar O'Donnell, organised the attack and called for immediate assistance from the local Volunteers. C company of 1st battalion received a despatch for assistance at very short notice. Patrick (Kit) O'Donnell, Anthony McGinley, Charlie Cole and Willie Sharkey went out onto the street in Dungloe and held up the first car that came along. They commandeered the car but none of them could drive so they had to get a driver at the local garage to bring them to Crolly. At the location Peadar O'Donnell had selected for the ambush the railway line ran along the bottom of a hill. The column took up position on the top of the hill and a scout was sent up the line with instructions to give a signal if there were no civilians on board. The train arrived at the station and the signal was given, and as soon as the train came within rifle range the ambush party opened fire. The four Volunteers from C company were approaching the ambush position when the firing started and came under fire from the train. They took cover and returned fire but the train managed to pass through.[11]

Shortly after that Joe Sweeney received a despatch from Henry McGowan, O/C 4th brigade, South-East Donegal, offering some of his men and weapons for active service in Sweeney's area if required. The Ballybofey and Stranorlar battalions were reluctant to engage in these areas for fear of reprisals due to the heavily garrisoned barracks in both towns. All weapons were collected and taken to Burtonport and given to Joe Sweeney on loan.[12]

Denis Houston of the 1st northern division, was brought before what the British called a field general court-martial on Wednesday 12 January charged under the Restoration of Order in Ireland Regulations (ROIR) with having a document relating to the affairs of an illegal organisation. Houston who had been arrested in December 1920 refused to recognise the court. A British officer gave evidence of accompanying a party of military to Dungloe on the evening of 4 December. He stated that a large party of civilians were in the town and a number of them began to run when the military arrived. The soldier said he ran down a side street where he was intercepted by a group of men. When the accused was found with the membership card of the Irish Volunteers dated 23 March 1919, Houston pointed out that the Irish Volunteers had not been proclaimed until November of that year and he asked if the court had sufficient evidence to connect him with the movement at that date. The prosecutor said there was nothing to show that the accused ceased to be a member of the Volunteers and even that could only be pleaded in mitigation of sentence. Houston was subsequently sentenced to six months' imprisonment.

The Donegal Town Company also suffered a blow on Wednesday morning with the arrest of Hugh Britton, company captain. A party of military and police raided his home at 5 a.m. and found Britton still in bed.[13] He was removed to Derry jail an a short time later interned at the Ballykinlar internment camp.

Volunteers who spent time in their local areas were always under threat of arrest as the RIC and British military had agents all over the county and were receiving information from various local sources. The commandant of the Carndonagh Company, Packie (P. H.) Doherty was a target of the RIC for some time and was aware that information on his movements was being passed to the police. This proved true in January when he attended a dance at his brother's dancehall in Carndonagh and the hall was suddenly surrounded by a large party of RIC and military. He made a hasty exit from the building but once outside discovered that all his escape routes were covered by RIC patrols. He then made his way towards the railway line in an attempt to cross the river, but there was a heavy flood that night and the only means of escape was via the railway bridge, which was also covered by an RIC patrol. A short time later the patrol moved along the line in the direction of the bridge and Doherty decided to follow them by crawling along a sunken footpath beside the rail. The patrol eventually passed over the bridge and he succeeded in crossing unnoticed. Now on the safe side of the river he proceeded along a garden hedge and accidentally kicked a tin can causing a bit of a racket. He moved quickly on and lay under a hedge and at that moment a party of RIC arrived carrying torches and with revolvers drawn. They searched thoroughly, but failed to locate Doherty's position and eventually moved on.

Doherty had been aware for some time that his movements were being reported to the police on a regular basis. If he stayed in a particular house one night the house was always raided the following day. He decided to move out of the area and cycled to Culdaff to stay with relatives. He stayed with his cousin on the Saturday night and decided to return to the Carndonagh area on Sunday evening. That night his cousin's house was raided and the RIC went directly to the bedroom he had slept in the previous night. Doherty reported the incidents when he returned to the Carndonagh Company and after a few days of analysing his movements concluded that the informer at Culdaff could only be a young man named O'Connell. He had been at the house on Doherty's arrival. O'Connell was the son of a retired RIC sergeant.

Some time later O'Connell was arrested by members of the Clonmany Company and brought before a republican court-martial where he was found guilty and sentenced to death. Packie Doherty was not called to give evidence and thought that the evidence against O'Connell was only circumstantial and, based on that assumption, that the sentence was too severe.

Doherty considered O'Connell to be a young man of low intelligence, who was possibly unaware of his actions, and that the information could have been passed on by his father. Fortunately for O'Connell he was handed over to Packie Doherty to be held until the sentence was to be carried out. As soon as Doherty was left alone with the prisoner he told him that he was free to go and to leave the area, never to return. O'Connell did as he was told.[14]

The hiring fair was held in Donegal town on Friday 14 January, drawing a very heavy military and police presence throughout that day and night. Checkpoints manned by soldiers were set on all roads leading to the town and all cars were stopped, searched and drivers questioned. People walking were also stopped and questioned throughout the day. The police brought four or five young men to the barracks, but these were later released, while all licensed premises were closed at 7 p.m. by order of the police.

Some excitement was caused at Buncrana railway station the following morning by the seizure of a mailbag by six Volunteers. There were two trains in the station and a number of people on the platform when Volunteers grabbed the mailbag from the parcel office and made a dash for the hills towards Tullydish. The police were informed and gave chase. Having run for over a mile, the Volunteers ditched the bag in an unoccupied house, where it was later found by the RIC.[15]

A party of military and police raided the house of Peter O'Donnell, Mullins, Donegal town, on the morning of Monday 17 January and questioned his son about posters that had been put up the previous morning. They then searched the house, but failed to find anything incriminating O'Donnell. The houses of James Boyle, a member of the Donegal Board of Guardians and a district councillor, and James Noonan, both from Letterfad, were searched by the military, but nothing was found. Charles McDaid, Tullynaha, vice chairman of the Donegal Board of Guardians, had a rather unique experience while out walking. He met a military raiding party who picked him up and gave him a lift to his house, which they subsequently searched. On the same day in Letterkenny a party of military raided the workhouse and searched the boardroom, taking away copies of the voting records of members and minute books.[16]

Later that evening the lighthouse at Fanad Head was raided by five Volunteers from the Fanad Company. There was only one man in the lighthouse looking after the lamp and he was held up at the point of a revolver. The Volunteers demanded rockets and explosives, but were told there were none in the building. The building was then searched and two telescopes and a Morse signal lamp were taken away.

The following day, in Buncrana, Patrick Fletcher, Charles McLaughlin, William Harkin and C. V. O'Donnell were charged with assaulting and robbing a corporal and a private, who they had relieved of 2 rifles and 200 rounds of ammunition. They were also charged with having a revolver not under effective military control. Fletcher, McLaughlin and Harkin stated that while they had no objections to the officers constituting the court, they declined to recognise it.

O'Donnell pleaded not guilty and was represented by a solicitor, T. E. Conaghan. The men were searched during a raid at Harkins' barbershop on 7 October 1920 and were arrested the following day.

215

Donegal County Councillor John E. Boyle was arrested at his home by a party of military and police on Wednesday 19 January. He was first taken to the former police barracks at Burtonport and later moved to Derry jail. The following day Joseph O'Doherty, TD, was removed from Derry jail and taken to Ballykinlar internment camp.[17]

Liam O'Duffy was tried before a court-martial in Derry on Saturday 22 January. He had been previously charged under the 1920 Restoration of Order Act for 'acting as a registrar of a court held under the Sinn Féin auspices', deemed an illegal organisation under the act. He was sentenced to one year's imprisonment with hard labour at Derry jail.[18]

The Dunfanaghy Company launched an attack on the police barracks near Dunfanaghy village at 4 a.m. the following morning. The local Volunteers were supported by the Creeslough and Falcarragh companies. A number of bombs were used in the attack, which lasted about an hour and which also featured sporadic firing from both sides. The attacking party had intended to seize the barracks and thought the bombs would cause enough structural damage to achieve their objective, but the explosives failed to give the desired effect. Neither the Volunteers nor members of the police were injured.[19]

The IRA's intelligence officers were quite resourceful in their methods of collecting information on enemy forces. One source of information on the movement of troops through Donegal was based at the Northern Counties hotel in Derry. Mary Molloy, a member of Cumann na mBan, was working there as a barmaid. The bar-room, a sort of private area separate from the main premises, was often frequented by British officers. Mary Molloy often overheard conversations between drunken officers which she passed on to Daniel Kelly. She had introduced Daniel Kelly to a major in the British army transport section. They used to have the odd drink together and Kelly was able to get information about troop movements between Derry and Donegal. It was Kelly who obtained the information that led to the Crolly ambush; he contacted two Volunteers, James Lynch and George Doherty, who cycled to Manorcunningham and made contact with William Holmes, who was to send someone to Letterkenny with information about the train.

However, by the time the two men reached Manorcunningham it was too late for Holmes to find anyone. The two cycled on to Letterkenny and made contact with Anthony Dawson. Dawson had a motorcycle and immediately set off for Creeslough to inform the captain of the Creeslough Company. Two of the Creeslough Company then drove to Burtonport and made contact with Joe Sweeney, who then mobilised a number of his men and with Peadar O'Donnell's flying column set off to ambush the troop train. At the selected site boulders were rolled on to the tracks. The ambush party positioned themselves in the hills above the tracks, however, the engine driver thought the boulders were sheep and slowed up. The Volunteers threw bombs into the train and began firing. The driver immediately drove the train back up the tracks until they reached Crolly station where a call was made for military reinforcements. A week later Daniel Kelly was having a conversation with a British major in the Northern Counties Hotel and he was told about the ambush. The major said, 'If the blighters had opened the pins of the bombs, there would not have been one of us left alive.'[20]

On Sunday 23 January a party of British troops billeted in Loughanure School were fired on by Volunteers from the Loughanure Company. The following day the train carrying the last detachment of troops returning from Burtonport to Derry was ambushed at Crolly by Volunteers from the Loughanure and Annagry companies.[21] A number of raids were carried out in the Kilcar area on Wednesday 26 January by police, resulting in the arrest of Dan Byrne and Joachim Murray who were handed over to military custody.

Miss Eileen D. McAdam, editor of *An Dáil*, published weekly in Ballyshannon, was also arrested that day. She was brought by train to Derry accompanied by armed military and a female searcher. She was then put into a first-class compartment and taken to Armagh jail, which was the female prison, but was released after a couple of days without charge. A few days later, three Volunteers – Francis O'Brien, Francis J. Murray and Charles Carr, all from Ardara – were arrested and taken by military escort to Derry jail.[22]

A party of sixteen military and one officer arrived in Burtonport on Saturday 5 February on the 12.30 p.m. train and carried out a number of raids and searches of houses in the area. They left again to join the 2.20 p.m. train at Meenbanad. The flying column was too far away to be notified, so Joe Sweeney organised the Dungloe Volunteers and set off on foot to Meenbanad. They arrived there several minutes late but were aware that the line would be blocked behind any military force so they set off in the direction the train had gone. Captain James Ward, with a party of the Loughanure Volunteers, had removed a portion of the track and blocked it with boulders earlier that morning. About two and half miles from Meenbanad the section under Sweeney came upon the train, which was wrecked, having run into the barricade of boulders. A railwayman informed them that the military had gone off in the direction of their base at Bunbeg. Sweeney had by now established contact with the flying column and both parties proceeded to a hill overlooking the British line of retreat but failed to locate them.

In the early hours of the following morning a troop train travelling very slow with a vanguard and flank guards arrived at the wrecked train and stayed there until daylight. A breakdown gang got to work and most of the military returned to Gweedore, leaving twenty men to guard the train.

Joe Sweeney, 1st brigade O/C, sent scouts out to the scene of the wreck during the morning and, learning of the small guard, ordered out the flying column and another twelve men drawn from those available from A, C, F and G companies. The O/C instructed the officer in command to get into position and attack. The attacking party were almost in position when a troop train accompanied by four lorryloads of RIC arrived at the scene, meaning that the Volunteers were now greatly outnumbered. Sweeney decided not to attack and waited at the scene to survey the military activities for some hours before withdrawing.

On Tuesday scouts reported that large numbers of military were still at the wrecked train and were using their own train as a patrol between the wreck and Gweedore station. An order was sent to the captain of the Dungloe Company, 2nd battalion, to cut the railway line at Dore to confine the patrol train. The O/C then selected a suitable position and the men lay in wait. About 4 p.m. the patrol train approached slowly with the wrecked train and as soon as it came within range rapid gunfire was directed at it; the driver put on all speed, saving the train by his prompt action.

The attacking party then moved up the line, but the lines had not been cut or blocked as ordered and the military escaped. Reports were later received from Volunteers in Derry that a number of ambulances full of wounded soldiers had arrived at the military hospital earlier that day.[23]

In a follow-up operation approximately 2,000 military advanced on the 1st brigade, West Donegal area in the early hours of Wednesday morning 9 February. They approached from four points and, having drawn a cordon, swept inside it and rounded up all men, young and old; only seven Volunteers were caught, however. Nine of the party which attacked the train were cut off inside the cordon, but got through under the cover of darkness to the hills with all arms and equipment. The military remained in the area until Friday when they left Burtonport by train with some of the prisoners.[24]

Shortly before this the members of the No. 1 flying column had made their way to Brockagh and were billeted in a large barn at James McKelvey's. McKelvey's was then used as a base by the column and they spent their time organising patrols in anticipation of British military passing through the area. However, they failed to locate any military or police after spending many days and nights in ambush positions. Peadar O'Donnell decided to move to Gortahork, where they made preparations for an attack on the RIC barracks in Falcarragh.[25]

The train carrying the prisoners from the Dungloe area had a military escort of approximately fifty soldiers and as a precautionary measure against attack, a pilot engine was sent out in front. As the engine approached Kincasslagh Road station it dashed into boulders on the line and was derailed and wrecked. The engine driver and fireman had a narrow escape. The train carrying the prisoners stopped and had to wait for three hours while the track was cleared and repaired. On proceeding, the train again hit boulders near Creeslough and the engine was damaged, causing further delay. The train eventually arrived in Derry in the early hours of Saturday morning and the prisoners were taken to Victoria barracks.

Joe Sweeney ordered two Volunteers to initiate an inquiry into the failure by the Dungloe Company to carry out orders to cut the railway track at Dore and later convened a court-martial. The inquiry team discovered that the issue concerned three Volunteers who bluntly refused to obey the order and the remainder of the company merely followed the insubordinates. The men of the Dungloe Company were rounded up. Sweeney presided over the court-martial of eleven men who disobeyed the orders and the three ringleaders were identified. The court-martial ordered the three men to leave the county, with the remaining eight receiving various sentences. Sweeney used members of all other companies of the 1st battalion to round up and guard the men to send out a message that such insubordination would not be tolerated. Following this court-martial a request was made to GHQ for a disciplinary code to deal with such insubordination in the brigade area. A staff memo was quickly issued detailing a variety of offences, including what were considered as serious, such as treason, cowardice and gross neglect of duty.[26]

Large numbers of military were again drafted into Dungloe and surrounding areas later that week; they were supported by the naval forces with sailors dressed in khaki searching the whole coastal area and adjacent islands. Reports at the time stated that several hundred young men were rounded up but after questioning many were released, with the exception of around sixty prisoners who were taken to Derry by train under heavy military escort. That evening the prisoners were taken to Ebrington barracks. Some were released and returned home on the train later that night. Further releases took place the following Monday with only twenty being detained. These included Patrick O'Donnell, Annagry; Charles Boyle, Loughanure, Annagry; John McFadden, Gweedore; Joseph Gallagher, Killendarragh, Crolly; Michael McBride, Meenalae, Annagry; Denis Doherty, Sheskinarone, Dungloe; John O'Donnell, Mín Doire Slua, Annagry, and Philip Sweeney, Guallagh, Annagry.[27]

The military and police concentrated on different areas of the county, an indication that the British were again increasing the pressure on the Volunteers and the general population. A large party of military arrived in Carndonagh by train from Buncrana on the morning of Friday 11 February. They apprehended a young boy called McLaughlin and marched him through the street at gunpoint. They thoroughly searched a number of houses and some arrests were made. Some literature relating to the St Vincent de Paul Society was seized as it was considered seditious material. Those arrested were James Lanigan, Sinn Féin county councillor, his brothers Bernard, Frank and Patrick, as well as William, Patrick and John Howel and Bernard Fitzsimons. Bernard Lanigan and Patrick Howel were later released while the others were conveyed to Buncrana for interrogation and then to Derry jail on Saturday morning.[28]

On the same day a party of police raided the house of Mrs Lafferty, Carrowreagh near Carndonagh and asked for the whereabouts of one of her sons. They ransacked the house and conducted a thorough search of the building, even examining school books and searching a twelve-year-old boy. They also raided and searched the house of Mrs Doherty, Glebe where an obsolete weapon was found. The raiding police removed a steel helmet belonging to one of Mrs Doherty's sons who had been in the British army since the beginning of the war and fought through the entire campaign. Mrs Lafferty had a son killed in the war and another had been a prisoner in Germany.[29]

A number of Donegal Volunteers were tried before a court-martial in Derry the following Saturday, 19 February with Patrick Gallagher, Donegal town being sentenced to five years commuted to two years. Four other men – Denis O'Neill, Thomas Gallinagh, John McDaid and Charles J. Harvey – were also sentenced at the same court and each received sentences of two years with hard labour. They were convicted of unlawful assembly and false imprisonment of an ex-soldier.[30]

On the same day solicitor C. A. Flattery, Letterkenny, who was looking after the affairs of P. J. Ward, TD, was arrested in Donegal town but was released after a brief detention. Later that day Volunteers raided the house of Commander Hobbart, RN, at Fintra, near Killybegs, removing several weapons and other items. The incident was reported by Hobbart and that evening a large group of military and police arrived in the area and carried out a number of raids.[31]

The RIC barracks at Mountcharles had been evacuated in September 1920 and the police usually deployed men from Donegal town to patrol the village on fair days. This gave the local Volunteers an opportunity to plan an ambush on the RIC on their next scheduled visit. The next fair day was Tuesday 22 February and eight local Volunteers – Brian Monaghan, Mick Dawson, Willie McGroarty, Michael Ward, Paddy Kelly, Andy Higginbottom, Joe Gallagher and Charles Murray – took up positions the previous evening in a thickly wooded area known as 'The Glen', just outside Mountcharles. At approximately 1 p.m. four or five police accompanied by a party of sixteen military came cycling along the road and as soon as they came into range the Volunteers opened fire. The police and military took whatever cover was available and returned fire. The exchange of fire lasted for about ten minutes, at which point the Volunteers retreated. One police officer was killed and a number of RIC and military seriously wounded. Two young men were arrested in follow up raids in the area, Thomas Waugh and Albert Griffin.

The remains of the dead policeman were brought back to Donegal town later that day and this prompted an angry response from the police and Tans stationed in the town. The mood among the RIC and Tans was one of vengeful anger, and soon they began firing shots at buildings in the town; shortly after 6 p.m. they ordered all businesses to be closed and shuttered. Shots could be heard at frequent intervals, causing great alarm among the inhabitants. Many people fled their homes for safety, taking shelter in outhouses and other places.

A substantial wooden structure, formerly used as a Sinn Féin hall, was set ablaze and completely destroyed. Shutters were battered in or pulled off, shop doors smashed and forced from their hinges and goods thrown on the streets. Many offices, licensed premises and shops, including the jewellery shop of William Britton, were looted and the interiors smashed up.

A mixed force of RIC, Tans, Auxiliaries and military returned to Mountcharles shortly after midnight the same night rampaging through the village and ransacking every house they entered. They broke into the houses of known republicans and sympathisers, setting some houses on fire. The mixed party fired indiscriminately at homes, businesses and anyone found outside. A party of raiders were smashing up McManus' in the village and starting fires in parts of the house when suddenly a drunken Auxiliary shot a policeman in the mistaken belief that he was Joe McManus, a brother of the woman who lived there. At that point a senior military officer commanding the murderous gang called the mixed forced together and ordered them to evacuate the village. In the aftermath of the night of terror a young woman was found dead in the yard of her uncle's farm. Mary Harley had been shot through the heart while trying to escape from

Bernard McGrory's house as the raiding party attempted to break in. Her family believed she had been in a safe place and were shocked to find her lifeless body next morning.[32]

At Donegal town another RIC man was killed on Wednesday morning when he was shot accidentally as the Black and Tans and police were shooting up the town. The next day businesses in the area remained closed, as did schools, and many residents stayed away from the town and their homes for fear of a repeat of the previous day's rampage and reprisals. The office of P. J. Ward, TD, received much attention during the rampage and was completely destroyed.

The reprisals continued with co-operative stores at Inver being burned to the ground on the night of Wednesday 23 February. Military and Tans had called there earlier in the day and instructed staff to remove all stock as they were returning to burn it. This policy of reprisal affected the local economy in various ways; co-operative stores were a source of local employment and their destruction would also impinge on the local farming industry.

The following day two shop assistants were compelled to remove republican graffiti, which read 'Stand Fast by the IRA' from the railway gates in Donegal town. At the same time Hugh Monaghan, Tirconaill Street, was taken from a house in the townland of Mullins by police and ordered to paint over graffiti on bridges and walls along the main road. The slogans 'Stand Fast by the IRA' and 'Informers Beware' had been painted at different points along the road.

The military and police remained active in the outlying areas and arrested a number of people in Ballintra on Wednesday evening. These included Fr Charles Boyce, Patrick McMenamin, boat merchant, James McMenamin, postman, and James Mangan, publican. They were taken to Finner camp for questioning and released the following morning.[33]

When the major raids began to ease the Volunteers from companies in the 1st battalion area and the No. 1 flying column were mobilised for an attack on Glenties RIC barracks. This barracks was in the 3rd brigade area and permission was granted by Seán Houston, the brigade O/C; arrangements for the attack and capture were in the hands of the officers of that brigade. The attack was planned for the night of Friday 25 February and, having mobilised the Volunteers, a number of cars were commandeered to transport equipment and men with the remaining Volunteers having to cycle the twenty miles to Glenties. The attacking party stopped for a short rest at Doochary, where other transport was commandeered.

When the party reached Glenties railway station they were informed that the operation was cancelled due to the heavy police presence in the area. It transpired that members of the Glenties Company were concerned for the safety of the local population and were busy all day warning townspeople of the impending attack. It was obvious that some of the businessmen and residents were worried about their property and informed the police. Glenties was described by Joe Sweeney in a report to GHQ as being notorious for its rottenness and he said the representatives of the IRA were a credit to the town. So all their trouble and hardship was in vain and they had to return to Dungloe.[34]

The mixed force of police and military returned to the Mountcharles area on Saturday morning as the funeral of Mary Harley was taking place. They drew a cordon around the village and all males attending the funeral were lined up, questioned and searched. Three men – John Harley, Pat McCahill and Dominic Boyle – were arrested. The funeral continued under the watchful eyes of the military and police, who remained in the area for several hours.

The military and police kept up the pressure, with further arrests and raids in south Donegal on Monday 28 February. Peter Cannon and Edward Carey from Glencolmcille and Patrick Bell, Donegal town were arrested and taken to the RIC barracks in Donegal town. They were searched and interrogated before being released the following morning.

In another military and police operation further west a Volunteer named Michael Heaney was shot dead by drunken Auxiliaries. A mixed party of British military, police and Auxiliaries raided his home at Malinbeg, near Slieve League. Michael Heaney was dragged from the house by two Auxiliaries and shot execution-style with his body also showing signs of a severe beating. The official report said he was shot while trying to evade arrest.

The military and police were also active in the Inishowen area that day. They raided the home of George Gill, Kindroyhead, Gleneely, but he was not at home at the time. A young man named Duffy was arrested at the house and taken to Carndonagh barracks. The prisoner was handcuffed at all times and the police refused to remove them even when local people brought food for him. The raiding party returned to George Gill's the following morning and he was arrested and removed to Carndonagh barracks. On their journey the raiding party stopped at the premises of William McConalogue and searched the building, but nothing was found. Further raids were carried out that day at Destertegney, near Buncrana. Three men were arrested – McGrory, Greaney and McLaughlin – and all were transferred to Derry jail.[35]

A Dáil session was held at Walter Cole's house at Mountjoy Square in Dublin on Friday 11 March. A number of decisions were made and decrees announced, including the prohibition of assistance in relation to the British census, a decree prohibiting the importation and sale of British goods, and a stipulation that £100,000 was to be provided in loans to local authorities from whom customary government grants had been withheld owing to the declaration of allegiance to Dáil Éireann. Austin Stack, the minister for home affairs, issued a warning to members of the local authorities who served both the republican administration and the English Local Government Board to desist or face the consequences. The correspondence was issued to all local authority officials:

In view of the gravity of the offence and the serious nature of the penalty with which it must in future be met, this Department thinks it proper to issue the following warning:

Where a local authority has by resolution declared allegiance to Dáil Éireann and has severed all relations with the English Local Government Board instructing its officials to cease communication with that institution, any such communication, written or verbal, direct or indirect, with that institution, or any of its officials, or any person acting on behalf of any of its officials, will be deemed a treasonable practice and dealt with accordingly. The Dáil Ministry is well aware that the great majority of the officials of local authorities are loyally accepting the instructions of their employing bodies and the issuing of this warning must not be interpreted as any reflection on the general body of local government officials. Those officials, however, who have been wanting in that loyalty (many of them are known and adequate steps are being taken to ensure that all of them will be known) should not take this warning lightly. It is not issued lightly.[36]

DOCTOR JOHNSTON'S MOTOR CAR

THE CHIEF OF staff, Richard Mulcahy, sent a despatch to Frank Carney, newly appointed O/C of the No. 1 Ulster division, outlining the new arrangements. On Monday 14 March, a meeting was held at Hugh O'Donnell's house in Dungloe at which representatives from all the brigades were present. The despatch from Mulcahy was forwarded to Joe Sweeney and read to the meeting:

> You (Carney) will proceed to Donegal and as arranged at the recent conference you will take temporary control over the new division for the purpose of the immediate cooperation of

the work of the four brigades concerned and for the purpose of developing and later on recommending the appointment of a divisional staff for the area to comprise a divisional commander, a divisional adjutant and a divisional quartermaster with attached officers. The division will be known as the No. 1 Northern Division, and the various brigades will be designated as follows:

No. 1 brigade (West Donegal) battalions: Burtonport, Falcarragh, Gweedore, Dungloe.
No. 2 brigade (North-East Donegal) battalions: Stranorlar, Strabane, Derry, Inishowen, Letterkenny.
No. 3 brigade (South-West Donegal) battalions: Ardara, Killybegs, Rosses.
No. 4 brigade (South-East Donegal) battalions: Donegal town, Ballyshannon (including Belleek), Ederney (including Pettigo), Castlederg, Ballybofey, Castlefinn.

You will arrange to put Captain Peadar O'Donnell in temporary charge of No. 2 brigade and you will arrange for the formation of a brigade staff there, the appointment of which you will later on be able to recommend. In the case of No. 3 brigade and No. 4 you will arrange for the temporary putting in charge of some person and for the formation of the brigade staff in each area which you can subsequently recommend for appointment. In the case of all brigades you will require to verify and where necessary define the various battalion areas. You will arrange for the cooperation of the commandant of the No. 1 brigade and the acting commandant of No. 2 brigade in your work, and you will further be assisted by the organiser at present in west Donegal, the organiser at present in Inishowen and the organiser who will be sent forthwith to assist you in the organisation of the two southern brigades. For the present and in order properly to control the munitions passed into the area, the QM of No. 1 brigade shall be regarded as the divisional QM and all material for the new divisional area will be forwarded to him.

The following were appointed onto the divisional staff: divisional commandant, Frank Carney; adjutant, Bernard Doherty; quartermaster, Frank Martin; divisional medical officer, Dr Farrell; director of training, John McCluskey; divisional engineer, Donncha McNelis.[37]

McNelis, a native of Glencolmcille, reported to Patrick Breslin at the divisional GHQ and Breslin arranged a place for him to stay at Caravan, Dungloe. McNelis was a first-class engineer and during his time in Donegal was known to his comrades as Seán Murray. He organised a good unit of engineers, who assisted him in the construction of dugouts for the storage of arms and equipment. He removed the wires from the Lough Swilly railway line and rewired the telegraph line from Dungloe to Doochary.

He constructed a dugout at Doochary and another on the outskirts of Dungloe on the Mill Road and connected both by telephone to be used in the event of the enemy approaching from the Doochary direction. From there brigade headquarters could be notified at Dungloe. McNelis had spent most of his early years as a Volunteer in County Cork, and in 1918 was the focus of an arrest operation at his lodgings at Leitrim Street in Cork city. He confronted the raiders with his revolver and defied them to search or arrest him. A struggle ensued and McNelis shot Head Constable Clarke and two RIC constables. Two other policemen were also wounded before McNelis and the owner of the house were overpowered and arrested. The No. 1 Cork brigade feared McNelis would be hanged if the head constable died and immediately began arranging for his escape. The plan was set for Monday 11 November 1918, which coincided with the ending of the war in Europe. Shortly after 3 p.m. six Volunteers arrived at the jail and were admitted in pairs. The prison allowed two people to visit a prisoner each day. Two of the Volunteers were admitted to the visiting cell and were greeted by McNelis, but the visit was a brief one. After a few minutes the two men said they had to hurry off again, which surprised McNelis. The warder inserted the key in the lock to let them out, at which point the Volunteers pulled small sandbags from their pockets and knocked him out. They opened the door and McNelis jumped the barrier separating the visitors from the prisoners. The three men moved swiftly into the prison grounds and McNelis was given a revolver. However, they had forgotten to close the door and one of them returned to do so. This turned out to be a fortunate oversight as three men leaving together would have aroused suspicion. The escape party had keys to the prison and locked the gates as they passed through so that no one could get in or out of the prison. The escape was successful and McNelis went back on active service in other parts of Cork prior to his arrival in Donegal in late 1920.[38]

A party of Volunteers carried out an attack on Milford police barracks at 2 a.m. on Monday 14 March; the attack continued for over an hour without any casualties on either side. A local solicitor named McConnell and his wife had a lucky escape when the occupants of the barracks returned fire. No fewer than twelve bullets entered their home, one bullet striking the pillow where Mrs McConnell had been sleeping moments earlier. The following Friday Neil Blaney, Rosnakill, Fanad, was arrested by a party of military and taken to Derry jail the next day under heavy escort. The military removed a Sinn Féin flag from the Kindrum Sinn Féin hall the same day.[39]

Meanwhile in Inishowen six Volunteers went to the RIC barracks at Moville at approximately 10.30 p.m. on Friday night on the pretext of applying for a permit. They knocked at the door but were prevented from entering by the local sergeant. They immediately opened fire but the sergeant managed to lock the door. The Volunteers then made a hasty retreat and moments later military and police piled on to the street but by then the Volunteers had gone. The military remained on the street for a number of hours and fired shots indiscriminately. Local residents were terror-stricken and many left their homes to seek refuge.

The following morning twelve Volunteers carried out a mail raid on the Derry train at Ballymagan. A number of them held up the station officials while the others checked the mailbags and removed all correspondence destined for the military and police.[40]

Over the same weekend in west Donegal the Volunteers from the Lettermacaward E company destroyed the signal cabin and coastguard station on Arranmore Island. They removed all the telephone apparatus and other useful articles before setting the place on fire. The Volunteers of D company, Doochary, on receiving information that a mixed party of Black and Tans, police and Auxiliaries patrolled the village of Doochary most evenings, planned an attack for Sunday 20 March. They arrived in the village the previous night and took up positions at various points. However, before the arrival of the larger patrol, three members of the local RIC were walking through the village when one of them heard a noise coming from a derelict house. Some of the Volunteers were inside the house and as the RIC man opened the front door a Volunteer fired at him, shooting him through the chin and killing him instantly. The other two policemen ran to the local barracks and began shooting in the direction of the house. The body of the policeman lay in the street until the following morning. The Volunteers evacuated the village shortly afterwards in anticipation of large numbers of military, police and Tans arriving.

The Volunteers of E company at Lettermacaward received instructions from Joe Sweeney to test the responses of the local RIC in their area. The Volunteers moved into the nearby hills and began carrying out military drilling. These manoeuvres were continued over a period of days, but failed to provoke a response from the RIC. The manoeuvres either gave the police the impression that the local Volunteers were nothing to fear or they feared such activities were a ruse to lure them into an ambush. Whatever the reason, the RIC remained in their barracks and seemed content to monitor the situation.[41]

A large party of military and local police arrived in Buncrana on Sunday morning 20 March and carried out extensive raids in the town and surrounding areas. Several Volunteers were arrested, including Daniel McGrory, Monaugh, Daniel McLaughlin, Doe, John Bradley, Glebe and Daniel O'Donnell and Patrick O'Donnell, Tondiff, who were taken to Ebrington barracks in Derry.[42]

Meanwhile the inactivity in the south-east of the county was attracting the attention of officers at GHQ in Dublin and questions were being asked about the lack of local involvement in the fight. The inactivity was the result of several factors, including the large number of military and police and the frequent raiding operations as well as the issue of weapons and men being loaned to the No. 1 brigade area under Joe Sweeney. Henry McGowan, acting O/C No. 4 brigade, received a despatch from GHQ enquiring about the lack of activity and he immediately began evaluating his command area. He decided that the weapons held by the No. 1 brigade should be returned to his area and any men should return also. He convened a meeting of the Ballybofey battalion and it was decided that they would travel to west Donegal for their weapons. However, a walk or cycle to Burtonport and back was considered too much and there were no cars or other vehicles at their disposal. They decided that it was necessary to commandeer a car in the area, but the only cars available belonged to Dr Johnston, a known loyalist, and Thomas McGinty, a local magistrate who also ran a hackney business. The Volunteers sent a telegram to Dr Johnston requesting him to call on a woman called Mrs Boyle who lived near Reelin Bridge. Mrs Boyle was already a patient of Dr Gormley and they knew Johnston would jump at the chance to take one of his patients. The Volunteers also decided that they should send a wire for McGinty, the local magistrate, as a backup. At Reelin Bridge, the Volunteers spread fence posts across the road to act as a type of barricade, prompting drivers to stop.

McGinty was unable to pick up the fare and asked Willie McClay, a neighbour, to do it. On reaching the spot where the fence posts were located, McClay stopped the car. He was about to exit when a Volunteer appeared and held him up at gunpoint. Then he and the car were taken to a spot farther down the road, as Dr Johnston was expected at any moment. Before long Johnston arrived accompanied by his wife and stopped at the point in the road where the fence posts were scattered. A Volunteer appeared and ordered the two out of the car at the point of a revolver. Johnston was incensed by this demand and initially refused to give up the car, with his wife pleading with him not to be so foolish. Johnston was having none of this and even tried to pull the mask from a Volunteer's face. The car was eventually commandeered and the three stranded pedestrians were instructed to call to a local farmer for a pony and trap to take them back to Ballybofey.

Henry McGowan, Charlie Doherty, Jim McCarron and Willie Tom McMenamin drove the two cars to Burtonport, collected their weapons and made their way back across country, on foot, to the No. 4 brigade area. The cars were kept by the 1st brigade command at Gortnasade, Kincasslagh and were hidden in sheds covered with various items including fish barrels.[43]

With the return of the weapons, the acting O/C was in a position to plan and execute attacks in the command area. Shortly after that McGowan set plans in motion to attack the RIC barracks at Castlederg, with the date set for Monday 21 March. There were no explosives available so the Volunteers decided to use a ladder to smash holes in the roof, through which they would pour petrol and set the barracks alight. A party of Volunteers from the Killygordon and Ballybofey companies were mobilised and made their way to Castlederg. McGowan sent men to various positions in the town and was on his way towards the barracks when a shot rang out. It was fired by one of the Volunteers and Henry McGowan was beside the barracks window at the time. He peered through a gap in the shutter and could see the RIC racing to take up defensive positions. He immediately cancelled the attack and later made enquires about the premature shot. The Volunteer concerned said that his rifle had a defective safety catch and the shot was accidental.[44]

Richard Mulcahy was not impressed when McGowan referred to the incident in his report to GHQ in early April. He replied:

> I was sorry to hear about the failure at Castlederg. Mistakes such as premature or accidental shooting of a rifle on an occasion like this should certainly never be made. They involve serious danger to men's lives and they involve our army in the discredit of a defeat. Every single man under your command must be made understand this. I hope now that your area is being definitely brought into the war area that we shall soon have evidence that every single member of your different units is using his brains and his eyes. I look to you and to your officers and men for the fullest and readiest cooperation with our now divisional command.[45]

As the large-scale raids by the military and police began to subside the west Donegal Volunteers were eager to get back to action. The RIC barracks at Falcarragh was selected as a target and intelligence was gathered on its layout and personnel. The No. 1 flying column, under Peadar O'Donnell, was notified and arrived at Dungloe to finalise the plans for the attack. The plan was to place a large mine at one of the gable walls. When detonated, this would cause most of the building to collapse, leading to shock and confusion among the RIC personnel and making it easier to attack and take the barracks.

Shortly after 8 p.m. on Monday 21 March, the No. 1 flying

column and Volunteers from the 1st, 2nd and 3rd battalions were mobilised and left Dungloe to carry out the attack on Falcarragh RIC barracks. The garrison at Falcarragh was composed mainly of Black and Tans and a small number of RIC. The barracks was a large two-storeyed building situated on the Dunfanaghy side of the village. It was difficult to approach from any angle and it was well protected, with barbed wire entanglements and apertures in the walls at various points for dropping grenades. After dark the column took up positions around the wall surrounding the barracks. William Doheny and Frank O'Donnell removed their boots and made their way over the wall. Hay, straw, petrol and oil were then passed over and placed against the gable wall along with the mine, which was connected to an electric detonator. A gun cotton charge of explosives was then placed against the wall and the whole thing was set on fire. The gun cotton charge exploded, but failed to cause any damage and then the mine was detonated, but this failed to work, leaving the Volunteers with the futile option of opening fire.

They fired into the barracks, but the doors and windows were so well protected with bulletproof steel shutters and sandbags that the bullets had little effect. One RIC man, James McKenna, who was in an outhouse in front of the barracks at the time of the attack, was shot in the neck and died from his wound about twenty minutes later. The Volunteers continued to fire at the building for over half an hour before retreating from the area and making their way back to Dungloe. The following day, British forces and Black and Tans visited the houses in the town and compelled a number of merchants and other local people to attend the dead RIC man's wake. Merchants were also ordered to close their doors and draw the blinds on their shop windows. People were threatened by the Tans that they would be shot if they failed to comply with the orders.[46]

Shortly after the failed Falcarragh attack, Joe Sweeney received information of a train leaving Dungloe carrying British military and quickly convened a conference to inform the Volunteers. The train, loaded with British troops, was due to pass through Creeslough, on the way to Derry. The decision was taken to hurriedly block the railway line in the hope of derailing the train. They did not have enough time to gather any weapons so made off to a point on the railway line. They had just enough time to roll a few rocks onto the line when the train came along. It crashed into the rocks and the engine and two carriages turned over on their sides. There was a sense of general confusion and had the Volunteers had time to gather weapons they could have inflicted further injuries. The British troops remained at the scene of the crash all night, firing volleys at intervals. As a reprisal the British invaded the village of Creeslough. From one end of the street to the others they smashed windows and battered doors with rifle butts, firing indiscriminately at houses. The occupants of the village were stricken with fear believing their houses would be burned over their heads. The military arrested a number of local men, none of whom were associated with the movement.[47]

In Inishowen the early train from Derry arrived at Ballymagan station on Saturday 26 February and was seized by twelve Volunteers. A number of them held up the station officials while the others went into the guard's van and removed any mail destined for the RIC and military. In response to the mail raid the military and RIC carried out a series of raids in the Buncrana area later that morning and arrested a number of men.

In the early hours of Monday 28 March, the military and police conducted a series of raids in south Donegal. These resulted in the arrests of Michael Ward, Letterfad, James Moohan, Letterfad and three brothers – John, Patrick and Manus Meehan from Drimaherk – one of whom was only fifteen. Ward and Moohan were released later that day. William Cunningham of Drimkeelin, Mountcharles, was also arrested. Patrick and Joseph Meehan from Ballymachill, near Frosses village, were released on the same day having spent nine days in military custody. At this time the Volunteers were also carrying out their own raids. One of their targets was Samuel Leaper, a draper from Meenagrave, who ignored a warning against purchasing goods from Belfast companies. Some drapery stored in his shop was thrown about and damaged.[48]

A lorryload of RIC arrived in the Annagry area on Wednesday 30 March and rounded up local men to remove a large stone barricade in the area. The captain of G company, Annagry, was informed about the incident and mobilised his men, but the police observed the Volunteer activity on the surrounding hills and cleared out before an attack could be launched, leaving the local men at the barricade.[49]

The No. 4 brigade acting O/C, Henry McGowan, continued to explore options to engage the police and military in his area and planned a number of raids in an effort to lure them to the outlying areas of Ballybofey. He first led a raid on the residence of Captain Rickey, a well known loyalist who lived approximately five miles outside the town. Volunteers took up ambush positions in anticipation of Captain Rickey reporting the raid. However, he failed to report it and the Volunteers remained in position for a day and a half waiting for military or police who never arrived.

Shortly after this they carried out a raid on Meenglass post office with the same intentions of drawing the military and RIC into an ambush. After the raid they took up positions along the road and Sam O'Flaherty, No. 4 brigade O/C, went with another Volunteer to take over the post office. The postmaster, named Bustard, and his brother-in-law were not pleased and the two started to fight with the Volunteers. All four ended up wrestling on the street and other Volunteers, mistaking the postman's uniform for that of the RIC, fired a number of shots but luckily failed to hit any targets. Meanwhile Henry McGowan spotted the RIC in the distance who, on hearing the shots, immediately halted and took cover. This ambush had also to be cancelled as one RIC man ran back to Ballybofey, returning later with a large party of military.[50]

237

UNREST IN THE RANKS OF THE 1ST NORTHERN DIVISION

THE No. 1 FLYING column left west Donegal as Peadar O'Donnell took up his new position as O/C for the No. 2 brigade area. He took all his men and three other men from the area for organising purposes. Seamus McCann and Peadar O'Donnell made plans to travel to Derry and left Dungloe and walked to Mullans' of Glendowan. There they met with Dr J. P. McGinley, who drove them to William Holmes of Drumoghill where they spent the night before cycling to Derry the following morning.[51] They arrived in Derry and it was while there O'Donnell, conscious of the state of the brigade area, considered the possibility of a recruitment campaign to bolster the ranks. He approached the local Cumann na mBan branch to discuss the idea and discovered that a bitter division existed between the local branch and the IRA battalion in the city. O'Donnell endeavoured to establish the root of this dispute as he felt the Volunteers in the city would suffer unnecessarily without the help of Cumann na mBan, who were adept in first aid and could offer valuable military assistance to the Volunteers.

O'Donnell met with Paddy Shiels, the local O/C, and representatives from Cumann na mBan to try to heal the rift. It seemed that the root of the problem lay in a disagreement between the O/C's fiancée and the local branch of Cumann na mBan and to add to the problem the new 1st northern division O/C, Frank Carney, was billeted at her home at the time. Carney pointed out to O'Donnell that he didn't have a proper understanding of the situation. O'Donnell admitted that he was unaware of the reasons for the dispute and requested an official position on the situation, but failed to receive an adequate response.

There were very few engagements with the enemy in Derry at the time and the following evening O'Donnell arranged a meeting in the Shamrock Hall in the Bogside where plans were discussed for a series of attacks on British military and RIC on patrol. Men were deployed to different parts of the city with instructions to shoot any RIC and military found on the streets. A number of shootings took place that night with the result that seven RIC were killed or injured; some of these were the result of accidental injuries, where men were shot by their own side or shot themselves by accident.[52] O'Donnell's initiatives in Derry were frowned upon by some of the officers in the city, something that later boiled over and caused further resentment.

Peadar O'Donnell, Seamus McCann and Jim Walsh were escorted out of Derry later that night by two Cumann na mBan girls, Mary McCormack and Nellie Sweeney, as far as Killea. They then walked to Manorcunningham and stopped off at Currans' for rest and food before carrying on towards Leck and then on to Quigleys' at Newmills. They were supplied with three bicycles at Quigleys' and cycled to McKays', which was the link between the 1st and 2nd brigades.[53]

A party of Volunteers from the Milford Company travelled to Ramelton village on the night of Friday 1 April to attack police there. A constable had a narrow escape when the two Volunteers fired nine shots at him as he walked along the street.[54]

About this time the unionist newspapers took an antagonistic attitude towards the British military authorities, with headings such as: 'Why subject the citizens to these hardships?' and 'The wild geese have flown, why don't you follow them?' The newspapers were reacting to attacks on them and other businesses as part of the Belfast Boycott. The military responded by sending the Gordon Highlanders, the Dorsets and the Northumberland Fusiliers to Donegal to support the garrisons based there.[55]

THE BIG BRITISH ROUND-UPS

Patrick Johnston, Thomas McShea and James O'Brien were arrested in the Bundoran area and taken to Finner camp on Saturday 2 April.

McShea was staying in the house of Thomas Mulhern when arrested. O'Brien was later released when it was discovered he was only in the area as part of his employment as an architect. Johnston and McShea were held at the camp and subjected to intense interrogation and beatings before being moved to Derry jail two weeks later.[56]

Meanwhile at Burtonport in the early hours of Tuesday 5 April a Volunteer knocked on Joe Sweeney's door to inform him that scouts had spotted columns of troops approaching Dungloe from Fintown, Glenties, Letterkenny and Gweedore. Sweeney immediately ordered the Volunteer to notify a flying column billeted in a house nearby and other Volunteers staying in the area. Many of the Volunteers escaped the sweep, but for some reason the members of the flying column in a house nearby were not informed. Later that morning a member of the column stepped outside the house and spotted a sentry a short distance away. The Volunteer ran back into the house, woke the others and they soon realised they were surrounded, causing a panic among some of the men. They decided to sit tight and prepared for a raid, but by midday the sentry had been removed and the column withdrew to the nearby mountainside. They remained there until darkness fell, at which time scouts were sent to find a way around the British cordon. A force of several thousand troops had set up a cordon between Dungloe and Crolly, supported with sentries at fixed points and with cars and motorcycle patrols operating along the road.

The British had been prepared for damaged roads and bridges and had brought iron girders so vehicles could cross over. A detention centre was set up at Dungloe and Burtonport and every man between the ages of seventeen and seventy was arrested and brought to the centres for identification. Those identified as harmless were given passes and released, while a few were held for questioning. Most of the Volunteers received the early morning warning and managed to avoid the round-up.

Meanwhile the flying column scout had discovered a sentry sleeping at his post, which allowed the column to move through the cordon and on to a friendly house at Crahyboyle. They then proceeded to Crovehy where they met with Peadar O'Donnell's flying column. Both columns crossed over to Brockagh and remained there for a few days until the military withdrew. The British stayed in the Rosses area for nearly a week patrolling and raiding houses and businesses, but they made no further arrests.[57]

Charlie McGuinness, Hugh Martin and Owen Callan, all members of the 1st brigade column, escaped the net and were temporarily posted to the 3rd brigade flying column, South-West Donegal, which was based initially a few miles outside Glenties at Straboy. They later moved to Rosbeg on the coast about seven miles north-west of Ardara where better training facilities and safe billets existed. The column moved there by night accompanied by a cover party from the No. 4 battalion. While waiting for backup from the Ardara battalion, members of the flying column decided to investigate the possibility of an attack on Ardara village as patrols regularly passed through from Killybegs to Glenties. Michael Sheer, Charlie McGuinness, Hugh Martin and Owen Callan proceeded towards Ardara on bicycles. Martin and Sheer were talking to Con Kennedy in his draper shop when they spotted two lorryloads of Black and Tans approaching, with a motorcycle leading the way. They were assured by Kennedy that this was a common occurrence, but they decided to go through the shop and out the back door. McGuinness and Callan spotted them and went into the Ulster Bank, locking the front door. The occupants of the bank were greatly alarmed, thinking it was a raid, and the two Volunteers had to restrain them until the Tans passed. The Volunteers then left Ardara and returned to Rosbeg.

Travelling on the Strand Road back towards their camp at Rosbeg the Volunteers were forced to cycle through small sandhills. McGuinness and Callan had dismounted from their bicycles and were walking, with Martin and Sheer cycling on ahead. As they were cycling through the sandhills Sheer's bicycle collapsed under him, followed almost immediately by a volley of shots. Sheer managed to peer over the sandhill and saw approximately twenty rifles pointed in their direction, blazing and smoking over a stone wall. They were coming under heavy gunfire from Black and Tans and the two men took cover behind a large boulder and returned fire. They could see Charlie McGuinness and Owen Callan leaving the strand and moving towards the sandhills to their right. Sheer and Martin then made their way around the cliff and were not pursued, emerging at the rear of the Black and Tans' position.

However, Charlie McGuinness was not so lucky and was hit twice as he turned to speak to Callan; despite this he instructed Callan to escape and he would cover him. Callan made his way along the sandhills until he got out of range. A member of the 3rd battalion, a fisherman, was out at sea and witnessed the incident from his boat. He brought his boat ashore near Dawross Bay and Callan jumped on board, but McGuinness was captured. He was badly wounded, having been hit several times while covering Callan's retreat.

That afternoon a report was received from the No. 4 battalion, Glenties, that the military were approaching their position at Straboy from Ardara and Glenties. They decided to evacuate the area by sea, and fishing boats were organised by the 3rd battalion, Ardara. After dark they boarded the boats at Loughros More Bay and sailed out to sea before turning back into the coast and landing at a small bay near Gull Island. They then made their way over the mountains towards Glengesh.

The following morning the Wiltshire Regiment and the Tans made another attempt to attack the column and battalions from the Glencolmcille area, but the 2nd battalion, Carrick, drew them off. The following day the column crossed the Glengesh Pass and stopped in the mountains south of Crowbane, but by the afternoon the Tans and the Wiltshire had caught up with them again and were chasing them over Crocknapeast. The next morning they stopped at Tullinteane where the 1st battalion arranged for them to billet.

The brigade had gone to great lengths to protect the column and had been forced to block roads, open roads, get food and billet the men. The brigade O/C was not pleased as he had lost at least ten trained men. It transpired that the whole pursuit was the result of the men being spotted, and their exact location at Rosbeg was reported to the military at Killybegs. The brigade intelligence section discovered that a Congested District Board's inspector named O'Kane had accidentally come across the column at Rosbeg and nobody had paid any attention to him. He immediately proceeded to Glenties on his motorcycle and brought the Tans to the spot where the column was billeted.

The brigade O/C decided that this man would have to be dealt with. The case was investigated and the sentence of death was passed, with Hugh Martin and Owen Callan being detailed to carry out the execution. The two Volunteers located O'Kane at the home of Falvey, a prominent loyalist and doctor, who lived on the outskirts of Ardara. There was a scene at the house, with women screaming and O'Kane protesting as the Volunteers removed him from the building.

They took him to a wood nearby where he began to pray and pleaded for a priest. As Owen Callan was very religious he decided to walk to Ardara to get the local priest. He proceeded to the parochial house and asked the priest to accompany him but the priest did not approve of the movement and refused. As Callan was trying to persuade the priest his attention was suddenly distracted by a series of shots coming from the direction of the woods. He immediately returned to find Martin searching through the wood for O'Kane. Having been on his knees praying, O'Kane had suddenly jumped up and run into the woods. Martin fired a number of shots at him, but he escaped. The two men received a select mouthful of words when they reported back to the O/C.[58]

In the No. 2 brigade area the enemy kept up the pressure when a large mixed party of military, police and Auxiliaries raided the house of James Duddy, Foxhall, a few miles outside Letterkenny on the morning of Saturday 9 April. They also raided three houses in the Churchill area, causing enormous damage to the properties, but no arrests were made and nothing was found in any of the houses raided.

In follow-up operations in south-west Donegal the police and a party of Black and Tans moved into the village of Inver, commandeering the house of Patrick Barry and using it as a barracks. Barry was the manager of the Inver creamery and co-operative stores that had been destroyed by military in February.[59]

The new 1st northern division O/C, Frank Carney, had yet to make an appearance in the county and it was now over a month since his official appointment. The officers and men of the county considered Carney's aloofness to be detrimental to the ongoing war campaign and were anxious for some form of communication and direction from the new commander. Joe Sweeney relayed the frustrations of the men to Gearóid O'Sullivan, adjutant general at GHQ in Dublin:

> We are being put in a rather peculiar position here by the non-arrival of the divisional commander. I would like to have a resumé of the proceedings at the recent conference at GHQ in connection with Donegal brigades so as to satisfy myself that certain suggestions which I have heard of were really made. Neither of the individuals who attended the conference has been able to give me a definite statement of the proceedings and a record would satisfy me. The state of my brigade is this. Previous to the arrival of the men of flying column from Derry we were unable to undertake any attack on troops or RIC owing to lack of arms. About the beginning of January I got loan of 18 Martini Carbines from east Donegal and sixteen rifles of various makes from the isolated Letterkenny battalion. With this armament we have got a very wide stretch of country clear of enemy forces. Now I have sent back to east Donegal the rifles

lent and O/C No. 2 brigade wants back the Letterkenny stuff as well as the stuff sent out from Derry ... I have repeatedly called to GHQ for rifles and got as a kind of sop small arms and gelignite and mines – the latter of which I already have. It is not fair to leave me in the position of telling my men that there are not arms for them, and if there is a falling off in the existing good spirit of the men, I can hardly be held responsible. I would make a last appeal for a consignment of at least twelve rifles for this brigade and I hope it will be seriously considered.[60]

Richard Mulcahy replied to Joe Sweeney's concerns in his despatch, stating:

I am very sorry that you have returned the Carbines to East Donegal. No other borrowed weapons should be returned by you until the whole question has been considered ... My attitude in the matter is that I am not willing to reduce the armament of that portion of Donegal whose initiative and activity have made Donegal what it is.[61]

The concerns of Joe Sweeney arose when Peadar O'Donnell requested the return of the borrowed weapons to the Letterkenny battalion to increase operations there. Richard Mulcahy also wrote to O'Donnell:

I am in receipt of a communication from O/C No. 1 brigade in which he mentions the proposed return of arms to the Letterkenny battalion. He has already returned some arms to the old East Donegal brigade. I am not satisfied to have the No. 1 area reduced in the strength of its armament at the present time ... This may perhaps interfere with some of your proposed immediate plans, but the spirit and initiative of the present No. 1 brigade have for a long time been our only hope and strength in Donegal. I am not prepared to weaken its strength until matters have further developed or been further appreciated.[62]

The No. 2 brigade O/C, Peadar O'Donnell was also putting pressure on GHQ about the lack of adequate armaments in the No. 2 brigade area. Frustration was being felt by the men at not being able to take RIC barracks due to the extreme fortification of all barracks throughout the area, and he relayed this to Richard Mulcahy in a despatch: 'I am quite satisfied I could capture at least three police barracks in my area, provided I had G.C. [gun cotton] or sufficient gelignite. Could HQ supply? You could consign to the address given by O/C No. 1 brigade, 1st northern division.'[63]

Glendowan was the dividing line between the 1st brigade in west Donegal and the 2nd brigade in the north-east and was the focus of much attention from the military. A large search operation was in progress early on Sunday 10 April and a large party of military and police were combing the hills in the area. James 'Ginger' McKee, a member of the No. 1 flying column, was billeted at McCormacks' farm and had just left the house when he was spotted by a small party of military about half a mile away. Ginger, who was accompanied by two dogs and carrying a rifle, didn't notice the military. The soldiers called on him to halt, but Ginger ran off, disappearing behind a hill. The soldiers proceeded to McCormacks' farm, searched the house and questioned the occupants. In the outhouses they found two rifles and 120 rounds of ammunition. Two members of the McCormack family were arrested and taken to Letterkenny. About two hours later Ginger McKee was spotted returning to the farm minus his rifle. He was immediately arrested and when questioned said his name was Joe McHugh of Loughbarrow and that he was paying a visit to his aunt, Mrs McCormack. As neither the military nor police could verify his identity he was taken to Letterkenny, where one of the soldiers identified him as the man seen that morning with the rifle. McKee was later taken to Derry jail and a few days later was transferred to Ballykinlar internment camp.[64]

The military concentration on the south-west continued and raids were carried out in the Ardara area on Monday 11 April resulting in the arrests of three Volunteers named Gallagher, Breslin and Ireland.

Meanwhile the Inishowen Volunteers kept up the pressure in their area on the same day and a raid was carried out on the Derry train at Ballymagan station with all official correspondence being removed. Earlier that morning a Volunteer officer from the area was arrested at Carrowreagh, Carndonagh, by a party of military and police. Leo Lafferty had arrived at his mother's house the previous night, which had been searched twice previously, but Leo was absent on both occasions. It was obvious the house was being watched, as the raiding party went directly to the bedroom he was sleeping in.

The mails taken in two recent raids at Drumfries and Ballymagan stations were returned to Drumfries on Tuesday and taken to Carndonagh. The postal officials at Carndonagh had to sort the mail for all areas between Ballymagan and Carndonagh as well as for Malin and Culdaff. Some letters had been opened and marked 'IRA' in pencil and in a few cases envelopes were empty while other letters were received without envelopes.[65]

On Thursday 14 April the 9 a.m. train from Stranorlar to Glenties was held up by Volunteers at Fintown station and two mailbags removed. All telegraph wires were cut, while many roads in the area were blocked by trenches. Following this raid the train service between Stranorlar and Glenties was closed to both passengers and goods.

The Crolly railway station was looted on Thursday by a number of individuals under the pretext of destroying goods from Belfast firms coming under the terms of the Belfast Boycott. It was discovered that those responsible were of the criminal element and were subsequently arrested and tried by a court-martial presided over by

Peadar O'Donnell. All were found guilty; two were sentenced to deportation from the area under penalty of death and the others were sentenced to various penalties.[66]

On Friday 15 April a train was held up at Falcarragh by Volunteers who took charge of the engine and ordered the driver to proceed in the direction of Burtonport. The train passed through Cashelnagore station, a scheduled stop, and stopped between there and Gweedore. During the journey the Volunteers went through the mail and removed all correspondence for the military and police, but nothing of importance was found.

As part of the Belfast boycott a number of Volunteers from the Creeslough Company visited the stationmaster at Creeslough station early on Sunday morning 17 April. He was woken and ordered to hand over the keys of the goods store. The Volunteers examined all goods and scrutinised the delivery books, but did not interfere with anything.

At about 3 a.m., seven Volunteers woke the gardener at Glenveigh Castle. They demanded tea, but when this was refused they produced their revolvers and were duly served with tea and food. They then proceeded to the garage and removed the car to dismantle it. They put the parts onto a cart and took the horses from the stables and made off. The tracks of the cart were traced by the RIC for about six miles to the burned-out RIC barracks at Churchill, at which the tracks became mixed with others and could not be followed further.

This was followed by similar actions when the goods store at Crolly station was raided by Volunteers on the night of Monday 18 April. A wagon of goods in a siding was also ransacked. The line between Letterkenny and Burtonport was subsequently closed by order of the British military. Kilmacrenan station was also raided the same night with the Volunteers compelling the stationmaster to hand over the keys, invoices and goods' delivery books, which were studied to identify the recipients of goods from unionist firms. Having broken open and examined several cases of goods the Volunteers removed and burned a box of tobacco and a case of plants consigned to local merchants. The keys of the signal box were also taken away.[67]

The Fanad Company O/C, Neil Blaney, was brought before a field general court-martial in Derry on Tuesday 19 April, charged with:

(1) Having a document containing a statement the publication of which would be likely to cause disaffection;

(2) Having a document containing statements the publication of which would be likely to prejudice the recruiting of persons to serve in the RIC;

(3) Having documents relating to the affairs of an unlawful association.

Neil Blaney declined to recognise the court because, he said, it was not constituted by the consent of the Irish people. Evidence was given that during a raid at his home on 18 February a search party found a printed handbook entitled *Introduction to volunteer training – Irish Republican Army – official publication* and a notebook containing in writing the heading 'Appeal for funds for the equipment of the Rosnakill Volunteers'. Another document contained the following:

> It has come to our knowledge that one or two members of our Sinn Féin cumann – I won't call them Sinn Féiners – one or two of them have offered themselves for sale to the British government. The British government wants as many traitors as it can get. It will pay them a big wage, feed the bruntees, put a black uniform on them, give them batons and guns and bayonets and hand grenades. It will do all this for any Irish traitor who is low enough to join the RIC. Royal! It is a grand name given by a grand country. These are the men who are spies and informers. They do the dirty work. They will knock

> a poor old Irish man or Irish woman senseless if they dare to speak a word publicly about Ireland's good; and here we are down in Fanad and right in our midst, aye in the midst of our Sinn Féin club, the nicknamed Sinn Féiner goes and applies for the job. What do you think of him? What should be done with him? Would it not be better to shoot him or drown him or poison him straight off than allow him to drag down the good name of Fanad Sinn Féiners?

In a statement Neil Blaney said he might as well be candid and let them know what he was. He declared that he owed no allegiance to any government except the government of the Irish Republic and as the Royal Irish Constabulary was an illegal force under that government he had the right to condemn and denounce that so-called force by speech, publication or any other means. As a soldier of the Irish Republic he had also the further right to have the documents that the witness said were found in his possession. The prosecutor said if the court considered the case proved, he would ask for an exemplary sentence. Neil Blaney was sentenced at a later date to five years' penal servitude and served his sentence at Dartmoor prison in England.[68]

Volunteers of the No. 3 brigade were planning an attack on the Glenties RIC barracks and a request was sent to Joe Sweeney for assistance from companies in the No. 1 brigade area. The 1st battalion was deployed to assist in the operation and a number of cars were commandeered to transport men and equipment to the Glenties area, although the majority of the Volunteers had to make the journey again by bicycle. The attack took place at midnight on Wednesday 20 April, with much the same tactics as were used in the attack on Falcarragh barracks; the result was also the same. A number of police received minor injuries, but such was the ferocity of the battle, which lasted for over an hour, that the Volunteers left a bag of bombs and ammunition behind and these were later seized by the police.[69]

On 20 April, a goods train left Derry at 10 a.m. heading for Burtonport. It was boarded by two Volunteers at Cashelnagore station, who ordered the driver to proceed. The train was then stopped between Cashelnagore and Gweedore where four more Volunteers were waiting. They searched a number of wagons trying to identify goods from unionist firms, but nothing was interfered with and the train was allowed to proceed to Burtonport. Gweedore, Cashelnagore and Falcarragh stations were visited during the night with goods being either seized or destroyed. On each occasion the Volunteers left notes on boxes that were opened: 'Nothing taken – IRA', and on other boxes: 'Disguised tobacco taken away – IRA'. Another raid was carried out on the mail train from Derry at Ballymagan station on the same day. On arrival six Volunteers boarded the train, took the mailbags and ordered the train to proceed. A consignment of money destined for the post office in Carndonagh was removed and used to maintain the flying column in cigarettes and food.[70]

The 8.30 a.m. mail train was held up at Inch Road station by a group of Volunteers on Thursday 21 April. Two undercover military on board immediately opened fire on the Volunteers, who returned fire while making a hasty escape.[71]

At a field general court-martial at Ebrington barracks, Derry on Friday 22 April, Charles Carr, Cashel, Gortahork was charged with incitement to commit arson. This was alleged to have happened at Gortahork the previous November where he 'unlawfully incited Edward Carr to burn Falcarragh RIC barracks ... with doing an act endangering the safety of members of his majesty's police force'. Carr refused to recognise the court or plead. The basis of the charge related to the content of a letter sent by him to his brother that said: 'I see you had some rough times since I left with raids and burnings. No arrests made yet. What is wrong with yous, when yous do not burn the Ballyconnell House as a reprisal for the college? If I was down there I would have it burned long ago. Now, see and get it out of the way at once ...' The letter was discovered during a raid on his brother's house. He was subsequently acquitted on both charges.[72]

A series of raids carried out on railway lines and stations on Sunday 24 April included Kilmacrenan and Dunfanaghy Road station, with the line being blocked in the south of the county at Barnes Gap with large boulders rolled from the nearby hills. The stations were raided as part of the general disruption of the railway, but on this occasion only tools were removed, which would delay any repairs on the line.

Early on Saturday 30 April, a number of Volunteers entered the residence of the Buncrana town clerk and took the books of the urban council, because of the council's continued recognition of the British Local Government Boards. Later that evening seven young men named McClean, Magee, Kelly, McGowan, Conway, Blee and Doherty, all from the Ballybofey area, were arrested by military, taken to Drumboe Castle and held for several days of interrogation. Meanwhile the Letterkenny Company carried out a raid on the post office in the town on Saturday night and removed four bicycles, while the telephone apparatus was also taken for use in the 1st brigade area.[73]

The Volunteers of the 1st brigade area were still active despite the large concentrations of military and police and the frequent raids. This did not go unnoticed and was even raising eyebrows in Whitehall, London. The British government was receiving reports from Dublin Castle that west Donegal was effectively operating as a 'Miniature Republic'.[74]

The large concentration of military activity in west and south Donegal was not only an annoyance to the Volunteers but also to the general population, and this was causing friction between the two. The divisional staff decided to address the issue and sent out directives to other areas less affected to organise increased activity in their areas. The directive resulted in a flying column, consisting of twelve Volunteers, being formed in Buncrana at the beginning of May to operate in the Inishowen district. Their instructions were to avoid large-scale operations and focus on harassing the enemy as often as possible to pin down a large number of British forces in Buncrana. This would ensure that attention was taken off the No. 1 flying column, which was already hard pressed in the Dungloe/Burtonport area. Philip Doherty, Buncrana, was the O/C of the Inishowen column. The other members of the column were: William Doherty and Joseph McLaughlin, Buncrana; Anthony Cassidy, Packie (P. H.) Doherty, James Diver and Owen McElany, Carndonagh; Mock (Stout) Doherty and Mick (Watt) Doherty, Illies; Charles Gilmartin, north County Leitrim; Cecil Doherty, Clonmany and David Quigley, Malin.

It was not considered feasible for a flying column to operate in the Inishowen area on a large scale for a number of reasons. First, there were strong detachments of British forces stationed in Buncrana and Derry, which could surround the area in a very short time, cutting off many escape routes. In addition, due to the mountainous nature of the area it was difficult to provide food for a large number of men for a lengthy period, and as a result the column operating in the area was confined to ten or twelve men armed with four rifles, shotguns and revolvers. The first job for the new column was to demolish the Drumandare Bridge. This was a high bridge and when demolished would compel the British forces to walk seven or eight miles to reach the Illies area. The Volunteers had no explosives and had to demolish it by hand, which took a couple of days.

Another of their early operations was an attack on an RIC patrol in Carndonagh. The patrol was fired on, but the night was so dark it was impossible to know whether there were any casualties. Some time later that night an RIC man named McLaughlin was fired at as he walked from his home to the barracks. Fortunately he was not hit as he was one of Michael Collins' agents and was very helpful to the local Volunteers, but only a select few knew. On several occasions McLaughlin had passed on information to the parish priest, Fr

Philip O'Doherty, about forthcoming raids. Fr O'Doherty was also very friendly with some of the British officers stationed at Buncrana and received invaluable information, which was always passed on to the Volunteers.[75]

About this time the Fanad Company decided to raid the bank agents at the next fair day to be held at Rosnakill. Agencies of the Belfast Bank and Northern Bank usually operated in areas where fairs and markets were held. The next fair day was Monday 2 May and the Volunteers waited until most of the day's business had been concluded before making a move. It was late afternoon and there were no police patrols operating in the area, giving the Volunteers a free reign. Just as business was concluding the Volunteers, working in two groups, held up both banking agencies. The Belfast Bank was relieved of £45 and the Northern Bank of over £700, but the Volunteers missed over £1,000, which was sitting on a table covered with documents.[76]

The British used various tactics to curtail the movements of Volunteers and cause annoyance to the general population. One of these was the closing of roads, and on Friday 6 May the order was issued prohibiting (except under special permit) motor traffic on all roads west of a boundary road running from Mulroy Bay, through Milford, Kilmacrenan, Letterkenny, Kilros, Stranorlar, Barnesmore Gap and Donegal town. The boundary road itself remained open for use.[77]

The Creeslough Company was also called on to increase activity and the vice-O/C, Bernard McGinley, convened a meeting of the company to discuss the possibilities of attacking police and military in the area. Their directive was similar to that delivered to other areas; they were to create any kind of disturbance to attract the attention of the enemy forces and they decided to launch a sniping attack on the Carrigart RIC barracks. This barracks was fortified in the usual manner and the Creeslough Company knew that the most they could do was to keep the RIC personnel out of their beds. The Volunteers arrived at Carrigart shortly after 1 a.m. on Thursday 5 May and began firing from selected positions. They fired intermittently at the barracks for up to two hours before withdrawing and returning to Creeslough. At daybreak a large party of military and police reinforcements arrived from Dunfanaghy and searched the hills. After a few hours they made their way to Creeslough and launched an attack on the village. This resulted in the arrest of three Volunteers, John and James McNulty and John McCaffery. They were taken to St Conal's hospital in Letterkenny, a wing of which had been taken over and occupied by British forces. During the raids ammunition, documents and IRA publications were found. The three prisoners were later transferred to Derry jail.[78]

The focus then turned to Inishowen and two trenches were cut in the road at Desertegney, Buncrana, on Saturday night 7 May in anticipation of military and police patrolling the area. Unfortunately, however, it was discovered the next morning when a grocer's van drove into one of the trenches. No one was injured and there was only slight damage to the van, but all the eggs were broken.[79]

Also on Saturday night four Volunteers were watching an RIC patrol near Clonmany and followed the two policemen as they walked along the coast. The Volunteers opened fire on Constables Clarke and Murdock, killing one instantly and seriously wounding the other, who was subsequently shot dead as he tried to run away. Their bodies were thrown into the sea; one was washed up the following morning but there was no trace of the second man and it was believed that his body was caught by the current and washed out to sea.

Members of the new Inishowen flying column established their headquarters at a disused cowshed near the Illies. They set out to commandeer essential items to make the place comfortable and liveable. At approximately 2.30 a.m. on Tuesday 10 May some members of the column knocked up the doorkeeper of the stores at the Buncrana railway station. On entering they seized about a dozen bundles of sheets and blankets as well as carpenters' tools and two bicycles.[80]

A large party of military and police left Letterkenny later that morning and made their way to the Glendowan area. With no scouts deployed, Peadar O'Donnell, Con Boyle and Mutt Walsh were caught off guard. They had been staying at John Mullan's when the military were spotted approaching. O'Donnell and Boyle made a run for it out the back door and up the Glendowan Mountains. Walsh decided to take his chances and hid in the rafters of the house; this proved to be a wise move as the British failed to find him when they entered and searched the place. Six soldiers gave chase to O'Donnell and Boyle, firing as they ran. O'Donnell was hit twice, in the arm and the hand, while Boyle was hit in the ankle and fell back down the hill. A local woman, Mrs Reilly, saw Boyle falling and ran to him to remove documents from his pockets before the military reached him. Con Boyle was dragged back down the hill and was roughly treated, being thrown into the back of a lorry without receiving any medical attention. Two other Volunteers billeted in the area heard the shooting and tried to get away. One succeeded, but the other was captured and beaten before being put into the lorry with Con Boyle. Peadar O'Donnell continued up the mountain with his arm hanging by the flesh as the bullet had broken the bone. He made his way to John Bonner's at Commeen and was suffering badly from shock. He was driven to Meenmore and met with Seamus McCann, who immediately arranged to have two Cumann na mBan nurses brought there.

Roisín O'Doherty and her sister-in-law were driven to the top of Glendowan where they were met by McCann. Having attended to the wounded man the entire party were taken to McKelveys' at Brockagh and O'Donnell was able to recuperate for a few days. The incident was reported by Joe Sweeney later that month to Richard Mulcahy, chief of staff:

> Six of the original flying column which operated in this area, one of whom is now acting O/C No. 2 brigade, were surrounded at

dawn by a large force of military at Glendowan on the border of this area. Four of them including O/C escaped in their shirts but two were captured and are receiving exceptionally bad treatment in Letterkenny military camp.[81]

Meanwhile the Inishowen Volunteers remained active and on Tuesday night the flying column launched an attack on the Carndonagh RIC barracks. They knew that they had no hope of inflicting serious damage or capturing the building so instead settled for a sniping attack. They took up positions around the barracks and fired at the building for up to an hour. The RIC and Tans stationed there returned fire and sent up several Verey lights for assistance. The Volunteers withdrew to the hills and crossed to the Illies area to their headquarters. They were resting at their base near the Illies when a sentry spotted a large force of military approaching. There was a heavy mist on the mountain and the military were within 150 yards of the base before they were spotted. The Volunteers were forced to make a dash for cover and ran to a turf cutting only to find that they were in the path of the advancing military and were forced to run into the open. They were spotted, but for some reason the British officer ordered his men to retreat instead of opening fire. The column continued up the mountain under a heavy mist, which compelled each member to hold hands to avoid becoming separated. They continued until they reached the summit of Slieve Snaght where they rested under the cover of the heavy mist. From this height they could see more military approaching and had only one gap open to them to escape. They made their way down the mountain in the direction of Clonmany and rested under cover near a road. Packie Doherty went to scout the area and met two farmers who had come down a by-road from the Clonmany direction, and they told Doherty that the road was clear of any military. He summoned the remainder of the column waiting in the hills, who proceeded to a house owned by a man call William Gill, Meenavogy where they received a welcome cup of hot tea.

The column had been running up and down Slieve Snaght for approximately eight hours trying to evade the large military party searching the entire area. This could have been avoided had the column O/C adhered to the information from Fr O'Doherty, who learned from military officers at Buncrana that they intended to carry out a large raid on the Illies area.[82]

On Wednesday 11 May, two officers of the No. 4 brigade, South Donegal were tried before a field general court-martial in Derry and charged with possession of a document relating to the affairs of the Irish Volunteers. The document, dated 2 September 1920, purported to be a charge against Joe Meehan, quartermaster 1st Battalion, South Donegal Brigade, for disobeying orders. The document was found on Thomas McShea and was signed by Patrick Johnston. Members of the Bundoran Company, McShea and Johnston had previously been charged with ordering the closing of shops for Terence MacSwiney's funeral in October 1920. A police witness said he had observed McShea, on the day of Terence MacSwiney's funeral in Bundoran, ordering traders to close their premises and this was later reported to the police. Both men refused to recognise the court and were sentenced to two years' hard labour.[83]

A Sinn Féin conference was held in Strabane the following day to select candidates for Donegal for the impending elections, called to elect members for the parliaments in the northern and southern counties under the Government of Ireland Act 1920. There were six seats for the entire constituency and the meeting unanimously decided to put forward Dr J. P. McGinley, P. J. McGoldrick, Joseph O'Doherty, Samuel O'Flaherty, Joseph Sweeney and P. J. Ward for election to the second Dáil.[84]

On Thursday night over thirty feet of track was lifted between Ballymagan station and Buncrana. It was discovered the next morning by a patrolman, who was able to stop the train in time. Half a dozen bridges on the roads between Buncrana and Clonmany were destroyed with explosives the same night, rendering the entire

Inishowen peninsula isolated. The next day Mr Hugh C. Cochrane, returning officer for the county, sat at Lifford courthouse to receive nominations for the Donegal constituency. As there were no other nominations, the six Sinn Féin nominees were declared elected. The local press reported: 'The elections for the Southern Parliament were over on the day of nominations as there was no opposition to the candidates in whom Ireland's destiny was safe and Donegal had, as it did in 1918, declared its allegiance to the cause of self-determination.'[85]

A few days after the Inishowen flying column's attack on the Carndonagh RIC barracks on 10 May, the column decided to ambush an RIC night patrol in the town. The column was particularly anxious to get one member of the patrol who had made himself conspicuous by his activities against the movement. They had just taken up positions in various parts of the town when one of the Volunteers fired a shot, supposedly by accident (there was a suggestion it had been a deliberate warning to the police). The Volunteers were forced to withdraw, having lost the element of surprise.[86]

BRITISH RAIDS AND INTERNAL TENSION

FRANK CARNEY, THE new O/C of the 1st northern division, decided to take action against Peadar O'Donnell for allegedly stirring up trouble in Derry in early April. Despite organising operations against the military and police in Derry, O'Donnell was to be reprimanded by his superior. However, the real reason for his reprimand was for his involvement in the ongoing friction between the Derry branch of Cumann na mBan and the IRA Derry battalion. Carney and O'Donnell had been at odds for some time, with O'Donnell critical of Carney's inactivity in his command area. O'Donnell was alleged to have said of Carney: 'Isn't it time he (Carney) visited his division instead of skulking in Derry?'

Carney sent a despatch to O'Donnell instructing him to attend a meeting in Derry scheduled for Monday 9 May and informed him that there was to be no further action taken against the enemy in Derry. O'Donnell had been operating in the Glendowan area at the time and was unable to attend the meeting as he was suffering from a bad dose of flu and the wounds to his arm. Despite his injuries, he had a few days earlier been scouting a military and police patrol and had to cross a river, becoming ill because of lying around in wet clothes.

Frank Carney finally arrived in Donegal to conduct a tour of the 1st northern division and arranged a meeting with the divisional staff in preparation for a tour of the area. Peadar O'Donnell received a despatch on Saturday morning, 14 May, stating that a flying column was being sent out from Derry with instructions on who was to take charge, etc. At that particular time O'Donnell was reluctant to receive any new columns until he was physically fit to command them and he instructed Paddy Shiels to keep them in Derry until he received further instructions from him. He also protested to Frank Carney about forcing men on him at a time of reorganisation. O'Donnell's protests were in vain, however, as the flying column had left Derry the previous day, four travelling by car and four by rail, on their way to Glendowan. It was becoming obvious that O'Donnell was being kept out of things, as the flying column attended a meeting with Frank Carney and Joe Sweeney the following day and discussed plans for operations in the No. 1 brigade area. O'Donnell sent two Volunteers out to locate the new flying column with instructions for them to return to Derry. They met the column at Dunlewey on Sunday evening and delivered O'Donnell's message. The two Volunteers were told that the column was not to take orders from Peadar O'Donnell but instead only from Frank Carney, and that Peadar O'Donnell had been suspended from his duties.

When O'Donnell learned of his suspension he immediately requested a conference with Carney, but this was refused. O'Donnell was of the opinion that news of his suspension had no foundation as it was conveyed to him through the O/C of the flying column. O'Donnell decided to seek intervention from GHQ and give his side of the story by sending a despatch to the adjutant general at GHQ in Dublin on Sunday morning. He used the opportunity to give his account of matters and requested an immediate investigation as he was of the opinion that the difficulties between him and Carney were having an adverse effect on the Volunteers of the No. 2 brigade. He stated in his despatch:

> You will remember my recent appointment as O/C of No. 2 brigade, 1st northern. The area to which I was appointed might be described as being a cold one, loosely organised, badly equipped and not yet definitely on the war map. I had under my own immediate command a flying column of well trained lads. Instead of attempting to run a flying column in my area I broke up the flying column and sent the lads into battalion and company areas for a lightning organisation campaign and a general tightening up of the company units ...
>
> I discovered that on the belt from Fanad to Castlefinn the morale of the people was poor ... there was no punch and the atmosphere was distinctly bad. It is immaterial to me whether I serve as brigade O/C or as a private, but if the divisional's [Carney] attitude towards the brigade O/C is truly what I suggest it has been, in this case I would request that an investigation should be held to prevent a mischief that I certainly don't want to see occur and which would do very much harm indeed in Donegal. I am sending this special messenger and would earnestly request a reply pending the arrival of a GHQ officer to investigate, that GHQ meantime sends at once for the waiting messenger instructions to be either to consider myself suspended pending investigation as God only knows what regrettable incidents will occur if divisional

O/C acts on the assumption that suspension can be effected by merely telling four or five privates that it has occurred.[87]

Prior to Frank Carney's arrival in County Donegal, Joe Sweeney heard of some friction between Carney and Peadar O'Donnell, and this was confirmed by Carney when he arrived in the county to conduct an inspection of the brigade areas. Frank Carney had left Derry with the divisional adjutant and quartermaster on Friday 13 May and made his way to Glendowan where he was met by Joe Sweeney and members of the new flying column.

The motor car earlier commandeered from Dr Johnston was taken out of storage and used to drive Carney around the area. The divisional command reviewed a number of companies of the 1st brigade area before the party returned to Sweeneys' hotel at Burtonport. This was about 2 a.m. in the morning of Monday 16 May and a few short hours later Joe Sweeney was awoken by the noise of the front door and windows being smashed in. He jumped out of bed and discovered that the house was surrounded by a party of military. Carney told Sweeney to escape, as he was the key man in the area. Sweeney decided to hide in a newly constructed wing of the house. The British carried out an extensive search but failed to find Sweeney. Among those arrested in the raid were Divisional Commandant Frank Carney, Divisional Adjutant Bernard and Divisional Quartermaster Frank Martin.

Later that morning a lorryload of military drove into a trench in the road at Gortnasillagh. A Volunteer who happened to be in the area took advantage of their predicament and sniped at the soldiers. Armed with a revolver, he fired intermittently from the hills above the road before moving away. This kept the military stationary for over an hour, as they were reluctant to proceed for fear of further attacks.[88]

Following the wounding of Peadar O'Donnell the No. 1 flying column was tasked with ensuring his safety and liberty. Members of the column blew up bridges and trenched all roads in the surrounding areas to prevent any military or RIC traffic moving through it. The night before the big round-up they made their way to O'Donnell's home for some well earned rest. The next morning Reddie, the local milkman, ran into O'Donnell's to tell Peadar O'Donnell's mother, Biddy that the Tans and military were coming up the road. Biddy O'Donnell alerted the members of the column to get up quickly. The IRA never anticipated that the British would land at Burtonport, so the members of the column were in no hurry to get up. Seamus McCann jumped out of bed and saw a large party of troops about half a mile away and shouted to the others. There wasn't even time to get dressed, as they had to make a run for it through the hills. As Seamus McCann recalled in his diary: 'Then the shirt tail parade started. A race up along the house then out across the Tully Mountains to Crovehy. It was tough going in the bare feet and bare arses.'

The column made its way to McKelveys' of Brockagh, where O'Donnell was staying and the nurses immediately got Peadar ready for travelling. They made their way to Commeen, hotly pursued by the military and arrived at O'Donnells' of Meenatinney just as the British were leaving after a raid. At O'Donnells' they were given food and stayed for a number of hours.[89] Joe Sweeney relayed the full details of the round-up in a report to the chief of staff, Richard Mulcahy:

> On the morning of Monday the 16 inst. a big drive was made by sea and land on this area taking all by surprise and resulting in the capture of the divisional commandant and his staff and also the commandant of my 1st battalion, his father and brother and I escaped only by hiding myself in the house from Monday until Thursday, then I got out and through the lines in disguise (wearing a woman's hat and coat). The military departed on Friday, but early on Saturday morning a lightning raid was made by a mixed force of police and military who effected the arrest

of a member of the flying column and an old man unconnected with any organisation, but in whose house was found a revolver, the property of the organiser who narrowly escaped – hiding himself under a bed. The military and police came into the 1st battalion area from Bunbeg, Glendowan, Fintown and Glenties or by all leading roads. The force that came by sea landed from a destroyer *Byfort* (D48) in Arran Road and came in small motor launches to Burtonport Quay. The first force raided my house and our first intimation of them was the noise of them coming through the windows …

Fortunately the alarm was raised and all prominent persons in the area escaped. I have been informed that a special flying column of police and military headed by Head Constable Duffy of Killybegs has been established to deal with our area. This head constable is the most dangerous man in the county and is subordinate only to General Tudor. He has unlimited sources of information and is indeed a man to be reckoned with … A direction to No. 3 brigade may serve to have him dealt with. The adjutant there is presently acting commandant. These big drives are beginning to tell on our men and when it is considered that there have been three of them since January it is little wonder. We seriously suspect those giving information, but we can obtain no proof whatever …[90]

The round-up was well organised, covering all approaches to the west of the county. The IRA never thought the British would land by sea at Burtonport and this served as a very valuable lesson.

In an attempt to relieve the pressure on the flying column operating in the west of the county during the British round-up, Peadar O'Donnell sent instructions to Anthony Dawson, adjutant, Letterkenny Company, for the Volunteers there to carry out an attack on British forces in the town. Dawson got in touch with Hugh McGrath, O/C, and they set about planning an ambush.

On the night of Thursday 19 May, Volunteers took up positions at a place called 'The Waltsteads' near the Literary Institute at Lower Main Street and lay in wait for a patrol. The attack took place just after 11 o'clock when a patrol of one RIC sergeant and three constables approached. The Volunteers opened fire when they came into range and two members of the patrol were hit. The sergeant was wounded in the hip and calf and a constable, Albert Carter, died having received a bullet to the throat. At the same time No. 2 police barracks was attacked by another active service unit.[91]

This had the desired effect, as the British turned their focus from west Donegal to Letterkenny in the belief that the column had moved and was operating there.

The police and Black and Tans at No. 1 barracks came onto the street and the reprisals began almost immediately, lasting for several hours. Two civilians were wounded, Anthony Coyle in the wrist and leg and Simon Doherty in the foot. McCarrys' hotel was also attacked and was badly shot up. All the windows, pictures and mirrors were smashed. A grenade was also thrown into the building, creating a large hole in the floor. Terror prevailed throughout the night and few people went to their beds.

The Black and Tans in Letterkenny had declared that they would be carrying out further reprisals by burning the houses of residents with national sympathies. District Inspector Walsh took command of the situation and with some difficulty prevented any further reprisals. About the same time local Volunteers taking advantage of the disturbance in the town took the opportunity to raid the post office and remove bicycles and new telegraph and telephone equipment.[92]

The round-up in west Donegal lasted for ten days and the British arrested a large number of men, but very few were involved with the IRA. The British then withdrew from that part of the county and the column decided to go back to Meenmore. Peadar O'Donnell and Seamus McCann considered it would be safer to remain out on the mountains for a while longer. The two men and their nurses spent

265

the night at Master Kelly's at the Corkskrew in Doochery while the column made its way to O'Donnell's family home at Meenmore. The following morning O'Donnell and McCann woke up to a big surprise when four military lorries stopped outside Kelly's house with a prisoner on board. One of the lorries had broken down and the occupants of the house had a tense twenty or thirty minutes while the lorry was examined. Luck was with them; the lorry was repaired and the convoy made off in the direction of Letterkenny. While McCann and O'Donnell were sweating, the rest of the column had arrived at O'Donnell's home and Mrs O'Donnell was none too happy to see them. She had gone through hell during the ten-day round-up when Tans and police arrived at her home twice with tins of petrol and threatened to burn it down. She gave the members of the column a good feed and then chased them out of the house. They had no sooner left when the Tans and police returned under the command of Head Constable Duffy.

By this time O'Donnells' health had deteriorated and he had been taken to Paddy Harkin's in Drumkeen to recuperate. He was there for over a week when Seamus McCann and Jim Walsh went to check on him. When they arrived Paddy Harkin lifted O'Donnell on to his back and was half way up the hill when the two men called on him to come back down. On hearing the noise of the old bicycles on the lane Harkin had thought it was the police or military so he ran into the house and lifted O'Donnell out of bed throwing him over his back and making a run for it.[93]

Frank Carney recorded his account of events while in custody at Burtonport barracks and the despatch was then smuggled out and given to Peadar O'Donnell, the first official notification he received suspending him as O/C No. 2 brigade.[94]

After the arrest of Frank Carney, Joe Sweeney was appointed acting divisional commandant of the 1st northern division. James McCole became O/C of No. 1 brigade and Frank O'Donnell was appointed vice-O/C.[95] Another casualty of the round-up was the discovery of Dr Johnston's car, which was taken away by the British and returned to the doctor in Stranorlar. Following an investigation into the circumstances surrounding the round-up, an intelligence report was sent to Mulcahy:

> The circumstances of the arrests were rather unfortunate. It now appears that all the converging forces were to reach their objectives at 7 a.m. on the morning of 16 May. The only force which did arrive to time was that landed from the destroyer and it was this force which affected all the arrests. In Burtonport a patrol takes up duty each night at 11 p.m. and goes off at 8 a.m. ... Investigation has shown that the patrol cleared home at 3.30 a.m. on that morning and had it been at its post not one man or woman would have been seized. The force coming from Letterkenny was held up at a broken bridge near Glendowan Mountain for three and a half hours and this force arrived in Doochary – its objective – at 11 a.m.
>
> The force coming from Glenties by way of Gweebara Bridge was held up at a trench at Gortnasillagh for one hour as, owing to the plucky action of an individual Volunteer firing at several lorries with a small bore revolver, the enemy was rather timorous of proceeding for a while.
>
> At both sides of Gweebara Bridge they encountered both trenches and barricades of large boulders which delayed them for four hours so that Dungloe was not reached until 12 noon. The men at Burtonport were the only crowd surprised, as those in other areas had every opportunity of getting warning, and outside those captured at Burtonport no men of importance were taken. The drive was a good if a dear lesson and we have established a coastal watch. At present there is great naval activity and a destroyer comes in at times quite close to the coast in 1st battalion area of No. 1 brigade and takes soundings. We are preparing to have her sniped in future.[96]

While west Donegal was dealing with the large military presence the Inishowen flying column continued with its harassment tactics and planned to remove the telephone equipment from the Carndonagh post office on Monday night 16 May. The post office was situated in the Market Square, almost opposite the RIC barracks. It was decided to post sentries around the square and enter the post office by the rear. The raiding party proceeded to the back door and when they knocked and called on the postmaster to open the door he immediately blew a whistle. The RIC were either informed of the raid or were anticipating a raid as they immediately opened fire from various houses around the square. The Volunteers made a hasty exit and got away safely. This action provoked a quick response from the enemy forces and at approximately 1 a.m. the police and Tans began firing shots and throwing grenades at houses in Carndonagh, continuing the onslaught for up to an hour. The following day they stated that their actions were in response to the attempted raid on the local post office.[97]

The military were in possession of information that certain fishing boats were being used to ferry Volunteers and equipment and that the crews were members of the movement. The military mounted an operation on Thursday morning 19 May and the crews of two fishing boats, totalling seventeen men, were arrested about a mile from Donegal town. The boats were thoroughly searched and the men held for about three hours before being released.

The military involved in the round-up in west Donegal switched their attention to the Buncrana area on Friday 20 May. They arrived in large numbers at approximately 8 p.m. and ordered everyone indoors before carrying out extensive raids throughout the town. Earlier that day up to twenty-eight prisoners from the west Donegal round-up arrived at Derry jail.[98]

Joe Sweeney's first task as acting O/C was to evaluate his former command area and direct the focus of the British to other parts of the county. Directives were sent out to all areas to organise and engage regular attacks on enemy forces. In response to the last major military operations the Volunteers considered it necessary to strike at the earliest opportunity and another attack was planned for Glenties barracks. This was to be carried out on Saturday 21 May by Volunteers from No. 3 brigade assisted by the 1st battalion of No. 1 brigade, along with the members of No. 1 flying column. Again cars were scarce, so many of the attack party had to cycle to Glenties. The flying column moved to an old house near Glenties and remained there until the Saturday night. This attack, under the command of General Joe Sweeney, O/C 1st northern division, was carried out on three sides, with the Volunteers being posted to various positions surrounding the building. Many of the same tactics were employed as in the previous attack on this barracks. When all the men were ready, Joe Sweeney gave the order to open fire. The men positioned in front of the barracks at the workhouse wall were armed with a bolt machine gun, one of the Derry city guns, but it failed to work when the order was given to open fire. Volunteers fired with rifles from all sides of the building for some time, with the police and Black and Tans returning fire. The battle continued for over thirty minutes, but the rifle fire made little impact on the barracks, which was protected with shutters and sandbags. This was considered a waste of ammunition and Joe Sweeney gave the order calling off the attack. No casualties were suffered by the Volunteers and it was not known if there were casualties on the British side.[99]

The 3rd brigade, South-West Donegal, set about organising an ambush on a regular police patrol in Ardara. The four-man ambush party were positioned at strategic positions on the edge of the village and opened fire on the four-man RIC patrol. Two members of the patrol were seriously wounded, but the police in the local barracks responded quickly, forcing the Volunteers to retreat.

In anticipation of a large-scale response, a large party of Volunteers had been put into ambush positions at Kilrean on the Glenties-Ardara road. Volunteers from the 3rd brigade flying column, 1st battalion, 3rd battalion and 4th battalion had been deployed in the area during the previous night. Hot beverages and food were provided by Cumann na mBan under Sis McGuire, who was also a nurse. Shortly after 2 p.m. the convoy's approach was signalled and the advanced positions occupied. These were staggered, with one on the left, one on the right and a central control position in the rear. The target was a convoy of lorries with police, military and Tans on board. The first vehicle came alongside the left section and fire was opened, hitting the driver, a Black and Tan. The vehicle came to a halt partly in the ditch, with some of the occupants falling out and the rest standing up holding their rifles above their heads in surrender.

The other two lorries stopped out of range of all sections, with the military dismounting and descending on the ambush positions in a flanking movement. This caused much confusion for the Volunteers as they were in no position to accept the surrender of the military in the first lorry with the occupants of the other lorries closing in. The Volunteers opened fire and began to withdraw section by section, with the enemy returning fire. Dan McTigh was seriously wounded early on and had to be carried to the rear, while a number of others were also slightly injured in the battle. They continued this step-by-step withdrawal until the entire party was safely away and they reached the foothills of the Blue Stack Mountains. They were pursued for the next two days by the Wiltshire Regiment and Black and Tans, but the weather was very bad and visibility poor. The morale of the Volunteers was high as they received reports of the large number of military and Black and Tan casualties from the ambush, with a Black and Tan dying of his wounds a number of days later.[100] The Black and Tan member was named Devine from Manchester, England and he was being treated at the hospital in Lifford where he died a few days later and was buried in a local cemetery. The dead man's mother travelled from England to attend her son's funeral, accompanied by a friend. Four policemen and the military Catholic chaplain were also present and when the grave was closed the dead man's mother said a few words:

> I want the Irish people to know that I did not send my son on this mission to Ireland and that I forgive the people who shot him. I have another son, and if he came on the same mission to Ireland, I should also forgive the people who would shoot him. I have the greatest sympathy with the Irish people and I wish them every success.[101]

The 3rd brigade, South-West Donegal column and battalions could move with relative freedom around the brigade area so long as they remained intact. Even if they became separated at any of the points on the coast they had the fishing fleet of the 2nd and 3rd battalions at their service. Inland they could always fall back into the Blue Stacks and it would take a large force to dig them out of these mountains, as most of the year they were covered in clouds and drenched with rain. There were plenty of animals around, such as mountain sheep and deer so there was no shortage of food.[102]

In late May Joe Sweeney received official notification from Richard Mulcahy of his appointment as divisional commander. He replaced Frank Carney, who had been captured during the last round-up. Sweeney had earlier criticised Carney's aloof attitude during his tenure as O/C. In fact Carney's first official tour of the divisional area ended abruptly, being arrested within three days of his arrival. Sweeney was now given the task of ensuring the war effort was spread throughout each brigade area.[103]

About that time the 3rd battalion of the 1st brigade called a staff meeting to discuss the possibility of an attack on the British forces in the area to relieve the pressure on their comrades further west in the Dungloe, Glenties and Burtonport areas. They decided to carry out a sniping attack on Carrigart RIC barracks, much the same as in the previous attack on that barracks. The 3rd battalion proceeded to Carrigart and began firing intermittently at the barracks from selected positions for approximately two hours; the RIC returned fire and sent up Verey lights. Shortly after daylight reinforcements arrived from Dunfanaghy, but by that time the Volunteers had withdrawn safely over the mountains.[104]

Sometime in mid May the Donegal prisoners at Ballykinlar received word from some of the new internees that the Volunteers in the 1st battalion, No. 4 brigade covering Ballybofey and the surrounding areas was experiencing problems due to the large numbers of military and RIC. They reported that the Ballybofey Company was not very active and as a result allowed the enemy forces to move around unhindered. The officers in the camp attached to the 1st northern division decided that action needed to be taken and it was decided that Jim McCarron, who was now a prisoner, should give the required undertaking to the British authorities to secure his release. The undertaking was to denounce all support for Dáil Éireann and the IRA, and as a former British soldier McCarron came across as more genuine.

McCarron had served with the British in Europe, suffered a leg wound during the war and was in receipt of a pension. He emphasised this point and the British believed him to be sincere. They released him on condition that he should report to the police on his return to Donegal. However, McCarron went on the run immediately and set about forming a small flying column in the Ballybofey area.[105]

The Inishowen Volunteers continued their harassment of the RIC and at times adopted less heroic and daring ways to keep the police on their toes. Two members of the Carndonagh Company were scouting the town at about 1.30 a.m. on Wednesday 18 May; there was very little activity, so one of them decided to test the police with a ruse. He blew a boy scout whistle to give the impression a raid was about to commence. The police in the barracks, assuming it was an attack, commenced shooting at ghosts and threw grenades onto the street; this was kept up for the next few hours. Neither of the two Volunteers was even armed, but it kept the police on their toes.[106]

The following day a police patrol was ambushed near Mullanmore. The small ambush party opened fire on the patrol and a policeman was injured. The patrol returned fire and a battle ensued with intermittent firing from both sides. Three soldiers patrolling a bridge a short distance away, on hearing the firing, drove in that direction. The Volunteers heard the approaching vehicle and, thinking it was reinforcements, decided to retreat from the area and split up. Volunteer Éamon Conaghan was spotted by one of the soldiers and ordered to stop. Conaghan ran towards the mountains; two shots were fired at him but missed. When he was a safe distance away and was out of sight of the military he hid his revolver and then continued on. The military and police searched the hills for the next two hours and eventually caught up with Conaghan, who said when questioned that he was tending to the sheep. He was arrested and later transferred to Derry jail.[107]

GHQ INVESTIGATES TROUBLE IN THE DONEGAL RANKS

IN RESPONSE TO Peadar O'Donnell's request for GHQ intervention in the dispute between him and other officers in the divisional area, Michael Collins sent Liam Archer, O/C 5 battalion, Dublin brigade, to investigate the circumstances surrounding the problem. Liam Archer arrived in Derry on Friday 27 May and began his investigations. He met with Joe Sweeney in Derry the following Tuesday and sent him back to Donegal to locate O'Donnell and arrange a meeting at Churchill the following day. Sweeney and Archer were at the designated location for the meeting at 5 p.m. but O'Donnell didn't arrive for another hour, at which point they had a brief meeting. O'Donnell cited that he was delayed due to the presence of a police patrol in the area, but Archer claimed in his report that he sent a scout out to locate the patrol but there was no sign of any. Peadar O'Donnell stated that the cause of the dispute originated from his efforts to secure the co-operation of the Derry city battalion with the local Cumann na mBan branch. He also referred to his attempts to engage with the enemy in the city as another reason for the dispute and stated that his efforts were the result of the lack of regular engagements by the Derry battalion. GHQ frowned upon any area entering into private treaties or ceasefires with the enemy. Peadar O'Donnell and Seamus McCann travelled to Derry regularly, organising operations with the members of the local battalion and engaging with the military and police. Rumours were being circulated, and were recorded in Archer's report, that O'Donnell was only in the IRA six months before his appointment as O/C No. 2 brigade. Archer recorded:

> The feeling is therefore prevalent that an injustice has been done, by the appointment to this position, of a man who is only some six months a member of the IRA, who was an organiser for an organisation regarded as being unfriendly to the IRA who possesses little Volunteer experience and whose ability has not yet been proved.[108]

This assertion was incorrect as O'Donnell had joined the IRA in early 1919 in County Monaghan while he was based there as organiser for the Irish Transport and General Workers' Union. He spread himself between the two organisations before becoming a full-time Volunteer, but there was no evidence that he was in any way hostile towards the IRA while in the ITGWU.[109]

Liam Archer also referred to O'Donnell's activities in Derry in his report:

> Recently a bombing attack was carried out in Derry. According to the O/C Derry, the O/C No. 2 brigade attended a company parade in Derry, announced to the full company what he

intended to do, and then selected from the assembled company the men for the work.

The O/C Derry was not consulted beforehand and only learned of the contemplated action at the company parade. The O/C brigade states the men were selected for him by Seamus McCann in conjunction with the company officer. Two banks have been robbed recently of some couple of hundred pounds by some officers and men of one of the companies recently organised by the O/C brigade. The explanation given for this by the O/C brigade is: he received instructions from Division Commandant Carney that brigade funds should be raised, by 'collection or otherwise'. This order was translated verbatim to the companies, who apparently placed a wide interpretation on the words 'or otherwise'. Peadar O'Donnell said he had placed the same interpretation on this order as his men had.

Archer then referred to the rumours being circulated and stated that the blame fell solely on Peadar O'Donnell and members of the No. 1 flying column. He said: 'To cite the only definite statement which I could get – Division Commandant Carney went to Dungloe because the O/C No. 2 brigade said: "Isn't it time he visited his division instead of skulking in Derry." This whole affair had created a division between the Derry battalion and the remainder of No. 2 brigade.'

Archer was of the opinion that O'Donnell was considered 'untrustworthy and incompetent' by the Derry battalion and that the O/C of the battalion would probably refuse to serve under him and request a transfer. Joe Sweeney the new O/C 1st northern division was of the opinion that 'He (O'Donnell) is well-meaning, but is unpractical.' Sweeney also suggested that Derry city should operate as a separate command area and that Peadar O'Donnell remain as O/C of the No. 2 brigade.[110]

In late May two members of the Ballintra Company approached Henry McGowan, acting O/C No. 4 brigade, to request permission for a raid on the office of Captain Hamilton, a land agent. He collected rents from tenants and forwarded the money to the trustees of Trinity College in Dublin. The Ballintra Company also requested the assistance of two experienced Volunteers. McGowan decided to go, bringing John Smith with him, and he put Jim McCarron in charge of the Ballybofey Company in his absence. They raided the office on the evening of Thursday 2 June, but only got £5 as Hamilton's wife had just left and was en route to the bank with a large amount of money.[111]

In McGowan's absence Jim McCarron decided to attack Captain McGregor and his fishing party if they ventured to Trusk Lough, a few miles outside Ballybofey. He joked with the other Volunteers that Henry McGowan would be both surprised and disappointed if they got McGregor in his absence as Henry McGowan often talked of ambushing his old adversary in the British army. McCarron received information on Thursday morning that McGregor had left Drumboe Castle with a small military escort and was going to Trusk Lough, approximately two miles from Ballybofey, to fish. Ballybofey and Stranorlar were heavily garrisoned by British troops, Black and Tans and RIC and the opportunities to engage them were limited.

On the morning of the attack McCarron could only secure the services of three other Volunteers, but decided to carry on with the attack as he was informed the military party was smaller than usual. The British party of three officers, a corporal and their driver arrived at the lough and before settling down to fish, McGregor placed some of his men at strategic positions around the lough. Unknown to McCarron, one of the soldiers was scanning the area with a pair of field-glasses, and spotted the Volunteers as they made their way to the lough. He informed the other officers and they immediately took up positions on higher ground, moving along a ditch parallel with the road. By this movement the military had successfully flanked the four Volunteers.

When they came into view McGregor called on them to surrender, but McCarron ordered the Volunteers to open fire in the direction of the voice, to which the British replied with heavy fire. Unable to locate the British, McCarron ordered the Volunteers to retreat, but in the process McCarron was shot in the hip. Patrick McAteer ran back to help him and was told to keep going, that McCarron would cover them. However, McAteer was also shot and was helped away by the other Volunteers. Jim McCarron was hit a second time, this time in the chin, and he died instantly. At this point the British returned to Drumboe Castle for reinforcements, giving the Volunteers enough time to clear out of the area. Local people arrived to assist them and some had the presence of mind to retrieve McCarron's rifle and any documents he had. When the British reinforcements arrived they put McCarron's body onto a lorry and drove back through Ballybofey shouting 'We got him, We got him' as they passed his home. The remainder of the ambush party made their way to a dugout near Kelly's Bridge and a doctor was summoned.

Afterwards the military, police and Tans were scouring the area for the three Volunteers and called at the residence of James Doherty. They smashed up the interior of the house in the normal fashion and interrogated James Doherty and his son Edward who had been working in the kitchen at his trade as a watchmaker. Two members of the Black and Tans began beating Edward Doherty and then suddenly one of them raised his rifle and shot the young man in the abdomen at point blank range. Edward Doherty was seriously wounded and was taken to the Stranorlar Infirmary where the doctors tended to his wound, but he died the following afternoon.[112]

About this time the members of the Inishowen flying column had contracted a severe attack of scabies and had to retire to a safe area where they could rest and bathe for a few days until the scabies attack had abated. The Volunteers serving in flying columns had to contend with many hardships and as a result of insanitation, irregular feeding and uncleanliness some would often suffer from scabies also known as the 'Column Itch'. An outbreak of scabies would seriously undermine the effectiveness of a flying column as mobility would be restricted and moral would also be affected. In such time a certain Napoleon maxim is fitting: 'health is indispensable in war and cannot be replaced by anything.'[113]

Once the scabies outbreak was dealt with the column returned to active service and their focus turned to procuring arms and ammunition. They decided to raid unionist households in the Inishowen area for weapons and set off in the direction of Moville. The raids would also attract the attention of the military and would keep them stretched across the Inishowen peninsula. The column divided into three raiding parties with Volunteers of the Moville Company acting as guides. Joe McLaughlin and Packie Doherty approached a house owned by a man called Campbell. They were told that Campbell had six hefty sons who were all armed and would likely put up some resistance. They knocked on the door and Campbell enquired who was there. When the Volunteers replied 'British military', the door was opened. Joe McLaughlin pounced on Campbell and Packie Doherty ran up the stairs to find the six hefty sons standing in their night clothing with their hands up and their knees shaking. Unfortunately the two men failed to procure any weapons as the British military had collected them some days earlier. They then made their way to the home of Colonel McNee, where they were treated to refreshments and conversed with their host about the political situation in the country. The colonel handed the two men a shotgun and a very good telescope.[114]

The war effort was intensified in the 3rd brigade area, south-west Donegal, and a large raiding party was made up from battalions in the area supported by the brigade flying column. They made their way towards Kilcar in preparation for an attack on the Teelin coastguard station nearby. On the night of Saturday 4 June they arrived in Kilcar, where they rested before continuing to the coastguard station. It was anticipated that the station would offer little or no resistance and the garrison would surrender. The attacking party was positioned at various points around the building and shortly after 2 a.m. began firing at the building. There was no immediate response from the garrison stationed there and they were then called on to surrender. Unknown to the Volunteers the garrison had been reinforced by a party of military the previous day and suddenly the garrison replied with a ferocious burst of gunfire. A fierce gun battle ensued for over an hour, with the Volunteers pinned down at some sections.

The garrison were showing no sign of surrendering and the command was then given to retreat. The Volunteers learned later that a soldier and a coastguard were killed in the battle.[115]

Joe Sweeney, division commandant, made a number of changes to the 1st northern division through the appointment of new commandants for the various brigades. The appointments were as follows: James McCole, O/C of No. 1 brigade; John Houston, O/C of No. 3 brigade; and Sam O'Flaherty, O/C of No. 4 brigade. The following instructions were also sent to the various officers commanding the four brigades:

> No. 1 brigade: battalion flying columns to be established each to operate in its own area.
> No. 2 brigade: three active service units to be established – one to operate in Derry city, another in the Inishowen peninsula and the third in the area of Fanad peninsula/Letterkenny/Lagan.
> No. 3 brigade: one active service unit to operate throughout the area for the present until the organisation in that area was perfected.
> No. 4 brigade: as soon as a semblance of organisation and control is established in this area an active service unit of full strength will be formed to operate along the enemy's

> main lines of communication. In the meantime a small
> unit will be formed to carry out small jobs. With a fair
> supply of munitions I believe that we will be able to tender
> a good account of ourselves next Winter and I hope by
> then to have the ground prepared for all emergencies ...[116]

Sweeney made a request to GHQ for rockets which could be used to give warning of approaching military or police. The rockets, to be fired from the top of a hill, would be seen for miles around, thus giving warning to all Volunteers in the area. He also wanted a grenade-making plant for the divisional engineer. Sweeney also made a request to GHQ for a standard scale of punishment for various offences:

> At present owing to there being no recognised penalties, it is
> very hard to maintain strict discipline and a directive in this
> matter is very badly needed. It is difficult, for instance, to know
> how to punish an offence such as the desertion of post which
> resulted in the capture of so many officers here on 16 May, and
> now that the IRA is rapidly developing into a regular army a
> scale of punishment is imperative.[117]

About the same time Peadar O'Donnell had recovered from his injuries to the extent that he could return to duty. He summoned the flying column to meet him in Letterkenny where he had arranged a meeting with the Letterkenny Company.

John Mullan gave him a lift in the sidecar of his motorbike and they travelled the back roads from Glendowan. They met some of the column at Glencar before walking through the fields towards the town. As the flying column was passing St Eunan's college, O'Donnell decided that it was as good a place as any to have a meeting to catch up on events.

The priests were not impressed with the sight of O'Donnell and other Volunteers walking in wearing trench coats, and bandoleers strapped around them filled with ammunition and weapons. In addition, they feared that O'Donnell's meeting would attract the attention of the Black and Tans to the college. Despite this, a meeting was convened; it lasted for over an hour, with various topics being discussed, including ways of intensifying the war campaign in that area.[118]

In the early hours of Wednesday 8 June, a large number of Volunteers were busy in the Mountcharles, Inver and Dunkineely areas with a series of raids on the post offices. The railway stations were also raided; large supplies from unionist firms were commandeered while some were destroyed.[119]

The saga of the difficulties between Peadar O'Donnell and other officers in the 1st northern division remained on the agenda at GHQ in Dublin, with Eamon Price, director of organisation sending his suggestions to Gearóid O'Sullivan, adjutant general, on the 9 June:

> I do not find it very easy to make up my mind from the report as to what would be the best thing to do. The whole difficulty is that O'Donnell's appointment appears to have been a mistake. This is true, whether the statements regarding his record are correct or not. He does not appear to possess the qualities necessary for dealing with a brigade command. I recollect that there was considerable trouble in Derry between the Transport Workers' Union and the Volunteers. You may remember the sheets of paper that the former incompetent commandant of this area covered on this and kindred subjects. If O'Donnell was the man who was mixed up in this trouble I can understand how the difficulty has arisen … I am inclined to discount some of the things that are said against the O/C of the 2nd brigade. The officer from headquarters appears to have been prejudiced against him from the beginning owing to his unpunctuality and possibly owing to having heard the other side of the story first. You will observe that the suggestion of

the inspector is that the O/C Derry be placed in charge of the area. If O/C division agrees, this should be tried.[120]

Following the Trusk Lough incident members of the Ballybofey Company frequently visited the dugout at Kelly's Bridge to keep an eye on the injured Volunteer, Patrick McAteer. On Friday 10 June, Henry McGowan, John Smith and Daniel Deery were visiting McAteer at the dugout when a large party of military, Black and Tans and RIC suddenly converged on the area, approaching the dugout from all directions. All four were arrested and arms and ammunition were found in a bag concealed approximately 80 to 100 yards from the dugout, which was on the side of a mountain several miles from Ballybofey.[121]

On the same day military discovered a bunker at Trusk near the location of the ambush, containing weapons and bicycles. The captured men were taken to Drumboe Castle before being transferred to Ebrington barracks the following morning, where they were held to await trial. Henry McGowan's brother Patrick was also at Ebrington barracks, waiting to be transferred to Ballykinlar. McGowan was concerned that he might be recognised as having taken part in the Drumquin barracks raid the previous year and would face a charge of murder. He switched identities with his brother and was subsequently transferred to Ballykinlar instead. On arrival at the camp McGowan reported to Joe McGrath, the camp commandant, who informed him that if a murder charge was preferred against him he could be lost in the camp. Losing a man in the camp was a regular occurrence and it would simply involve moving a man, resembling the prisoner, from another hut and each man would answer to the other's name. In some instances the prisoners would resort to shaving their heads and growing beards etc., to make identification difficult. Henry McGowan was the acting brigade O/C when captured at the dugout at Kelly's Bridge. GHQ in Dublin ordered an inquiry into the circumstances surrounding the raid as they received information to the effect that an agent on the estate of Lord Caledon, near Kelly's Bridge, may have given information to the British, which led to the raid on the dugout. The arrest of Henry McGowan and Daniel Deery created an anxious situation for the staff of the No. 4 brigade and raised concerns at GHQ in Dublin. Michael Collins instructed Sam O'Flaherty to immediately return to Donegal and take command of the No. 4 brigade area; Joseph Murray had reluctantly taken temporary charge since McGowan's arrest. O'Flaherty had been appointed O/C of the brigade area by Joe Sweeney, but had been held up in Dublin with his work for GHQ. O'Flaherty arrived back in Donegal with a directive from Collins that Joseph Murray was to carry out an investigation into the circumstances surrounding the arrests and discovery of the arms dump.

O'Flaherty arranged for those involved in the investigation team to dress in British military uniforms, which had been collected from deserters some time previously. Michael Doherty, the Ballybofey Battalion O/C, selected men to assist in the investigation; these included Joseph Hannigan, adjutant and Andrew Doherty, company captain. There was still a large military and police presence in the area and Murray decided to travel from Bundoran to Pettigo as a pilgrim on his way to Lough Derg. He was then taken to Kelly's Bridge by Owen O'Donnell, posing as a sheep dealer. He met with the members of the Ballybofey Battalion, but with no British military uniforms, as they had met a lorryload of military and police, forcing them to abandon the uniforms in a ditch. Despite this setback they carried on with the investigation and Murray was satisfied beyond doubt that the estate manager played no part in either spying or informing the British about the activities of the Volunteers. They also questioned a number of people before deciding that it was impossible to reach any conclusion as to the identity of the informer. It transpired after further investigation that the men made no effort to conceal the existence of the dugout and everyone in the area was aware of its location. Empty food and cigarette cartons were scattered around the place, which was sure to attract attention as there were no houses in the immediate area. However, Henry McGowan believed that the location was disclosed to the British by the doctor who was brought to attend to McAteer's injury.[122]

The Volunteers from the Ballybofey battalion arrived back from their mission to Kelly's Bridge and found that Joseph Hannigan's house had been raided by the military. On one of the lists captured from Mulcahy's briefcase the previous year was the name J. Hannigan, and as a result Joe Hannigan's brother, James was arrested and later interned in Ballykinlar. James had not been associated with the Volunteers.[123]

Joe Sweeney, the new divisional commandant, decided to tour his command area to gauge the strengths and weaknesses of the organisation. He began with an inspection of east Donegal and later made his way by bicycle to Sam O'Flaherty's home near Castlefinn. Following a conversation with O'Flaherty, Sweeney was convinced that the poor state of armaments in the division was a matter of concern and warranted a visit to GHQ in Dublin. He stayed the night at O'Flaherty's and was woken early the next morning by the growls of an old Labrador dog outside. Sweeney jumped out of bed, grabbed his clothes and ran out the back door to the bottom of the garden. He jumped into the River Finn, which flowed behind the house, and swam across to the other side, where he put his clothes on.

The house was surrounded by a mixed party of military and specials. They entered the house and asked for Sweeney by name. When they eventually left, Sweeney returned to the house. Having dried his clothes, he set off again on his bicycle. He was cycling down a steep hill when the front forks of the bicycle collapsed, sending him into the air. Sweeney received deep cuts to the face and was forced to return to O'Flaherty's house and the doctor was called to attend to his wounds. Ned Gallon arrived at O'Flaherty's on his way to Lough Derg and Sweeney travelled with Gallon to Lough Derg, spending most of the week there before going to Enniskillen. He stayed there for a couple of days with Michael Dawson from Letterkenny, who was working as an engineer in Enniskillen. When his wounds had completely healed, Sweeney made his way to Dublin by train.

Sweeney met with Michael Collins, Eoin O'Duffy and Richard Mulcahy at Batt O'Connor's house in Donnybrook. He outlined the problems experienced in Donegal and made a plea for weapons and explosives to bolster the war effort in the county. He received guarantees that more emphasis would be put on the north-west and it was left at that. A few days later Mulcahy arranged a meeting with Cathal Brugha, then minister for defence, who instructed Sweeney to secure Volunteers to go to London to shoot members of the British cabinet. Sweeney was a little perturbed by the idea and was relieved a day later to learn that de Valera had heard of the plan and pressured Collins to cancel the order. While in Dublin, Sweeney had come to the conclusion that there was friction between Collins and de Valera. It transpired that the assassination plot against the British cabinet was cancelled due to the secret negotiations that were in progress with the British.[124]

In Donegal the Ardara Company attempted a raid on the Ulster Bank at Ardara on Thursday 16 June. Staff members were closing the premises when five Volunteers entered. They searched the building for any cash before demanding the keys of the safe from the manager; he refused, and the Volunteers were forced to leave empty-handed. As they were leaving they ran into a party of police and Tans on patrol from Glenties. A running battle ensued with the Volunteers being chased for several miles through the sanddunes along the coast in the direction of Rosbeg. Two Volunteers were shot and badly injured and the pursuing police and Tans surrounded the two men and found Charles Hennessey from Drogheda injured and concealed behind a rock a short distance away. All three were arrested and taken back to Ardara.[125]

British reinforcements arrived from Glenties and a large-scale search of the surrounding area followed. Two dugouts were discovered containing blankets, literature, lamps and other provisions; these were seized and the dugouts burned. The police and military made their way up the coast towards Kiltoorish, where two Volunteers were seen running. The police and military gave chase and eventually discovered the two men hiding in a growth of bushes. Volunteers Francis Gallagher and Patrick Reilly were unarmed and were being marched back to Harkins'. As the British and their prisoners appeared over the hill Patrick Harkin was spotted leaving his house carrying two rifles and a bandolier. A soldier fired a shot, prompting Harkin to stop, and he was then ordered to walk towards them. The military and police conducted a thorough search of his house, discovering a substantial cache that included 4 rifles, 500 rounds of ammunition, bombs, trench coats and various other items. All men were removed to Derry jail later that day.

Buncrana was once again the focus of British military attention on the night of Friday 17 June when military based in the town, backed up by reinforcements from Derry, put the local population under siege. Several houses were raided and searched including those of J. McLaughlin, J. Porter, P. Porter, J. O'Donnell and Hugh Doherty. The military dragged three men out of their homes and marched them to the Belfast bank where they forced them to paint over graffiti on the wall. John O'Hagan was arrested during the raids and was later transferred to Ebrington barracks in Derry.

Some time during the night members of the Black and Tans stationed in Buncrana painted slogans on the walls of local residences, including: 'No Pope here' and 'Up Craig'. The following morning, to their embarrassment, they were publicly reprimanded by the military officers and ordered to paint over the graffiti.

The Volunteers of the Letterkenny Company were also active on Friday evening when an RIC man was attacked as he was walking from the police barracks at Lower Main Street to his lodgings. It had been a market day and the town was still quite busy when the two

Volunteers attacked the policeman, relieving him of his revolver. The officer immediately reported the incident at the barracks and a large party of police were soon in the hunt. In a follow-up operation two men, John Glackin and Charles McDaid, were stopped at Newmills and arrested.[126]

The Inishowen flying column continued to harass the British in their area and a game of tit-for-tat was slowly developing. On Saturday morning the Volunteers held up a lorry carrying food supplies to the military based at Lough Swilly forts. The lorry and the food were burned. The flying column kept up the pressure and set off from Buncrana in a commandeered car in the direction of Moville on Friday night 16 June. The target was the coastguard station. The Volunteers, aware that a garrison of British marines were stationed on a gunboat in the bay, approached the coastguard station with caution and discovered the building was empty. They broke in and saturated the interior with petrol and oil found in a store room. On setting the building on fire, they immediately left the area. When a safe distance away they stopped to observe the fruits of their labour and could see the building in flames with the roof blowing completely off in the first burst of petrol fumes.[127]

The towns of Carndonagh and Buncrana were the targets of British reprisal, beginning on Saturday night and continuing through to Sunday morning. A mixed party of military, Tans and police arrived into both towns late on Saturday night and terrorised the local population into the early hours. They raided and searched a number of houses and business premises, making two arrests – Hugh McLaughlin and Edward O'Donnell. McLaughlin was released a short time later, but O'Donnell was taken to Ebrington barracks because the police claimed he had seditious material, which was Gaelic literature, in his possession. O'Donnell was not involved with either Sinn Féin or the Volunteers and was described as an ardent Gaelic student. On Sunday morning a large party of military and police set up road blocks on either side of Cockhill Road, forcing anyone going to mass to endure a barrage of abuse. All men were stopped, questioned and searched, and were roughly treated in the process; no arrests were made.[128]

Meanwhile in Letterkenny on the same day two young men were stopped at a military and police barricade as they cycled through Newmills. When a revolver cartridge was found in one of their pockets, James Friel was taken to the RIC barracks at Letterkenny. He was subjected to a severe interrogation and beaten so badly that he required medical treatment. He was released the following evening.[129]

The following morning in Buncrana the local Volunteer company used a postman to lure a police patrol into their trap. The postman was stopped near the town by two Volunteers and his mailbag taken. Two policemen patrolling nearby spotted the two men running away and gave chase, only to run into their trap. The two Volunteers had hidden behind a wall, where a third man was waiting, and when the police approached they jumped out with revolvers drawn. They ordered the two RIC men to raise their hands and relieved them of their weapons and ammunition before escaping in a waiting car.[130]

The inquiry into the difficulties between the divisional staff in Donegal was finally concluded by the officers at GHQ in Dublin. Eamon Price, director of organisation wrote to Chief of Staff Richard Mulcahy on Tuesday 21 June, with his recommendations:

> The only difficulty now is the command of the No. 2 brigade of which O'Donnell is new O/C. GHQ inspector recommends the appointment of O/C Derry battalion for this position. I would not think this is wise just now and would be inclined to ask the opinion of the acting O/C division on the following proposal ... Separate Derry city battalion from No. 2 division and place the present O/C in charge and put O'D in charge of remainder of that brigade, each to report separately to the O/C division. This is to be only a temporary arrangement pending

further developments. If Derry city battalion is given to O'D just now the new divisional O/C will have local difficulties to attend which might hamper him in the rather responsible work he has undertaken.[131]

Meanwhile in Donegal the harassment of the local population continued when the Black and Tans arrived in the village of Killgordon early on Wednesday morning, 22 June. They came in two lorries accompanied by an RIC sergeant, who was there to point out selected houses to be searched. They subsequently raided the homes of Dr Kerrigan, Mrs McGroarty, James McNulty, John Bonar, Mrs Hannigan, J. J. Doherty and James McGranaghan, smashing through the houses in an aggressive manner and terrorising the occupants in the process. Following further raids, two young men – Charlie Doherty and Patrick Hannigan – were arrested and taken to Drumboe Castle for interrogation; later that week they were transferred to Ballykinlar internment camp.[132]

Also on Wednesday 22 June, the Northern Ireland Parliament was being officially opened by King George V in Belfast. He delivered what was, in the circumstances, a remarkable appeal for peace, concluding with:

> ... I speak from a full heart when I pray that my coming to Ireland today may prove to be the first step towards the end of strife among her people, whatever their race or creed. In that hope I appeal to all Irishmen to pause, to stretch out the hand of forbearance and conciliation, to forgive and forget, and to join in making for the land they love a new era of peace, contentment and goodwill ...

Partition was now cast in stone, signalling a victory for the unionists of the six counties of Derry, Antrim, Armagh, Down, Fermanagh and Tyrone.[133]

The appeal for conciliation was not quite on the agenda in Inishowen where the flying column joined forces with the Carndonagh Company and set plans in motion to ambush a British military patrol that regularly travelled by lorry on the Malin Road. In preparation for the ambush the Volunteers partially dismantled a bridge at a blind bend on the road and took up positions. Eventually the patrol was observed approaching, but before it reached the bridge a young man ran on to the road waving his arms. The British pulled up and he informed them that the bridge was damaged. The military immediately dismounted and proceeded in an encircling movement towards the ambush position. The Volunteers had now lost the element of surprise and were mostly armed with shotguns, which were no match for the enemy fire power. The order was given to fall back and they safely retreated from the area.[134]

In late June James McCole, O/C No. 1 brigade, informed Joe Sweeney that many of his officers and men had declared that they intended travelling to Scotland and England for the harvest season. This was an annual exodus from west Donegal and was the result of economic necessity. Sweeney was faced with his first big dilemma and decided to write to Michael Collins for advice on how to keep the men in the area:

> The O/C No. 1 brigade informs me that difficulties are arising in his area through most of his best officers and men having notified him that they are migrating to Scotland. You are probably aware that up here the holdings are all uneconomic and every year the young men migrate to the mines and other works in Scotland while the older men and young boys and girls go to the potato-digging in the same country. The end of summer and all the autumn is for us a bad time of year as during that period the numbers of the organisation are very small and generally the best men are absent.

The truce between the IRA and the British would be declared before the GHQ decided on a resolution to address this problem.

While the annual migration served to weaken the numbers on the ground, in the county it was also beneficial in other respects. When they arrived in the different parts of Scotland and England they made contact with the local Volunteers and joined the ranks there. They proved useful in the procurement of arms and explosives. These were then sent back to the local areas by various means and were greatly welcomed by the local Volunteers.

The report continued:

> No. 1 area is especially concerned and particularly the 1st battalion of that area. The battalion and company officers are absent for six months so that the companies have to be reorganised periodically. Could you suggest anything to hold on to the existing officers? The countryside of the 'Rosses' here is being greatly affected by the coal strike and there will be great privation unless employment can be obtained for the young men. I mentioned the whole circumstances to Messrs France, Spicer and Drew of the 'American Committee for Relief in Ireland' delegation who passed through here last week.[135]

The Volunteers of the Falcarragh Company organised a joint operation with the Cloganeely Company to prevent military movement through the area. They began late on Saturday night 25 June, constructing three large barricades at various points along the road between Falcarragh and Gortahork; each barricade was four feet high and six feet deep. This would also present ambush opportunities later and they were watched over the coming days, but the British used extreme caution and rounded up local men in Falcarragh to clear a path. This was a typical tactic and prevented any opportunity of attack for the Volunteers.[136]

Joseph Blee, Ballybofey, was arrested on Sunday night near

Stranorlar and taken to Drumboe Castle for interrogation. While there he was identified by a soldier as one of two men who approached him in early May and coerced him to steal weapons from Drumboe Castle to be purchased by the Volunteers. Patrick McAteer, who had been injured at Trusk Lough and later arrested at Kelly's Bridge, was the other man. Blee was transferred to Derry jail and charged before a field general court-martial on Tuesday 28 June with soliciting a soldier to sell rifles and ammunition, but he refused to recognise the court. The soldier gave evidence that he met Joseph Blee and Patrick McAteer in McMenamins' public house in Ballybofey. He was asked by McAteer if he could get rifles and ammunition from Drumboe Castle, for which he would be paid. As McAteer was wanted by the military and police he arranged with the soldier to meet with Blee to get the money. Joseph Blee was sentenced to one year's imprisonment with hard labour.

The No. 3 brigade flying column set out to raid the bank agents at the Kilcar fair on Tuesday 28 June. They arrived on the outskirts of Kilcar about midday and sent scouts out to survey the area. The scouts reported back that there was a large number of military from Killybegs and some police in the village. They discussed a change of plan and decided to attack the military on their return journey to Killybegs. The column moved off in the direction of Killybegs and took up ambush positions a few miles outside Kilcar. They were in the ambush positions for a couple of hours when a car approached. Someone recognised that it was the manager of the Ulster Bank in Killybegs, and the car was stopped. The manager, who was returning from the fair with his accountant, was relieved of his day's takings, approximately £200. The Volunteers immobilised the car before retreating from the area.

The trial of John and James McNulty, Feymore, Creeslough, was held on the same day in Derry. The two were charged with having documents relating to the affairs of an unlawful association – the Irish Republican Army. Both refused to recognise the court. Their home had been raided on Thursday 5 May 1921 and the following items were found: 'Form 3 – Intelligence Department IRA' – *Pamphlet No. 7 Cyclist Training IRA Official Publications* – a copy of *An t-Óglach* and an IRA drill book. Ammunition was also allegedly found in a shed at the back of the house. The officer in charge of the raiding party said John McNulty told him at the time of the arrest that he knew nothing about the ammunition, to which McNulty replied: 'You never mentioned you found anything until the next day at Letterkenny.' The officer reiterated: 'I informed both of the accused at the time that the ammunition had been found.' John McNulty said the premises belonged to him and that he was responsible for anything found there. He was sentenced to three years' imprisonment with hard labour with his brother receiving a six month sentence.[137]

Owen McCarron, Buncrana, was shot dead by military on Thursday 30 June near Cockhill chapel, Buncrana. He had left his home to fetch a cow from a nearby field when he was spotted by a military patrol. McCarron was sixty-eight years old and very hard of hearing. The military called on him to stop a few times and then fired a shot, killing him instantly. McCarron's wife Rose and daughter Annie, on hearing the shot, ran to the scene.[138]

The following day P. H. Doherty, O/C Inishowen flying column, was returning from Carndonagh to meet with the rest of the column. About two miles on the Clonmany Road he spotted a military patrol approaching and immediately threw his bicycle into a manure pit at the side of the road. He then ran to an old outhouse for cover, but found himself exposed and could be seen from the road. Three young boys sitting on a wall on the opposite side of the road served as a distraction as the patrol passed without noticing Doherty. He had mail addressed to the police and military in his pocket and would have been in trouble had he been caught. This same patrol shot Owen McCarron the previous day and was under the command of a ruthless officer.[139]

A military convoy was travelling towards Bunbeg on Saturday

morning when one of the lorries broke down. The convoy continued on its journey and left a number of soldiers behind to guard the lorry and its contents. Dan Green, O/C Ranafast Company, was informed of the incident and decided to attack the guarding party with the prospect of possibly finding armaments in the lorry. Six Volunteers were hurriedly mobilised and ran to the scene. When they arrived they found ten soldiers, but decided to attack. They opened fire from high ground and five soldiers were hit on the first strike with the remainder taking cover and returning fire. The two sides engaged in a brief battle, but the Volunteers were forced to retreat due to lack of ammunition.[140]

During the same week a number of other incidents occurred: an RIC man was badly wounded in an ambush in the Glenties area; the main road between Letterkenny and Manorcunningham was rendered impassable after Volunteers of the Letterkenny Company used explosives to put a large crater in the road; a police patrol travelling in a Crossley Tender through Killybegs was ambushed by Volunteers, with one RIC man being hit in both thighs and four Volunteers wounded; the bridge at Beltany outside Gortahork was destroyed by explosives.[141]

THE BRITISH AGENT

THE VOLUNTEERS ENJOYED the support and assistance of the general population, who acted as an invisible force, for example as scouts and as hosts. However, a portion of the population served a similar role for the British military and RIC. Anyone considered loyal to the British was continuously monitored and information passed on to Volunteers and officers in various parts of the county. If it was considered that certain people had become conspicuous in their dealings with police, and more obviously with the military, it would be recorded by the local company and passed on to the brigade staff. The local brigade would then compile a list that would be forwarded to GHQ in Dublin where enquiries would be made through the agents at Dublin Castle. Confirmation of those suspected as being agents of the military or police would then be sent to the brigade area. Those identified were listed in monthly reports from brigades to GHQ and information relating to their activities was recorded. Individual suspects were identified in many parts of Donegal, including Burtonport, Annagry, Lettermacaward, Gweedore, Arranmore Island, Ramelton, Raphoe, Ballybofey, Dunfanaghy, Creeslough, Kilmacrenan, Letterkenny, Killybegs, Ardara, Carrick, Buncrana and Carndonagh. The brigade reports also included lists of suspected agents employed at post offices and railway stations, and employees of the British civil service, excise officers, land commissioners, etc.[142]

One such agent was identified by GHQ in Dublin as operating in County Donegal and the information was passed to the divisional staff. The agent was a man called John Collins who had been travelling through the county for several months with a horse and van under the guise of a fishmonger. Collins was an ex-British soldier who had served with the British army during the war in Europe. After leaving the army he lived for some time at Ramelton with his wife. He had initially joined the Auxiliary section of the RIC and shortly after began working for the intelligence division, reporting on a regular basis to the intelligence section at Enniskillen. His contact in Donegal was Head Constable Duffy, head of RIC intelligence in the county, based at Killybegs. Duffy had a reputation for being a ruthless man and was known for his viciousness when commanding raiding parties. The problem was that no one could actually identify Collins; however, he was to expose himself when he took part in a raiding party at Dungloe.

Head Constable Duffy led a raiding party of military and RIC to Dungloe on the morning of Sunday 3 July and Collins was there, dressed as an Auxiliary, to identify Volunteers. They stopped at Cloughwilly; some set up a road block while the remainder walked into Dungloe and began searching and questioning every man attending the chapel. Denis (Donncha) McNelis, divisional engineer, had been working through the night with a few others completing a telephone connection between a dugout and safe houses in the area. He was on his way to the chapel at Dungloe when he spotted the RIC and took a sudden detour. Collins was seen pointing him out to Duffy and McNelis was pursued, captured by the police and subjected to a severe beating.

McNelis was left on the side of the road and a number of locals and a doctor removed him to a place of safety where he was treated for his wounds. It was obvious Collins was identifying people and locations, as brigade headquarters was also raided, although nothing was found. This was a building attached to a house, which was also raided. Anthony McGinley had been sleeping there, but concealed himself under a bed and evaded capture. However, his revolver was found and Henry Glackin, the house owner, was arrested.

John Boyle had been visiting his family at Caravan, Dungloe, and was in bed when the police entered the house and discovered a rifle lying against the window sill and a bandolier containing fifty rounds of ammunition. Boyle was severely beaten and questioned before being marched to the military vehicle and held there. Daniel Walsh was also arrested and was badly beaten at his home. Walsh was a district justice of the republican courts.

Patrick Breslin was staying in a house at Quay Road, Dungloe, and was getting ready for mass when he heard of the raids. Luckily for him the house he was in was overlooked, while the houses on either side were raided. Breslin sent word to James McCole, brigade O/C, to prepare Volunteers for an attack, but by then the RIC had left the area. Breslin thought it would be possible to attack them as they returned to their lorries, but McCole decided against it due to lack of men and weapons. When the raiding party had left the area some of the Volunteers felt safe to return to their homes. John O'Gorman was feeling quite satisfied with having evaded capture when two lorries suddenly pulled up outside his home. The front and back of the house were covered, the front door forced open and O'Gorman arrested by Head Constable Duffy.

It was now clear that Collins, who had been collecting information on the Volunteers in the area, was the reason for the raids. The order was given to Denis Houston, intelligence officer, to have Collins arrested. Houston discovered that Collins was in the habit of returning to his wife in Ramelton at weekends and sent a despatch to the intelligence officer in Milford to have Collins arrested as soon as he made an appearance at his home. Some time later the Milford Volunteers made contact with Houston, telling him that Collins had been arrested and they were instructed to have Collins conveyed to brigade headquarters in Dungloe. To Houston's surprise he was now face to face with a man who had been a criminal prisoner in Derry jail during his time there. Houston used his prior acquaintance to engage in conversation with Collins and told him he was glad to see him again, but was sorry to meet him as a prisoner of the Volunteers.

Collins was held for over a week, but failed to give any information about his activities as an agent and Houston informed him that he was anxious to save his life, but he would have to reveal the names of other agents in the county. Collins eventually started to talk and gave information about a man called McKeown, a vagrant, who had given him regular information, naming men who were active Volunteers. He gave the names of others who, he said, he had been instructed to make contact with by his superior officers. Collins said that McKeown was an agent of Head Constable Duffy and had received substantial sums of money for the information. Volunteers were sent out to locate and arrest McKeown and he was also brought to brigade HQ. Both prisoners were blindfolded and Collins was told to repeat his statement of McKeown's activities, at the conclusion of which the blindfolds were removed. The two men were face to face and McKeown made no effort to deny the account given by Collins.

Collins then made a full statement about his activities as a British agent, revealing contacts and names of people already suspected and others that surprised the Volunteers. Collins told how he concealed his reports in the bodies of fish which were then forwarded to Colonel McClintock, British intelligence, based in Omagh. Collins was subsequently court-martialled and sentenced to death while McKeown was ordered to leave the county. However, Collins was reprieved following the announcement of the Truce a few days later and was ordered to leave the county.[143]

TALKS AND TRUCE

THE CAPTURE OF the British agents led to a large influx of military and police returning to the Dungloe area a few days later in search of Collins and McKeown. Patrick Breslin was at brigade headquarters just outside Dungloe when he noticed a British officer and a party of soldiers approaching the front door. He ran out the back door and through a field, but he was spotted on the Carnmore Road. They called on him to stop and fired a series of shots but Breslin kept running until he reached Chapel Road and saw another group of military searching a man on Diamond Road. Breslin sheltered at the chapel wall until the road was clear and then made his way to Caravan where he met Dinnie McCole. The two stayed at a house there until dark before proceeding to O'Donnells' at Crohyboyle, where they found officers and Volunteers who had also escaped the net. They decided to split up and move to different locations. McCole and Breslin made their way to Gweedore across the bogs and arrived at Denis Conaghan's house at Tor where they received food and a bed for the night. Meanwhile the remainder of the men made their way from Crohyboyle to Meenbanad. Breslin and McCole were woken at 5 a.m. and told that a large party of military was approaching from the Crolly direction. The two men dressed and crossed the mountains towards Brockagh, where they saw the military raiding houses in the area. While waiting up the mountain they could hear the officer in charge ordering all men and women from the area to gather at a nearby bridge. Here he made a remarkable speech, calling on the Volunteers to cease fighting. He added that he would petition the British government to make an offer of peace and that he was opposed to this form of interference with the Irish people.

After this McCole and Breslin made their way back to Dungloe and arrived just as the British were preparing to move out. No Volunteers were arrested during the raid, but a large number of civilians were taken into custody and brought to Derry jail, but were released the following day.[144]

In early 1920 moves were being made to explore a possible peace agreement between Dáil Éireann and Westminster. This was advanced by July 1921 with envoys and representatives from both sides presenting various suggestions and formulas to establish a truce. Less than a month after the speech of King George V in Belfast, a peace conference at the Mansion House in Dublin, made up of representatives from Sinn Féin and southern unionists, was concluding. The conference had been held between 4 and 8 July and concluded with a message from Éamon de Valera that the platform for negotiations had been established and he declared his intention to meet with Lloyd George to discuss peace. The following statement was handed to the press:

> President de Valera informed the conference of the terms in which he proposed to reply to the British prime minister's invitation. At its previous session the conference had expressed the view that it would be impossible to conduct negotiations with any hope of achieving satisfactory results, unless there was a cessation of bloodshed in Ireland ...[145]

A letter to Lord Midleton from Lloyd George was read, concurring in this view and indicating the willingness of the British government to assent to a suspension of active operations on both sides: 'It is expected that an announcement of a truce, to take effect from Monday next, will be made early tomorrow.'

De Valera subsequently wrote to Lloyd George indicating his willingness to end the conflict between Ireland and Britain:

> Mansion House, Dublin
> July 8, 1921
>
> The Right Honourable
> David Lloyd George
> 10 Downing Street
> London
>
> Sir
> The desire you express on the part of the British government to end the centuries of conflict between the peoples of these two islands and to establish relations of neighbourly harmony is the genuine desire of the people of Ireland. I have consulted with my colleagues and secured the views of representatives of the minority of our nation in regard to the invitation you have sent me. In reply, I desire to say that I am ready to meet and discuss with you on what basis such a conference as that proposed can reasonably hope to achieve the object desired.
> I am, Sir, faithfully yours
> Éamon de Valera.[146]

On the previous day, Thursday 7 July, in Donegal the British military and police were continuing with large-scale manoeuvres against the Volunteers, with the focus this time on the south-west of the county. The Dorset Regiment were involved and were putting the railway line into commission, clearing barricades and filling in trenched roads. The No. 3 brigade column received information about the movements of the British breaking through to Castlefinn from Stranorlar and decided to mount an attack at the west end of Lough Finn. The No. 3 flying column with the support of the 3rd and 4th battalions crossed the Glenties glen and moved on to the Agha Mountains where billets had been arranged for the night. This continued for the next few days with the Dorset Regiment being observed making steady but slow progress, but for no apparent reason they halted as they approached Brockagh on Sunday 10 July. They began to pack up and soon evacuated the area. While the Volunteers were considering their options a messenger arrived to inform them that a truce had been arranged and all units would soon be ordered to cease operations.[147]

About the same time Joseph Murray had summoned a meeting of the brigade and battalion staffs in the No. 4 brigade area for Sunday 10 July in Bundoran. There had been no official confirmation of the Truce, due to come into operation the following day at noon. However, the next morning the staff of the No. 4 brigade awoke to witness the British forces based in the town withdrawing from their outposts to their headquarters at Finner camp and soon after they received official confirmation that a truce had been arranged and was operative from noon that day.[148]

The following was issued on Friday night in London:

Press Notice:
In accordance with the prime minister's offer and Mr de Valera's reply arrangements are being made for hostilities to cease from Monday next July 11 at noon.
10 Downing Street, July 8 1921

The following telegram was despatched by Lloyd George to de Valera:

É. de Valera, Mansion House, Dublin
I have received your letter of acceptance and shall be happy to see you and any colleagues whom you wish to bring with you at Downing Street any day this week. Prepare date of your arrival in London.
D. Lloyd George.

On Saturday 9 July a typed order was despatched from GHQ, Irish Republican Army to various parts of the country and also appeared in the *Irish Bulletin*:

Óglaigh na hÉireann,
GHQ

General Order to officers commanding all units.

In view of the conversations now being entered into by our government with the government of Great Britain and in pursuance of a mutual understanding to suspend hostilities during these conversations, active operations by our troops will be suspended as from noon, Monday, July 11.
Risteárd Ua Maolcatha
Chief of staff
9–7–21

The following proclamation was issued by de Valera through the national press on Monday 11 July:

Fellow Citizens – During the period of the Truce each individual, soldier and citizen must regard himself as a custodian of the nation's honour. Your discipline must prove in the most convincing manner that this is the struggle of an organised nation. In the negotiations now initiated your representatives will do their utmost to secure a just and peaceful termination of this struggle. But history, particularly our own history, and the character of the issues to be decided are a warning against undue confidence. An unbending determination to endure all that may still be necessary and fortitude such as you have shown in all your recent sufferings – these alone will lead you to the peace you desire. Should force be resumed against our nation you must be ready on your part, once more, to resist. Thus alone will you secure the final abandonment of force and the acceptance of justice and reason as the arbiter.

The terms to the Truce were decided on Saturday at 3 p.m. at British military HQ, Parkgate Street, Dublin. British officers represented the British government and Commandant R. C. Barton, TD, and Commandant E. J. Duggan, TD, represented the army of the Republic:

On behalf of the British army it is agreed as follows:

1. No incoming troops, RIC, Auxiliary police and munitions and no movements for military purposes of troops and munitions, except maintenance drafts.
2. No provocative displays of force, armed or unarmed.
3. It is understood that all provisions of this Truce apply to the martial law area equally with the rest of Ireland.
4. No pursuit of Irish officers or men or war material or military stores.
5. No secret agents noting descriptions or movements and no interference with the movement of Irish persons – military or civilian – and no attempt to discover the haunts of Irish officers and men.
Note – This supposes the abandonment of curfew restrictions.

6. No pursuit or observance of lines of communication or connection.
7. No pursuit of messengers. (Note – there are other details connected with court-martial, motor permits, and ROIR to be agreed later.)

On behalf of the Irish army it is agreed:

(a) Attacks on crown forces and civilians to cease.
(b) No provocative displays of force – armed or unarmed.
(c) No interference with government or private property.
(d) To discountenance and prevent any action likely to cause disturbance of the peace which might necessitate military interference.

The following is the communiqué issued on Saturday 9 June from Belfast military headquarters in Ireland:

Mr de Valera having decided to accept the prime minister's invitation to confer with him in London is issuing instructions to his supporters.

(a) To cease all attacks on crown forces and civilians.
(b) To prohibit use of arms.
(c) To cease military manoeuvres of all kinds.
(d) To abstain from interference with public or private property.
(e) To discontinue and prevent any action likely to cause disturbance of the peace which might necessitate military interference.

In order to co-operate the British directed that:

(a) All raids and searches by military or police shall cease.

(b) Military activity shall be restricted to the support of the police in their normal civil duties.
(c) Curfew restrictions shall be removed.
(d) The despatch of reinforcements from England shall be suspended.
(e) The police functions of Dublin shall be carried out by the DMP.

In order to give the necessary time for these instructions to reach all concerned the date for which they shall come into force has been fixed at 12 noon, Monday, July 11, 1921.

Some time after the Truce announcement the Dáil executive accepted an invitation to send delegates to London for negotiations 'with a view to ascertaining how the association of Ireland with the community of nations known as the British Empire may be reconciled with Irish national aspirations'.[149]

CONCLUSION

THE WAR OF Independence ended with the Truce, which came into effect on Monday 11 July, ending the six-year campaign against the British establishment in Ireland and Britain. This conflict was the product of a determined effort by the Irish people to dismiss the authority of the British government in Ireland. This determination was borne out of the idea of Arthur Griffith's *The Resurrection of Hungary*, which became the blueprint for the Sinn Féin organisation. This organisation gradually spread the new idea throughout the country and in its infancy small pockets of interest began sprouting up in the towns, villages and parishes of County Donegal. The new wave of thinking was a countermeasure to the wavering Home Rule movement fronted by the Irish Parliamentary Party, which became more diluted from its original perception, with the objections of unionist politicians, and would inevitably lead to the division of the island.

The establishment of the Ulster Volunteer movement as a paramilitary force in opposition to the introduction of Home Rule brought about the birth of the Irish National Volunteers to counter the threat. However, the war in Europe not only witnessed the suspension of the Home Rule Bill, it also created a split in the Irish National Volunteers and the formation of the Irish Volunteers. The Irish Volunteers were composed of those who were opposed to fighting in the British army. In the early days the Volunteers attracted a large number of young men with different ideas of what membership of the Volunteer organisation represented. For some it was a safe haven from the threat of conscription and for others it was an army to strike against the British occupation in Ireland. This proved correct on both counts; numbers declined as the conscription threat subsided for the moment, due to the lack of proper armaments and the lure of the British shilling to fight for the British army in the war in Europe, while the other faction, though small in number, remained and continued to organise, awaiting their opportunity to strike. This opportunity came about in Easter 1916, but in the absence of a clear objective the unity of the organisation fractured, causing confusion and friction throughout the country. Although the Easter Rising did not produce the desired outcome, its aftermath created the platform of a more united and determined enterprise. Following the Rising, the Irish Volunteers and the Sinn Féin organisation had a parallel existence, establishing the army of the Irish Republic and Dáil Éireann, which existed as the authority of an underground government, an independent state within a colonial state.

The two organisations developed military and political pockets in the towns, villages and parishes of Donegal. These helped to spread the principles of the Republic, leading to the election successes in 1918 despite British proclamations banning both organisations and the imprisonment of many leaders through the so-called German Plot.

This election witnessed the demise of the Irish Parliamentary Party and unionist dominance, and the election of three Sinn Féin representatives in County Donegal to serve as TDs in the new native parliament, Dáil Éireann. Coincidently the first actions of the War of Independence occurred on the day of the first sitting of Dáil Éireann on 21 January 1919. This was not a planned manoeuvre and attracted criticism from leaders within the Sinn Féin organisation, including Éamon de Valera and Arthur Griffith. The die was now cast and the way forward was paved by the men of the South Tipperary brigade. Although some have alluded to the rescue of two British army deserters in January 1918 as the first actions of the war, what was considered to be the official declaration was published in *An t-Óglach* in October 1918:

Passive resistance is no resistance at all. Our active military resistance is the only thing that will tell. Any plans, theories, or doubts tending to distract the minds of the people from the policy of fierce, ruthless fighting ought to be severely discouraged.

The War of Independence was now official and in a sense conflicted with the operations of the national parliament and interrupted the political emergence of the Irish Republic as many politicians were also Volunteers of the army of the Irish Republic.

In the early stages of the war in Donegal the Volunteers were tasked with procuring weapons wherever they could, and in the meantime a campaign of disruption witnessed the destruction of many roads, railways and communication lines, causing great annoyance and discomfort for the Royal Irish Constabulary (RIC) and British military. This was coupled with the operation of the Belfast Boycott with the wholesale seizure of goods from unionist firms and any goods destined for the British and RIC barracks in the county. The British countered the increase in Volunteer activity through wholesale raids initially on the homes of republicans, those involved, their supporters and also the general public in an attempt to deter support. Despite these efforts the campaign continued and the first official operation was carried out by the west Donegal Volunteers in December 1919 with an ambush on a party of RIC near Dungloe.

This was followed by further elections, with Sinn Féin representatives winning seats on local councils and boards. Within months of the first sitting of Dáil Éireann a new justice system – the Sinn Féin courts – was put in place, signalling the end of the British legal system in Donegal. In advance of this the Volunteers set about destroying buildings that housed the British courts, and this was followed by the resignations of peace commissioners and justices throughout the county with the local population availing of the Sinn Féin courts to adjudicate in disputes.

CONCLUSION

The Volunteers of the 1st northern division were responsible for what was described as the first daylight arms raid ever carried out in the country when they raided an RIC barracks at Drumquinn, County Tyrone. The aftermath of this raid caused some concern for the Volunteers of the Letterkenny Company when local RIC District Inspector Walsh informed Dr J. P. McGinley that some of the Volunteers, including him, were identified, but this took another twist when Walsh also declared that he was one of Michael Collins' spies and he proved to be a valuable asset for the local Volunteers.

The Donegal Volunteers continued with raids on barracks and coastguard stations in Fermanagh and Donegal in pursuit of weapons and ammunition. While all this was going on the British were busy raiding and arresting Volunteers and sympathisers in an effort to undermine the Volunteers' activities. The ranks of the British military and RIC were later bolstered with the addition of the Black and Tans and the Auxiliaries, who operated with no regard to the codes of war. These two factions were responsible for general destruction and were vicious when raiding the homes of known Volunteers and Sinn Féin members. Another measure to counter the activities of the Volunteers was the introduction of internment, and with interment camps in County Down and County Kildare pressure mounted on the Volunteers to avoid capture.

The addition of the flying column in January 1921 introduced a new dynamic to the war in Donegal, and they were soon put into action with local Volunteers during an attack on a train containing British military at Meenbanad. Other flying columns were established in different areas of the county and before long the war effort was spread evenly across the county.

With further large-scale operations Donegal was soon recognised as a 'hot' area and even attracted the attention of British MPs at Westminster, with west Donegal being referred to as 'a miniature Republic'. Widespread raids followed, putting further pressure on the Volunteers, and soon the British were employing destroyers and aeroplanes in their pursuit of the IRA. This pressure was compounded by internal friction between officers in the divisional area, which only served to distract attention from the war. It could be argued that this facilitated the British in the capture of the divisional command staff at Burtonport in May and in some ways solved the problem for the officers at GHQ in Dublin who were forced to resolve the dispute.

Despite the raids and friction in the ranks, the Donegal command was faced with the annual problem of seasonal migration to Scotland and England, resulting in the regular restructuring of companies in the west Donegal command area. The loss of experienced men biannually affected the companies of west Donegal in many ways and prevented that area from giving a proper account of itself during the war. Despite these pressures, west Donegal was the most prominent part of the county throughout the entire campaign. The Volunteers of the Donegal brigades continued to operate throughout 1921 despite the increased pressure from the British in all areas of the county. Unknown to the Volunteers the leaders of Sinn Féin were working behind the scenes with the aid of intermediaries to bring the conflict to an end. The British had exhausted almost every option to defeat the Volunteers and eventually succumbed to entering into peace talks in July 1921, ending the six-year war.

APPENDIX 1

1ST ULSTER DIVISION 1919:

Donegal East Brigade:
1st Battalion – Strabane
2nd Battalion – Castlefinn

Donegal West Brigade:
1st Battalion – Dungloe
2nd Battalion – Gweedore
3rd Battalion – Creeslough

Donegal South Brigade:
1st Battalion – Ballyshannon
2nd Battalion – Donegal town
3rd Battalion – Inver
4th Battalion – Killybegs
5th Battalion – Ardara

Inishowen Brigade:
1st Battalion – Carndonagh
2nd Battalion – Buncrana
3rd Battalion – Moville

Letterkenny Brigade:
1st Battalion – Letterkenny
2nd Battalion – Rosnakill/Fanad
3rd Battalion – Churchill

APPENDIX 2

1ST ULSTER DIVISION (1ST NORTHERN DIVISION) 1920:

No. 1 Brigade – West Donegal:
1st Battalion – Dungloe Companies:
Dungloe
Burtonport
Meenacross
Doochary
Lettermacaward
Mullaghduff
Annagry
Kincasslagh
Inishfree
Ranafast
Arranmore Island

2nd Battalion – Gweedore Companies:
Gortahork
Meenlaragh
Cloghaneely
Derrybeg
Crolly
Tory Island

3rd Battalion – Falcarragh Companies:
Creeslough

Glen
Kilmacrenan
Loughkeel
Dunfanaghy
Falcarragh

No. 2 Brigade – North East Donegal:
1st Battalion – Strabane Companies:
Strabane
Sion Mills
Lifford
Ballindrait
Raphoe
Convoy

2nd Battalion – Inishowen Companies:
Malin
Culdaff
Moville
Greencastle
Carrowmenagh
Clonmany
Carndonagh

3rd Battalion – Inishowen / Derry Companies:
Buncrana
Derry city
Bridge End
Burnfoot
St Johnston
Carrigans
Manorcunningham
Newtowncunningham

4th Battalion – Letterkenny Companies:
Letterkenny
Breenagh and Glenswilly
Churchill
Drumkeen
Ramelton
Stranorlar

5th Battalion – Fanad Companies:
Fanad
Cranford
Carrigart
Rosnakill
Milford
Downings
Kerrykeel
Ray

No. 3 Brigade – South-West Donegal:
1st Battalion – Ardara Companies:
Ardara
Glenties
Rosbeg
Kilrean

2nd Battalion – Carrick Companies:
Carrick
Killybegs
Kilcar
Glencolmcille
Malin More
Malin Beag
Teelin

3rd Battalion – Rosses Companies:
Rosses
Dunkineely
Bruckless
Mountcharles
Croagh
Inver

No. 4 Brigade – South-East Donegal:
1st Battalion – Donegal town Companies:
Donegal town
Laghy
Ballintra

2nd Battalion – Ballyshannon Companies:
Ballyshannon
Belleek
Bundoran
Kinlough
Cliffony
Tullaghan
Pettigo

4th Battalion – Ballybofey Companies:
Ballybofey
Barnesmore
Cloghan
Fintown
Castlefinn (Liscooly/Killygordon)
Castlederg

APPENDIX 3

IRA GENERAL HEADQUARTERS DESPATCH, MARCH 1921

The Division will be known as the No. 1 Northern Division, and the various Brigades will be designated as follows:

No. 1 brigade: (West Donegal)
Battalions: Burtonport / Falcarragh / Gweedore / Dungloe.

No. 2 brigade: (NE Donegal)
Battalions: Stranorlar / Strabane / Derry City / Inishowen / Letterkenny.

No. 3 brigade: (SW Donegal)
Battalions: Ardara / Killybegs / Rosses.

No. 4 brigade: (SE Donegal)
Battalions: Donegal town / Ballyshannon (including Belleek) / Ederney (including Pettigo) / Castlederg / Ballybofey / Castlefinn.

APPENDIX 4

DONEGAL INTERNEES – BALLYKINLAR CAMP 1920–1921:

East Donegal:
P. Kelly, Killygordan
John McElhinney, Raphoe
Tom McGlynn, Liscooly
J. J. Kelly, Clady
H. McGowan, Ballybofey
M. Hannigan, Brockagh
F. Marley, Killygordan
H. McBrearty, Killygordan
J. D. McLaughlin, Ballybofey
Patrick McGowan, Ballybofey
Paddy Hannigan, Killygordon
Charlie Doherty, Killygordon
Jim Hannigan, Ballybofey
Jim McCarron, Ballybofey
H. Gallagher, Ballindrait, Lifford
F. Devine, Castlefinn
C. Gordon, Ballybofey
C. Crawford, Ballybofey
Jim Dawson, Letterkenny
James McMonagle, Letterkenny
Hugh Deery, Letterkenny

West Donegal:
J. E. Boyle, Burtonport
John Gorman, Dungloe
Hugh Doherty, Dungloe
? Forker, Dungloe
John Boyle, Dungloe

South Donegal:
Patrick Meehan, Frosses
Charlie Haughey, Dunkineely
John Molloy, Dunkineely
John Bonner, Summerhill, Donegal
George Meehan, Donegal town
James Boyle, Drimarone, Donegal
Con McShane, Teelin, Glencolmcille
Dan Byrne, Kilcar
Mick Byrne, Carrick
John Kane, Ballyshannon
F. J. Murray, Kilcar
Jim Campbell, Donegal
Owen Gallagher, Bundoran
Hugh Britton, Donegal
Seamus Ward, Ballyshannon
F. J. Morgan, Ballyshannon
Binny Ryan, Bundoran
D. Meehan, Inver
John O'Hara, Kilcar
Charles Cunningham, Killybegs
P. J. Brennan, Ardara
D. Green, Glenties
John J. McIntyre, Kilcar
H. Byrne, Kilcar,
Joe Gallagher, Ardara

Thady Higgins, Inver

North Donegal:
J. Hinnell, Carndonagh
Willie McGoldrick, Buncrana
Manus Higgins (Unknown)

NOTES

1   The New Political Aspiration Versus the Old
1. Brian Feeney, *Sinn Féin: 100 Turbulent Years* (O'Brien Press Ltd, 2002).
2. *Donegal News*, 18/2/2005.
3. *An Phoblacht*, 20/1/2005.
4. T. W. Moody & F. X. Martin, *The Course of Irish History* (Mercier Press, 2000) p. 248.
5. *Ibid.*, p. 249.
6. Major-General Joseph A. Sweeney, 'Donegal and the War of Independence', in *The Capuchin Annual* 1970, p. 425; Bureau of Military History (BMH WS) Brian Monaghan p. 3, Military Archives (MA).

2.   The Obstacles to Revolution
1. BMH WS, Eamon Broy, p. 27, MA.
2. Major-General Joseph A. Sweeney, 'Donegal and the War of Independence', *The Capuchin Annual*, 1970, p. 425.
3. *Derry Journal*, 23/7/1915; *Donegal News*, 'The Way We Were', 29/9/2006.
4. *Donegal News*, 29/9/2006.
5. Tim Pat Coogan, *1916 – The Easter Rising* (Cassell & Co., 2001), p. 50.

3.   Home Rule Suspension and the Birth of the Irish Volunteers
1. BMH WS, Daniel Kelly, pp. 7–9, MA.
2. Bureau of Military History – Lot 6.
3. Major-General Joseph A. Sweeney, 'Donegal and the War of Independence', *The Capuchin Annual*, 1970, p. 425.
4. *Derry Journal*, 15/1/1916.
5. BMH WS, Daniel Kelly, pp. 9–10, MA.

6. *Derry Journal*, 15/1/1916.
7. *Daily Ireland*, 'Today in History', 18/8/2005, p. 19.

4. 1916 – Leaders in County Donegal

1. Casement Collection, Ms. 22,317, National Library of Ireland.
2. Some Casement Associations with Donegal, *Donegal Annual*, 1966, pp. 59–65.
3. BMH WS, Eamon Broy, p. 44, MA.
4. P. J. McGill, 'Pádraig Pearse in Donegal', *Donegal Annual* 1966, pp. 67–88.
5. *Derry Journal*, 2/2/1916.
6. *Derry Journal*, 5/5/1916.
7. P. J. McGill, 'Pearse Sculpture in St. Eunan's Cathedral', *Donegal Annual*, 1966, pp. 78 & 87.

5. Organising the IRB in Donegal

1. Ernest Blythe Papers, P24 / 1002, UCD Archives Department (AD).
2. Earnán de Blaghd, 'Organising the IRB in Donegal', *Donegal Annual*, 1966, pp. 41–44.
3. BMH WS, Brian Monaghan, pp. 4–5, MA.

6. Donegal and 1916

1. BMH WS, Daniel Kelly, p. 16, MA.
2. Tim Pat Coogan, *1916 – The Easter Rising* (Cassell & Co., 2001), pp. 89 & 135.
3. BMH WS, Daniel Kelly p. 17, MA.
4. Tim Pat Coogan, *1916 – The Easter Rising*, p. 128.
5. Major-General Joseph A. Sweeney, *Capuchin Annual*, 1970, p. 425.
6. Peter Hegarty, *Peadar O'Donnell* (Mercier Press, 1999), p. 34; *Derry Journal*, 1/5/1916.
7. Seán Ó hÉinne, 'Donncha MacNiallghuis', *Donegal Annual*, 1966, pp. 32–33.
8. BMH WS, Daniel Kelly, pp. 18, 20–27, MA.
9. *Derry Journal*, 1/5/1916.

10. *Derry Journal*, 8/5/1916.

7. 1917 – Developing the Military and Political Organisations

1. Kenneth Griffith and Timothy O'Grady, *Curious Journey – An Oral History of Ireland's Unfinished Revolution* (Mercier Press, 1988), p. 113.
2. *Irish Times*, 6/1/1917.
3. BMH WS, Daniel Kelly, p. 27, MA.
4. BMH WS, Anthony Dawson, p. 1 & Dr J. P. McGinley, p. 2, MA.
5. BMH WS, James McCaffery, p. 2, MA.
6. *Derry Journal*, 23/4/1917.
7. *Derry Journal*, 28/5/1917.
8. *Derry Journal*, 25/5/1917.
9. *Derry Journal*, 20/5/1917.
10. *Derry Journal*, 22/5/1917.
11. *Derry Journal*, 29/6/1917.
12. *Derry Journal*, 18/7/1917.
13. *Ibid.*
14. *Derry Journal*, 27/7/1917.
15. *Derry Journal*, 20/8/1917.
16. Major-General Joseph A. Sweeney, *Capuchin Annual*, 1970, p. 427.
17. *Derry Journal*, 21/9/1917.
18. *Derry Journal*, 26/10/1917.
19. BMH WS, Patrick Breslin, p. 4, MA.
20. BMH WS, Joseph Murray, p. 2, MA.
21. BMH WS, Daniel Kelly, p. 32, MA.
22. BMH WS, Eithne (Coyle) O'Donnell, p. 1, MA.
23. Niall MacFhionnghaile, *Dr. McGinley & his Times* (An Crann, 1985), pp. 19–21.
24. *Derry Journal*, 4/1/1918.
25. *Ibid.*
26. *Derry Journal*, 7/1/1918.

8. 1918 – Sowing the Seeds of Revolution

1. Major-General Joseph A. Sweeney, *Capuchin Annual*, 1970, pp. 427–428.
2. *Derry Journal*, 21/1/1918.
3. *Derry Journal*, 28/1/1918.
4. *Derry Journal*, 11/2/1918.
5. BMH WS, Anthony Dawson, p. 2 & Thomas McGlynn, p. 2, MA.
6. BMH WS, Daniel Kelly, p. 33, MA; *Derry Journal*, 15/2/1918.
7. BMH WS, Eamon Broy, p. 55, MA.
8. BMH WS, Eithne (Coyle) O'Donnell, p. 1 & Brighid O'Mullane, p. 3, MA.
9. *Derry Journal*, 15/2/1918.
10. *Derry Journal*, 7/3/1918.
11. *Derry Journal*, 20/3/1918; BMH WS, Daniel Kelly, pp. 33–34, MA.
12. *Derry Journal*, 29/2/1918.
13. *Derry Journal*, 5/4/1918.
14. Major-General Joseph A. Sweeney, *Capuchin Annual*, 1970, p. 429.
15. *Derry Journal*, 12/4/1918.
16. *Derry Journal*, 17/4/1918.
17. *Derry Journal*, 22/4/1918.
18. Niall Mac Fhionnghaile, *Dr. McGinley and His Times*, p. 21.
19. *Derry Journal*, 22/4/1918.
20. *Derry Journal*, 17/4/1918.
21. Niall Mac Fhionnghaile, *Dr. McGinley and His Times*, p. 22; *Derry Journal* 13/5/1918 & 20/5/1918.
22. BMH WS, Frank Henderson, pp. 40–41, MA.
23. *Derry Journal*, 20/5/1918.
24. Seán Ó Lúing, 'The German Plot 1918', *Capuchin Annual*, 1968, p. 378.
25. BMH WS, Patrick Breslin, p. 5, MA.
26. *Derry Journal*, 14/6/1918.
27. *Derry Journal*, 24/6/1918.
28. *Dawson Collection* – Pat Dawson, Letterkenny, Co. Donegal.
29. *Derry Journal*, 5/7/1918.
30. *Derry Journal*, 9/8/1918.
31. *Derry Journal*, 23/8/1918.

32. BMH WS, John O'Gorman, p. 2, MA.
33. BMH WS, Annie O'Brien and Lily Curran, p. 17, MA.
34. BMH WS, Henry McGowan, p. 2, MA.
35. Major-General Joseph A. Sweeney, *Capuchin Annual*, 1970, p. 430; *Derry Journal*, 9/9/1918.
36. *Derry Journal*, 11/9/1918.
37. *Derry Journal*, 16/9/1918.
38. BMH WS, Seamus Robinson, p. 19, MA.
39. *Derry Journal*, 23/11/1918.
40. *Derry Journal*, 25/11/1918.
41. *Derry Journal*, 29/11/1918.
42. BMH WS, Joseph Murray, p. 2, MA.
43. *Derry Journal*, 4/12/1918.
44. *Derry Journal*, 6/12/1918.
45. BMH WS, Joseph Murray, pp. 4–5, MA.
46. *Derry Journal*, 11/12/1918.
47. *Derry Journal*, 13/12/1918.
48. *Derry Journal*, 16/12/1918.
49. BMH WS, Anthony Dawson, p. 2, MA.
50. BMH WS, Thomas McShea, p. 4, MA.
51. *Derry Journal*, 30/12/1918.
52. *Derry Journal*, 13/1/1919.
53. *Derry Journal*, 1/1/1919.
54. BMH WS, Henry McGowan, p. 2, MA.
55. *An t-Óglach*, 16 December 1918, MA.

9.   1919 – Government and War

1. Ernie O'Malley, *On Another Man's Wound* (Anvil, 2002), p. 103.
2. BMH WS, Liam O'Duffy, p. 4, MA.
3. BMH WS, Thomas McShea, p. 5 & Joseph Murray, p. 6, MA.
4. BMH WS, James McMonagle, p. 3, MA.
5. BMH WS, Eamon Broy, p. 58, MA.
6. Major-General Joseph A. Sweeney, *Capuchin Annual*, 1970, p. 431.

7. *Derry Journal*, 8/1/1919.
8. *Derry Journal*, 8/1/1919.
9. *Derry Journal*, 15/1/1919.
10. *Derry Journal*, 17/1/1919.
11. Mulcahy Papers – P7C/42 – UCD AD.
12. BMH WS, Seamus Robinson, p. 27, MA.
13. BMH WS, Seamus Robinson, pp. 19 & 30, MA.
14. BMH WS, Eamon Broy, p. 38, MA.
15. BMH WS, Charles McGinley, pp. 3–4, MA.
16. BMH WS, James McMonagle, p. 4, MA.
17. *Derry Journal*, 29/1/1919.
18. BMH WS, Bernard McGinley, pp. 2–3 & Charles McGinley, p. 3, MA.
19. *Derry Journal*, 7/2/1919.
20. *Irish Times*, 13/2/1919.
21. *Derry Journal*, 24/2/1919.
22. *Irish Times*, 19/2/1919.
23. *Derry Journal*, 26/3/1919.
24. *Derry Journal*, 31/3/1919 & 11/4/1919.
25. Michael Hopkinson, *The Irish War of Independence* (Gill & Macmillan, 2004), p. 26.
26. *Derry Journal*, 20/6/1919.
27. *Derry Journal*, 2/7/1919.
28. *Derry Journal*, 5/9/1919.
29. *Derry Journal*, 15/9/1919.
30. *Derry Journal*, 26/9/1919.
31. *Derry Journal*, 6/10/1919; BMH WS, Michael Doherty, pp. 3–4, MA.
32. *Derry Journal*, 3/11/1919.

10. Donegal Engages with the Enemy – December 1919

1. *Derry Journal*, 15/12/1919 and 17/12/1919.
2. BMH WS, Patrick (Kit) O'Donnell, pp. 2–3 & Denis Houston, pp. 5, 6, 7–8, MA.
3. Niall Mac Fhionnghaile, *Dr. McGinley & his Times* (An Crann, 1985), p. 29.

4. Major-General Joseph A. Sweeney, *Capuchin Annual*, 1970, p. 432; *Derry Journal*, 17/12/1919.
5. *Derry Journal*, 22/12/1919.
6. *Derry Journal*, 5/1/1920.

11. 1920 – The Guerrilla Soldiers and the Donegal Gun-runner

1. BMH WS, Eamon Broy, p. 38, MA; Michael Hopkinson, *The Irish War of Independence*, p. 28.
2. *Derry Journal*, 19/1/1920.
3. *Derry Journal*, 4/2/1920.
4. *Derry Journal*, 9/2/1920.
5. *Derry Journal*, 11/2/1920.
6. BMH WS, James W. Cunningham, pp. 1–2, MA.
7. *Derry Journal*, 5/3/1920.
8. *Derry People and Tirconaill News*, 12/3/1920.
9. *Derry Journal*, 10/3/1920; *Irish Times*, 11/3/1920; *Daily Herald (London)*, 13/3/1920.
10. *Derry Journal*, 10/3/1920.
11. BMH WS, James W. Cunningham, pp. 3, 4, 5 & 7, MA.
12. *Derry Journal*, 24/3/1920.
13. *Derry People and Tirconaill News*, 4/4/1920.
14. Major-General Joseph A. Sweeney, *Capuchin Annual*, 1970, pp. 432–434.
15. *Derry Journal*, 31/3/1920.
16. BMH WS, Thomas McShea, p. 7, MA.
17. *Derry Journal*, 4/5/1920.
18. BMH WS, James McMonagle, pp. 3–4, MA.
19. BMH WS, Seamus McCann, pp. 2–3 & Patrick Breslin, pp. 10–11, MA.
20. *Derry Journal*, 5/4/1920.
21. *Derry Journal*, 19/4/1920.
22. BMH WS, James W. Cunningham, pp. 10, 11 & 13, MA.
23. BMH WS, Michael Doherty, pp. 4–5, MA.
24. *Derry Journal*, 26/4/1920; 2/5/1920.

NOTES

25. Mulcahy Papers – P7/A/17 – UCD AD.
26. BMH WS, Patrick Breslin, pp. 14, 15 & 30, MA.
27. *Daily Herald (London)*, 10/5/1920.
28. *Derry People and Tirconaill News*, 15/5/1920.
29. BMH WS, Denis Houston, p. 10, MA.
30. *Derry Journal*, 31/5/1920.
31. *Derry Journal*, 28/5/1920.
32. Michael Hopkinson, *The Irish War of Independence* (2004), p. 43.
33. *Derry Journal*, 21/6/1920.
34. BMH WS, P. H. Doherty, p. 5, MA.
35. BMH WS, Joseph Murray, pp. 6–7, & Thomas McShea, p. 10, MA.
36. *Derry People and Tirconaill News*, 12/6/1920.
37. BMH WS, P. H. Doherty, pp. 6–7, MA.
38. *Derry Journal*, 2/7/1920.
39. *Derry People and Tirconaill News*, 26/6/1920.
40. Captain E. O'Baoighill, 'An Incident of the Anglo-Irish War', *An t-Óglach*, October 1927, MA. My thanks to Dr Connell Cunningham, Spiddal, County Galway for this source.
41. BMH WS, Liam O'Duffy, p. 6, MA; John B. Cunningham, 'The struggle for the Belleek-Pettigo Salient 1922', *Donegal Annual*, 1982, p. 40.
42. BMH WS, Thomas McShea, p. 9, MA.
43. *Derry Journal*, 7/7/1920.
44. *Derry Journal*, 9/7/1920.
45. *Derry Journal*, 14/7/1920.
46. *Derry Journal*, 16/7/1920.
47. *Ibid.*
48. *Derry Journal*, 19/7/1920.
49. BMH WS, P. H. Doherty, p. 6, MA.
50. Mulcahy Papers – P7/A/40 – UCD AD.
51. Charles Townshend, *The British Campaign in Ireland 1919–1921 – The Development of Police and Military Policies* (Oxford University Press, 1975), pp. 110–111; BMH WS, Eamon Broy, p. 27, MA.
52. *Derry Journal*, 23/7/1920.

53. *Ibid.*
54. *Derry Journal*, 26/7/1920.
55. *Derry Journal*, 23/7/1920.
56. *Derry Journal*, 28/7/1920.
57. *Derry Journal*, 30/7/1920.
58. *Derry Journal*, 2/8/1920.
59. Bureau of Military History 1913–1921 – Chronology Parts I & II.
60. *Derry People and Tirconaill News*, 14/8/1920.
61. *Derry Journal*, 6/8/1920.
62. *Derry Journal*, 9/8/1920; BMH WS, Patrick Breslin, pp. 12–13, MA.
63. *Derry Journal*, 9/8/1920.
64. BMH WS, Patrick Breslin, p. 14, MA.
65. *Derry Journal*, 18/8/1920
66. BMH WS, Patrick Breslin, pp. 13–14, MA.
67. *Derry Journal*, 20/8/1920.
68. *Derry Journal*, 30/8/1920.
69. BMH WS, Anthony Dawson, p. 4, Henry McGowan, p. 3 & Dr J. P. McGinley p. 4, MA.
70. BMH WS, Dr J. P. McGinley p. 5, Henry McGowan p. 6, Michael Doherty p.6 & James McMonagle pp. 6–7, MA; *Derry Journal*, 1/9/1920.
71. BMH WS, Henry McGowan, p. 6, MA.
72. *Derry Journal*, 29/8/1920.
73. BMH WS, Brian Monaghan, pp. 5–6, MA.
74. *Derry Journal*, 6/9/1920
75. BMH WS, Henry McGowan, pp. 6–7, MA.
76. BMH WS, Dr J. P. McGinley, p. 11, MA.
77. BMH WS, Thomas McShea, p. 11, MA.
78. *Derry Journal*, 3/9/1920.
79. *An t-Óglach*, 1 September 1920, MA.
80. *Derry Journal*, 3/9/1920.
81. Niall MacFhionnghaile, *Dr. McGinley and His Times* (1985), p. 34.
82. BMH WS, Anthony Dawson pp. 5–6, Dr J. P. McGinley pp. 8–9 & James McMonagle pp. 9–11, MA.

NOTES

83. Niall MacFhionnghaile, *Donegal Ireland and the First World War* (An Crann, 2nd edition, 2005), p. 390; *Derry Journal*, 6/9/1920.
84. BMH WS, Joseph Murray, pp. 10–11, MA; John B. Cunningham, 'The Struggle for the Belleek-Pettigo Salient 1922', *Donegal Annual*, 1982, p. 40; *Derry Journal*, 8/9/1920.
85. *Derry Journal*, 10/9/1920.
86. BMH WS, James McMonagle, pp. 11–12, J. P. McGinley, pp. 9–10, MA.
87. BMH WS, John O'Gorman, p. 4, MA.
88. *Derry Journal*, 15/9/1920.
89. BMH WS, Joseph Murray, p. 11, MA.
90. *Derry Journal*, 17/9/1920 and 20/9/1920.
91. *Derry Journal*, 24/9/1920.
92. *Derry Journal*, 27/9/1920.
93. *Derry Journal*, 3/10/1920.
94. *Derry Journal*, 1/10/1920.
95. BMH WS, Patrick Breslin, p. 17, MA.
96. *Derry Journal*, 4/10/1920.
97. *Derry Journal*, 6/10/1920 and 8/10/1920.
98. BMH WS, Liam O'Duffy, p. 7, MA.
99. *Derry Journal*, 15/10/1920.
100. *Derry Journal*, 15/10/1920 and 18/10/1920.
101. *Derry Journal*, 29/10/1920.
102. Kenneth Griffith & Timothy O'Grady, *Curious Journey – An Oral History of Ireland's Unfinished Revolution* (Mercier Press, 1988), p. 162; BMH WS, Thomas McShea, p. 14, MA.
103. *Derry Journal*, 1/11/1920.
104. Michael Hopkinson, *The Irish War of Independence* (2004), pp. 80 & 94.
105. *Derry Journal*, 5/11/1920.
106. *Derry Journal*, 10/11/1920.
107. *Derry Journal*, 15/11/1920.
108. *Derry Journal*, 26/11/1920.
109. *Derry Journal*, 22/11/1920.
110. *Derry Journal*, 31/11/1920.

111. *Derry Journal*, 29/11/1920.
112. BMH WS, Michael Doherty, p. 8, MA.
113. BMH WS, Denis Houston, p. 12, MA.
114. BMH WS, Patrick Breslin, p. 17, MA.
115. *Derry Journal*, 6/12/1920.
116. BMH WS, James McMonagle, pp. 12–13, MA; Col. Declan O'Carroll, *Lt. Col. James McMonagle 1898–1986* (Roughpark, Letterkenny, 2008).
117. Derry Journal, 8/12/1920.
118. Michael Hopkinson, *Irish War of Independence* (2004).
119. *Derry Journal*, 8/12/1920.
120. BMH WS, Thomas McGlynn, pp. 9–10, MA.
121. Dawson Collection – Pat Dawson, Letterkenny, Co. Donegal.
122. BMH WS, Thomas McGlynn, p. 9–10, MA.
123. BMH WS, James McMonagle, p. 14–15, MA.
124. *Derry People and Donegal News*, 1/1/1921.
125. *Derry Journal*, 15/12/1920.
126. *Derry Journal*, 10/12/1920.
127. *Derry Journal*, 18/12/1920 & 31/12/1920.
128. BMH WS, Patrick Breslin, p. 17, MA.
129. *Derry Journal*, 3/1/1921.
130. Mattie Lennon, 'The Story of how a Burtonport man came to die in Wicklow', *Donegal News*, 6/1/2006.
131. *Derry People and Donegal News*, 8/1/1921.

12.   1921 – The Donegal Flying Column

1. Michael Hopkinson, *The Irish War of Independence* (2004), p. 139.
2. Mulcahy Papers – P7/A/17 – UCD AD.
3. McCann Collection – Seamus McCann, Letterkenny, County Donegal; BMH WS, Seamus McCann, pp. 9–12, MA.
4. BMH WS, Patrick Breslin, pp. 23–24, John O'Gorman, p. 5, MA.
5. McCann Collection.
6. BMH WS, Patrick Breslin, pp. 18–19, MA.
7. *Derry Journal*, 7/1/1921; Liam O'Duffy, p. 9, MA.

NOTES

8. McCann Collection.
9. Major-General Joseph A. Sweeney, *Capuchin Annual*, 1970, pp. 436–437; Seamus McCann Diary; BMH WS, John O'Gorman, p. 5, Patrick Breslin, pp. 19–20, Seamus McCann, pp. 13–14, Patrick (Kit) O'Donnell, p. 5, MA.
10. 'Some valuable hints can be gained from the train fight in Donegal' *An t-Óglach* 15 March 1921, MA.
11. BMH WS, Patrick (Kit) O'Donnell, p. 5, MA.
12. BMH WS, Henry McGowan, p. 7, MA.
13. *Derry Journal*, 14/1/1921; *Derry People and Donegal News*, 15/1/1921.
14. BMH WS, P. H. Doherty, pp. 7–9, MA.
15. *Derry Journal*, 17/1/1921.
16. *Derry Journal*, 19/1/1921; *Derry People and Donegal News*, 22/1/1921.
17. *Derry Journal*, 21/1/1921.
18. *Derry Journal*, 24/1/1921; Liam O'Duffy, p. 9, MA.
19. *Derry Journal*, 24/1/1921.
20. BMH WS, Daniel Kelly, p. 39, MA.
21. BMH WS, Patrick Breslin, p. 23, MA.
22. *Derry Journal*, 28/1/1921.
23. Mulcahy Papers – P7/A/39 – Monthly Report from Donegal No. 1 Brigade to GHQ Dublin – March 1921 – UCD AD.
24. *Ibid.*
25. McCann Collection.
26. Mulcahy Papers – P7/A/39 – UCD AD.
27. *Derry Journal*, 14/2/1921.
28. *Derry Journal*, 21/2/1921; *Derry People and Donegal News*, 12/2/1921.
29. *Derry Journal*, 23/2/1921.
30. *Ibid.*
31. *Derry People and Donegal News*, 26/2/1921.
32. Brian Monaghan, pp. 8–9, MA.
33. *Derry Journal*, 2/3/1921.
34. BMH WS, Philip Boyle, p. 4, Patrick Breslin, pp. 24–25, MA; McCann Collection.

35. *Derry Journal*, 2/3/1921.
36. Mulcahy Papers – P7/A/39 – UCD AD.
37. Major-General Joseph A. Sweeney, *Capuchin Annual*, 1970, pp. 436–437; Mulcahy Papers – P7/A/17 – UCD AD.
38. Seán Ó hÉinne, 'Donncha MacNiallghuis', *Donegal Annual*, 1966, pp. 30–34.
39. *Derry Journal*, 16/3/1921; *Derry People and Donegal News*, 26/3/1921.
40. *Derry People and Donegal News*, 19/3/1921.
41. Mulcahy Papers – P7/A/39 – Monthly Report from Donegal No. 1 Brigade to GHQ Dublin – UCD AD.
42. *Derry Journal*, 28/3/1921.
43. Joe McGarrigle, 'O.C. Describes Capture of Johnston's Motorcar', *Donegal Democrat*, 9/3/1968; Henry McGowan, pp. 7–8, MA.
44. BMH WS, Henry McGowan, p. 8, MA.
45. Mulcahy Papers – P7/A/17 – UCD AD.
46. BMH WS, Patrick Breslin, p. 26, Seamus McCann, pp. 15–16, Charles McGinley p. 5, James McCaffery pp. 10–11, MA.
47. BMH WS, Bernard McGinley, pp. 4–5, MA.
48. *Derry Journal*, 30/3/1921.
49. *Derry Journal*, 1/4/1921.
50. Mulcahy Papers – P7/A/39 – UCD AD.
51. BMH WS, Seamus McCann, p. 17, MA.
52. *Ibid.*, p. 18, MA.
53. *Ibid.*
54. *Derry Journal*, 6/4/1921.
55. BMH WS, Michael Sheer, p. 20, MA.
56. BMH WS, Thomas McShea, p. 14, MA.
57. Major-General Joseph A. Sweeney, *Capuchin Annual*, 1970, pp. 439–440.
58. BMH WS, Michael Sheer, pp. 21–25, MA.
59. *Derry Journal* 11/4/1921.
60. Mulcahy Papers – P7/A/17 – UCD AD.
61. Mulcahy Papers – P7/A/17 – UCD AD.
62. Mulcahy Papers – P7/A/17 – UCD AD.

63. Mulcahy Papers – P7/A/17 – UCD AD.
64. *Derry Journal*, 27/4/1921.
65. *Derry Journal*, 13/4/1921 & 15/4/1921.
66. *Derry Journal*, 20/4/1921; Mulcahy Papers – P7/A/20 – UCD AD.
67. *Derry Journal*, 20/4/1921.
68. *Ibid.*
69. BMH WS, Patrick Breslin, p. 29, MA.
70. *Derry Journal*, 20/4/1921.
71. *Derry Journal*, 22/4/1921.
72. *Derry Journal*, 25/4/1921.
73. *Derry Journal*, 2/5/1921 & 4/5/1921.
74. Kenneth Griffith and Timothy O'Grady, *Curious Journey – An Oral History of Ireland's Unfinished Revolution* (Mercier Press, 1988), p. 210.
75. BMH WS, P. H. Doherty, pp. 10–11, MA.
76. *Derry Journal*, 6/5/1921.
77. *Derry Journal*, 9/5/1921.
78. BMH WS, James McCaffery, p. 10, MA; *Derry Journal*, 9/5/1921.
79. *Derry Journal*, 11/5/1921.
80. BMH WS, P. H. Doherty, pp. 11–12, MA.
81. *Derry Journal*, 11/5/1921; McCann Collection; Mulcahy Papers – P7/A/18 – UCD AD.
82. BMH WS, P. H. Doherty, p. 11–13, Patrick Lynch, p. 2, MA.
83. *Derry People and Donegal News*, 21/5/1921; Thomas McShea, p. 15, MA.
84. *Derry Journal*, 13/5/1921.
85. *Derry Journal*, 16/5/1921; *Derry People and Donegal News*, 21/5/1921.
86. BMH WS, Patrick Lynch, p. 3, MA.
87. Mulcahy Papers – P7/A/18 – UCD AD.
88. Major-General Joseph A. Sweeney, *Capuchin Annual*, 1970, p. 442.
89. BMH WS, Seamus McCann, pp. 21–22, MA.
90. Mulcahy Papers – P7/A/19 – UCD AD.
91. BMH WS, Anthony Dawson, p. 7, MA.
92. *Derry Journal*, 20/5/1921.
93. BMH WS, Seamus McCann, pp. 21–22, MA.

94. Mulcahy Papers – P7/A/18.
95. BMH WS, Patrick Breslin, p. 31, MA; Major-General Joseph A. Sweeney, *Capuchin Annual*, 1970, p. 442.
96. Mulcahy Papers – P7/A/20 – UCD AD.
97. BMH WS, P. H. Doherty, pp. 13–14, Patrick Lynch, p. 4, MA.
98. *Derry Journal*, 23/5/1921.
99. BMH WS, Seamus McCann, pp. 20–21; Patrick Breslin, p. 29, MA.
100. BMH WS, Michael Sheer, pp. 27–29, MA.
101. BMH WS, Rev. Father E. J. Mullen, MA.
102. BMH WS, Michael Sheer, p. 30, MA.
103. Major-General Joseph A. Sweeney, *Capuchin Annual*, 1970, p. 442.
104. BMH WS, Bernard McGinley, p. 6, MA.
105. BMH WS, Thomas McGlynn, pp. 11–12, MA.
106. Mulcahy Papers – P7/A/19 – UCD AD.
107. *Derry Journal*, 20/5/1921.
108. Mulcahy Papers – P7/A/18 – UCD AD.
109. Peter Hegarty, *Peadar O'Donnell* (Mercier Press, 1999), p. 56.
110. Mulcahy Papers – P7/A/18 – UCD AD.
111. BMH WS, Henry McGowan, p. 10, MA.
112. *Derry Journal* – 6/6/1921; Henry McGowan, pp. 10–11, MA.
113. *An t-Óglach* – 1 May 1921, MA.
114. BMH WS, P. H. Doherty, pp. 15–16, MA.
115. *Derry Journal*, 6/6/1921.
116. Mulcahy Papers – P7/A/20 – UCD AD.
117. *Ibid.*
118. McCann Collection.
119. *Derry Journal*, 10/6/1921.
120. Mulcahy Papers – P7/A/18 – UCD AD.
121. *Derry Journal*, 15/6/1921; BMH MS, Henry McGowan, pp. 11–12, MA.
122. BMH WS, Joseph Murray, pp. 15–16, Henry McGowan, pp. 11–12, Michael Doherty, p. 10, MA.
123. BMH MS, Michael Doherty, p. 11, MA.
124. Major-General Joseph A. Sweeney, *Capuchin Annual*, 1970, pp. 443–444.

125. Mulcahy Papers – P7/A/18 – UCD AD.
126. *Derry Journal*, 20/6/1921.
127. *Derry Journal*, 22/6/1921; BMH MS, P.H. Doherty, p. 16, MA.
128. *Derry Journal*, 22/6/1921.
129. *Derry Journal*, 24/6/1921.
130. *Derry Journal.* 22/6/1921.
131. Mulcahy Papers – P7/A/18 – UCD AD.
132. *Derry Journal*, 27/6/1921.
133. Dorothy Macardle, *The Irish Republic* (Wolfhound Press, 1999), p. 466.
134. BMH WS, Patrick Lynch, p. 4, MA.
135. Mulcahy Papers – P7/A/22 – UCD AD.
136. *Derry Journal*, 1/7/1921.
137. *Derry Journal*, 8/7/1921.
138. *Derry Journal*, 4/7/1921.
139. BMH WS, P. H. Doherty, pp. 17–18, MA.
140. *Derry Journal*, 4/7/1921.
141. *Ibid.*
142. Mulcahy Papers – P7/A/10 – UCD AD.
143. BMH WS, Denis Houston, pp. 17–19, Patrick Breslin, pp. 31–34, MA; Major-General Joseph A. Sweeney, *Capuchin Annual*, 1970, pp. 444–445.
144. BMH WS, Patrick Breslin, pp. 34–37, MA.
145. *Derry Journal*, 11/7/1921.
146. *Derry Journal*, 11/7/1921 and 13/7/1921.
147. BMH WS, Michael Sheer, pp. 30–31, MA.
148. BMH WS, Michael Doherty, pp. 11–12, MA.
149. *Derry Journal*, 13/7/1921.

REFERENCES

REFERENCES FROM THE following publications were used in the writing of this book I would like to take this opportunity to thank the following publishers, research institutes and others for their kind permission to reproduce certain material.

Mercier Press:
Peter Hegarty, *Peadar O'Donnell*, 1999.
T. W. Moody & F. X. Martin, *The Course of Irish History*, 2000.
Kenneth Griffith & Timothy O'Grady, *Curious Journey – An Oral History of Ireland's Unfinished Revolution*, 1988.

Gill and Macmillan:
Michael Hopkinson, *Irish War of Independence*, 2004.

Anvil Books:
Ernie O'Malley (Cormac K. H. O'Malley), *On Another Man's Wound*, 2002.

Wolfhound Press:
Dorothy Macardle, *The Irish Republic*, 1999.

Cassel and Company:
Tim Pat Coogan, *1916 – The Easter Rising*, 2001.

Oxford University Press:
Charles Townshend, *The British Campaign in Ireland 1919-1921 – The Development of Police and Military Policies*, 1975.

O'Brien Press:
Brian Feeney, *Sinn Féin – A Hundred Turbulent Years*, 2002.

REFERENCES

An Crann:
Niall Mac Fhionnghaile, *Dr. McGinley and His Times,* 1985.
Niall MacFhionnghaile, *Donegal Ireland and the 1st World War,* 2005.

Bureau of Military History:
Witness Statements 1913-1921/ An t-Óglach / Lot 6.

UCD Archives Department:
Coyle Papers
Ernest Blyth Papers
Mulcahy Papers

Derry Journal:
1906–1921.

Derry People and *Donegal News:*
1920 & 1921

Declan O' Carroll:
Col Declan O'Carroll, *Lt. Col James McMonagle 1898–1986,* 2008.

Donegal Annual:
'Bliainiris Thir Chonaill – Tirconaill and 1916', in *Journal of the County Donegal Historical Society,* Vol. VII, No. 1, 1966.

Capuchin Archives, Church Street, Dublin:
Capuchin Annuals 1941, 1968 & 1970.

Newspapers:
Irish Times
Daily Herald (London)

INDEX

A

Aiken, Frank (Armagh) 111
Altadoo (Donegal town) 183
Ancient Order of Hibernians (AOH) 17, 18, 19, 20, 38, 45, 65, 66, 68, 73, 80, 82, 84, 89, 116
Anderson, Robert (Lord Mayor of Derry) 111
Andrews, Sergeant (RIC) 143
Annagry (West Donegal) 56, 76, 84, 90, 166, 217, 221, 237, 295, 312
Archer, Liam 273, 274, 275
Ardaghey (South Donegal) 72, 104, 154, 178
Ardara (South Donegal) 33, 67, 73, 77, 85, 104, 107, 131, 159, 169, 180, 183, 191, 200, 218, 228, 241, 242, 243, 247, 269, 285, 295, 311, 314, 316, 318
Ardglass (Co. Down) 24
Arranmore (West Donegal island) 56, 70, 73, 231, 295
Asylum Road (Letterkenny) 133
Auxiliary division (Auxiliaries) 149, 223, 226, 231, 243, 295, 303, 309

B

Balbriggan (Dublin) 185, 187
Ballindrait (Lifford) 313, 317
Ballintra (South Donegal) 27, 85, 104, 155, 169, 179, 182, 224, 276, 315
Ballybofey (South-East Donegal) 37, 41, 46, 56, 65, 66, 67, 68, 71, 77, 106, 109, 112, 155, 161, 167, 168, 212, 228, 232, 233, 237, 252, 272, 276, 277, 282, 283, 284, 291, 292, 295, 315, 316, 317
Ballyconnell (Falcarragh) 251
Ballydesken (Fanad) 35
Ballydevitt (Donegal town) 200
Ballykinlar internment camp 193, 194, 195, 196, 213, 216, 247, 272, 282, 284, 289, 317
Ballylar (Fanad) 190
Ballyliffin (Inishowen) 34, 54, 58, 110

Ballymachill (Frosses) 236
Ballymagan (Inishowen) 231, 236, 247, 251, 258
Ballyshannon (South Donegal) 31, 61, 66, 71, 85, 89, 94, 104, 129, 139, 143, 152, 169, 173, 174, 192, 217, 228, 311, 315, 316, 318
Bangor (Co. Down) 20, 24
Barnesmore Gap (South Donegal) 130, 183, 191, 254, 315
Barry, Patrick (Dunkineely) 138, 178, 184, 244
Barton, R. C. 303
Belleek (Co. Fermanagh) 168, 173, 174, 228, 315, 316
Beltany (Gortahork) 110, 294
Belvin (South Donegal) 198
Bigger, Francis Joseph 24
Birkenhead, Lord 20
Black and Tans 16, 120, 149, 159, 170, 177, 181, 182, 184, 185, 186, 187, 189, 190, 192, 199, 200, 204, 205, 207, 223, 224, 231, 235, 241, 242, 243, 244, 257, 263, 265, 266, 268, 269, 270, 276, 277, 281, 282, 285, 286, 287, 289, 309
Blaney, Neil (O/C Fanad Company) 171, 182, 230, 249, 250
Blee, Joseph (IRA Vol. Ballybofey) 252, 291, 292
Bloody Foreland 21
Blythe, Ernest 29, 36, 37
Bogan, Michael 111, 165
Bogan, Patrick 78
Bogside (Derry city) 202, 238
Boland, Harry (IRA GHQ staff) 79
Bomany (Letterkenny) 191
Bonner, Jim (IRA Vol. Burtonport) 61
Bonner, John (IRA Vol. Burtonport) 61, 256, 318
Bonner, Michael (Sinn Féin Councillor/IRA Vol. Buncrana) 137
Bonner, Richard (Sinn Féin Cumann, Donegal town) 103
Boyle, Bernard, G. (Sinn Féin West Donegal Executive) 76

INDEX

Boyle, Charles (Loughanure) 221
Boyle, Con (IRA Vol. West Donegal) 210, 256
Boyle, Dominic (Mountcharles) 225
Boyle, Felix (Castlefinn) 78
Boyle, Fr (Cloghaneely) 28
Boyle, Hugh (Castlegrey/South Donegal) 198
Boyle, J. C. (Burtonport/Dungloe) 136
Boyle, Jack 208
Boyle, James (Drimarone) 138, 215, 318
Boyle, James (Dungloe) 210
Boyle, John (Caravan, Dungloe) 296, 318
Boyle, John E. (Burtonport) 33, 216, 318
Boyle, Mrs (Reelin Bridge, Ballybofey) 232
Boyle, Patrick (IRA Vol. West Donegal) 193
Boyle, Patrick (Rate Collector, Donegal town) 180, 187
Boyle, Philip (Meenacross/West Donegal) 135, 208, 209, 210
Boyle, William (Letterkenny) 121, 122, 123
Bracen, Lieutenant (Dorset Regiment) 206, 207, 208, 211
Bradley, John (Glebe/Buncrana) 57, 232
Bradley, Maisie (Letterkenny) 177
Brady, Sarah (Killybegs) 145
Breen, Dan (Tipperary Brigade) 100, 101
Breenagh (Glenswilly) 27, 130, 314
Brehon Law 15, 134, 135
Brennan, Patrick James (P.J.) (Bundoran) 71, 109, 144, 318
Breslin, Charlie (Derry city) 42
Breslin, John (Bunbeg) 84
Breslin, Patrick (Burtonport/Dungloe) 53, 55, 76, 115, 116, 157, 159, 192, 205, 206, 208, 209, 210, 229, 247, 296, 298, 299
Brett, Major (Magistrate) 118
Bridge End (Donegal/Derry border) 111, 313
Bridgetown (South Donegal) 174
Britton, Hugh (Donegal town) 110, 212, 213, 318
Britton, William (Donegal town) 223
Brockagh (Glenfin) 130, 219, 241, 256, 263, 299, 301, 317
Broy, Eamon (RIC Dublin Castle/IRA spy) 75
Bruckless (South Donegal) 85, 315
Brugha, Cathal (TD/Minister for Defence) 55, 74, 100, 285

Bunbeg (West Donegal) 84, 166, 179, 180, 192, 218, 264, 293
Buncrana (North Donegal/Inishowen) 31, 49, 50, 53, 73, 88, 106, 114, 131, 137, 147, 148, 149, 153, 155, 160, 169, 170, 171, 172, 175, 178, 182, 183, 184, 186, 187, 188, 190, 198, 214, 215, 221, 226, 232, 236, 252, 253, 254, 255, 258, 268, 286, 287, 288, 293, 295, 311, 313, 319
Bundoran (South Donegal) 56, 61, 71, 83, 85, 89, 94, 104, 117, 129, 139, 143, 144, 155, 169, 173, 174, 175, 186, 188, 239, 258, 283, 301, 315, 318
Burnfoot (North-East Donegal) 114, 115, 117, 147, 153, 199, 313
Burt (North-East Donegal) 27, 73
Burtonport (West Donegal) 56, 60, 61, 64, 73, 76, 81, 110, 115, 124, 136, 137, 140, 144, 147, 150, 157, 159, 166, 174, 175, 176, 179, 184, 186, 193, 198, 204, 208, 211, 212, 216, 217, 218, 219, 228, 232, 233, 240, 248, 251, 253, 262, 263, 264, 266, 267, 271, 295, 310, 312, 316
Bustard (UVF Ballybofey) 56, 237
Butt Hall (Ballybofey) 167
Byrne, Connell (Donegal town) 200
Byrne, Dan (IRA Vol. Kilcar, South Donegal) 217, 318
Byrne, H. (IRA Vol. Kilcar, South Donegal) 318
Byrne, John (IRA Vol. Liscooley, East Donegal) 111, 165
Byrne, Mick (IRA Vol. Carrick, South Donegal) 318

C

Caledon, Lord (Kelly's Bridge) 283
Callaghan, Barney (Killybegs) 183
Callan, Owen (No.1 Brigade Flying Column) 241, 242, 243
Campbell, Bernard (Glenties) 79
Campbell, James (JP) (Milford) 159
Campbell, Jim (IRA Vol. Donegal town) 318
Cannon, Peter (Glencolmcille) 225
Caravan (Dungloe) 229, 296, 298
Carberry, Conal (Letterkenny) 37
Carberry, Michael (Kilmacrenan) 29
Carberry, Patrick (Packie) (IRA Vol. Letterkenny) 74
Carey, Edward (Glencolmcille) 225

339

Carndonagh (Inishowen) 27, 63, 82, 88, 105, 110, 111, 114, 118, 140, 147, 149, 155, 158, 169, 180, 182, 213, 214, 221, 226, 247, 251, 253, 257, 268, 272, 287, 290, 293, 295, 311, 313, 319
Carney, Frank (O/C Fermanagh Brigade/ O/C 1st Northern Division 1921) 168, 173, 174, 202, 227, 229, 238, 244, 259, 260, 261, 262, 266, 271, 275
Carr, Charles (Ardara) 218
Carr, Charles (Gortahork) 251
Carr, Edward (Gortahork) 251
Carr, Johnny (Fanad) 171
Carrick (South Donegal) 33, 85, 104, 107, 123, 141, 142, 156, 242, 295, 314, 318
Carricknashane (East Donegal) 78
Carrigans (East Donegal) 53, 130, 175, 313
Carrigart (North-West Donegal) 62, 73, 104, 107, 174, 254, 255, 271, 272, 314
Carroll, P. (JP) (Letterkenny Board of Guardians) 44
Carrowreagh (Carndonagh) 221, 247
Carson, Edward (Unionist Politician) 33, 44, 50, 100, 109, 118
Casement, Roger (1916 Leader/executed in London) 20, 31, 32, 43
Cashel, Alice (Cumann na mBan organiser) 99
Cashelard (South Donegal) 85, 104
Cashelnagore (West Donegal) 37, 40, 41, 64, 166, 167, 174, 248, 251
Cassidy, Anthony (IRA Vol. Carndonagh/ Inishowen Flying Column) 253
Cassidy, James (Drimfin) 198
Cassidy, John (IRB, Ballybofey) 37, 41, 110
Castlecaldwell (Co. Fermanagh) 131
Castlederg (Co. Tyrone) 106, 164, 228, 233, 234, 315, 316
Castlefinn (East Donegal) 27, 50, 57, 65, 66, 67, 73, 78, 105, 111, 132, 133, 161, 162, 164, 183, 228, 261, 284, 301, 311, 315, 316, 317
Castlegrey (South Donegal) 198
Castlehill (East Donegal) 27
Castle Street (Donegal town) 200
Castle Street (Letterkenny) 193
Cavanagh, William (IRA Vol. Buncrana) 131
Chapel Road, Dunloe 298
Childers, Erskine (Howth Gun-running) 24, 25
Citizen Army 39, 141

Clady (Donegal/Tyrone border) 105, 133, 161, 317
Clancy, Mrs M. J. (Cumann na mBan) 67
Clar (South Donegal) 85, 191
Clarendon Street (Derry city) 113
Clarke, Constable (RIC Cork city) 229, 255
Clarke, James (Unionist) 137
Cliffony/Cliffoney (Leitrim/South Donegal IRA brigade area) 94, 143, 315
Cloghan (South West Donegal) 315
Cloghaneely (West Donegal) 27, 28, 31, 32, 33, 57, 63, 64, 73, 76, 107, 141, 189, 312
Cloghglass (West Donegal) 60
Clonmany (Inishowen) 53, 54, 63, 88, 91, 110, 147, 148, 169, 214, 253, 255, 257, 258, 293, 313
Cloughwilly (Dungloe) 295
Cockhill, Buncrana 287, 293
Cole, Charlie (Dungloe) 211
Cole, Patrick, J. (Carndonagh) 105
Cole, Walter (Mountjoy Square, Dublin) 226
Coll, Jimmy (Fanad) 171
Collins, Aggie (Letterkenny) 67, 177
Collins, John (British agent/spy) 295, 296, 297, 298
Collins, Michael 43, 93, 101, 102, 125, 132, 140, 168, 253, 273, 283, 285, 290, 309
Colquhoun, T. J. Trew (Buncrana) 50, 121
Commeen (West Donegal) 256, 263
Conaghan, Denis (Tor) 298
Conaghan, Éamon (IRA Vol. Glenties) 273
Conaghan, T. E. (Solicitor) 215
Con Colbert Sinn Féin Cumann (Castlefinn) 50, 57
Connolly, Con (IRA Vol. Tipperary, Member of No. 1 Flying Column) 210
Connolly, Jim (Sinn Féin Cumann, Letterkenny) 54, 67, 68, 133, 188
Conscription 70, 74, 91
Convoy (East Donegal) 27, 117, 130, 313
Corkskrew, Doochary (West Donegal) 266
Cosgrave, William T. 52, 75
Coyle, Anthony (Letterkenny) 265
Coyle, Edward Thomas (Liscooley) 111, 165
Coyle, Eithne (Cloghaneely) 57, 66
Coyle, Patrick (Kilmacrenan) 175
Crawford, C. (Ballybofey) 317

INDEX

Creeslough (North-West Donegal) 27, 32, 37, 39, 40, 46, 62, 63, 81, 103, 104, 105, 107, 166, 167, 176, 216, 217, 220, 236, 248, 254, 255, 292, 295, 311, 312
Croagh (South Donegal) 33, 85, 315
Crohyboyle (West Donegal) 298
Crolly (West Donegal) 90, 110, 115, 147, 184, 205, 208, 211, 217, 221, 240, 247, 248, 298, 312
Crossan, Tom 73
Crossroads (Killygordon) 112
Crovehy (Dungloe/West Donegal) 207, 208, 211, 241, 263
Crowe, Berkely (British army/Buncrana) 154
Crowe, Tadhg (Tipperary Brigade) 101
Cruckaughrim Hill, Ballyliffin 34
Culdaff (Inishowen) 61, 73, 88, 118, 130, 131, 169, 213, 214, 247, 313
Cullen, William (Derry) 202, 210
Culmore (Derry) 31
Cumann na mBan 16, 57, 66, 67, 69, 71, 72, 73, 77, 80, 82, 96, 99, 107, 133, 136, 177, 205, 216, 238, 239, 256, 259, 270, 274
Cunningham, Charles (Killybegs) 194, 318
Cunningham, Fr (PP Glenties) 88
Cunningham, Fr Bernard (Clar) 191
Cunningham, James (Carrick & Birmingham) 123, 125, 126, 132
Cunningham, Mrs F. (Killybegs) 183
Cunningham, William 236
Curragh camp 194, 196
Curran, James (IRA East Tyrone) 163, 165
Curran, John (Letterkenny) 54, 121, 122, 203

D

Daly, Paddy (O/C Liverpool/Gun-runner) 125, 132
Dartmoor prison, England 250
Davitt, Michael (Fenian, Land League) 107
Dawson, Anthony 162, 164, 165, 171, 177, 217, 264
Dawson, James (Jim) (Letterkenny) 46, 56, 57, 65, 68, 69, 71, 74, 77, 130, 165, 168, 183, 193, 317
Dawson, Michael (Mick) (Mountcharles) 77, 94, 222
Dawson, Michael, Jnr (Letterkenny) 285

Dawson, Michael, Snr (Letterkenny) 19, 57
Deeney, Edward (Rathmullan) 137
Deery, Hugh (Letterkenny) 193, 317
Defence of the Realm Act (DORA) 18, 28, 29, 109, 127, 188
Derry 239, 240, 244, 245, 247, 249, 251, 253, 255, 258, 259, 260, 262, 268, 269, 273, 274, 275, 279, 281, 282, 286, 288, 289, 292, 297, 299, 313
Derrybeg (West Donegal) 166, 179, 181, 312
de Valera, Éamon 51, 52, 55, 62, 63, 64, 65, 66, 67, 75, 81, 108, 197, 285, 299, 300, 301, 302, 304, 307
Devine, F. (Castlefinn) 317
Devlin, Joe (Irish Party) 17
Diver, James (Carndonagh) 140, 253
Doaghbeg (Fanad) 131
Dobbyn, Seamus (IRB organiser) 37
Doe (Killybegs) 73, 107, 232
Doe Castle (Creeslough) 39
Doheny, William (Bill) (Tipperary) 202, 210, 235
Doherty, Andrew (Ballybofey) 283
Doherty, Bernard (Adjutant – Divisional Staff 1st Northern Division) 229, 262
Doherty, Cecil (Clonmany) 253
Doherty, Charlie (Ballybofey) 233
Doherty, Charlie (Killygordon) 289, 317
Doherty, Cissy (Dungloe) 205
Doherty, Denis (Dungloe) 221
Doherty, Edward (Ballybofey) 277
Doherty, George (Derry) 217
Doherty, Hugh (Buncrana) 286
Doherty, Hugh (Donegal town) 200
Doherty, Hugh (Dungloe) 318
Doherty, J. J. (Killygordon) 289
Doherty, James (Ballybofey) 277
Doherty, James (Cashel, Inishowen) 110
Doherty, John (Culdaff Sinn Féin) 61, 121
Doherty, Johnnie (Letterkenny) 123, 177
Doherty, Michael (IRA O/C Castlefinn) 111, 162, 165, 200, 283
Doherty, Michael (Scotland) 78
Doherty, Mick (Watt) (Illies, Inishowen) 253
Doherty, Mock (Stout) (Illies, Inishowen) 253
Doherty, Mrs (Glebe, Inishowen) 221, 222
Doherty, P. H. (Packie) (Carndonagh) 137, 139, 140, 213, 214, 253, 257, 278, 293
Doherty, Patrick (Bundoran) 94

341

Doherty, Simon (Letterkenny) 265
Doherty, William (Sinn Féin Councillor/IRA Vol. Buncrana) 50, 121, 153, 182, 253
Dolan, James N. (Manorhamilton, Co. Leitrim) 72
Donaghadee (Co. Antrim) 20
Donegal Board of Guardians 44, 178, 184, 215
Donegal town 27, 33, 37, 48, 53, 69, 72, 73, 81, 85, 87, 94, 96, 103, 104, 108, 110, 126, 131, 137, 138, 150, 157, 158, 159, 160, 165, 169, 177, 179, 180, 181, 183, 185, 186, 187, 190, 191, 194, 199, 200, 207, 212, 214, 215, 222, 223, 224, 225, 228, 254, 268, 311, 315, 316
Donovan, John T. (Irish Party) 29, 89
Doochary (West Donegal) 56, 76, 88, 130, 131, 179, 204, 225, 229, 231, 267, 312
Doorin (South Donegal) 179
Doran, James (Croveigh) 208
Dore (West Donegal) 219, 220
Downings (North-West Donegal) 24, 314
Drimarone (South Donegal) 72, 104, 187, 318
Drimfin (South Donegal) 198
Drumboe Castle (Stranorlar) 168, 252, 276, 277, 282, 289, 292
Drumbologue (Letterkenny) 27
Drumfries (Inishowen) 160, 247
Drumkeen (South-East Donegal) 27, 112, 266, 314
Drumoghill (North-East Donegal) 27, 105, 238
Drumquinn (Co. Tyrone) 161, 162, 163, 164, 165, 168, 309
Dublin Castle 23, 32, 41, 75, 77, 145, 156, 190, 210, 252, 295
Duffy (RIC Head Constable) 126, 264, 266, 295, 296, 297
Duffy, Hugh (Dunfanaghy) 138
Duffy, Jimmy (Meenbanad/West Donegal) 60
Duffy, Leo (IRA Dublin 3rd Battalion) 123
Duggan, Charlie (Gola Island) 25
Duggan, E. J. (TD) 303
Dunfanaghy (North-West Donegal) 103, 105, 138, 159, 174, 180, 205, 216, 235, 252, 255, 272, 295, 313
Dungannon Clubs 19
Dungloe (West Donegal) 5, 27, 33, 37, 53, 55, 60, 64, 75, 81, 84, 86, 88, 95, 102,

103, 110, 111, 113, 114, 115, 116, 117, 125, 127, 130, 135, 136, 140, 144, 145, 146, 147, 150, 159, 169, 170, 176, 179, 186, 192, 193, 198, 199, 202, 204, 205, 206, 207, 208, 209, 211, 212, 218, 219, 220, 221, 225, 227, 228, 229, 234, 235, 238, 240, 253, 267, 271, 275, 295, 296, 297, 298, 299, 308, 311, 312, 316, 318
Dunkineely (South Donegal) 94, 126, 138, 177, 198, 281, 315, 318
Dunleavy, Anthony (Donegal town) 131
Dunnion, George (Donegal town) 187
Dunnion, Michael (Donegal town) 138
Dwyer, Paddy (Co. Tipperary) 101

E

Easter Rising 13, 14, 31, 32, 39, 40, 41, 42, 43, 45, 51, 57, 130, 136, 141, 307
Ederney (Co. Fermanagh) 228, 316
Enniskillen (Co. Fermanagh) 149, 285, 295
Enniskillen Fusiliers 42
Errigal, Mountain (West Donegal) 21

F

Fahan (Inishowen) 27, 73, 170
Fairhill (Dungloe) 115
Falcarragh (West Donegal) 57, 105, 156, 157, 159, 160, 180, 185, 220, 228, 234, 235, 248, 250, 251, 291, 312, 313, 316
Fanad (North-West Donegal) 21, 31, 35, 83, 96, 107, 114, 131, 138, 168, 171, 172, 181, 190, 215, 230, 249, 250, 254, 261, 279, 311, 314
Fanavolty (Fanad) 83
Farrell (RIC Sergeant) 116, 117
Farrell, Dr (1st Northern Division IRA Medical Officer) 229
Farren, James (Buncrana) 50
Ferguson, Mary (Dunkineely) 126
Feymore, Creeslough 292
Fianna Éireann (Boy Scouts) 81
Figgis, Darrell (Sinn Féin Executive) 190
Finlay, Peter (Bundoran) 143
Finner Camp (South Donegal) 56, 61, 66, 71, 85, 94, 127, 139, 145, 168, 169, 181, 182, 224, 239, 301
Finn Valley (Stranorlar) 133
Fintown (South-West Donegal) 84, 146, 240, 247, 264, 315

INDEX

Fintra (Killybegs) 222
Fitzsimons, Bernard (Barney) (Carndonagh) 140, 221
Flattery, Mrs C. A. (Letterkenny) 57, 67, 69, 222
Fletcher, Patrick (Buncrana) 154, 182, 215
Foxhall (Glenswilly) 27, 243
Friel, Bernard (Mountcharles) 138
Friel, Daniel (Inishowen) 121
Friel, E. (Nationalist Councillor Milford Area) 137
Friel, Éamon (Edward) (President Fanad Sinn Féin Cumann) 83
Friel, James (Glenswilly/Churchill) 288
Frongoch prison camp 15, 40, 42, 43, 46, 47
Frosses (South Donegal) 72, 104, 110, 179, 184, 187, 236

G

GAA 18
Gaelic League 18, 77, 84, 194
Gallagher, A. F. (Dunkineely) 138
Gallagher, Anthony (Crovehy) 208
Gallagher, Charles (Ballyshannon) 175
Gallagher, Dan (Glenswilly/Churchill) 73
Gallagher, Daniel (Laghey/South Donegal) 138
Gallagher, Éamon (IRA Vol.) 165
Gallagher, Francis (IRA Vol. Letterkenny) 74, 286
Gallagher, H. (Ballindrait, Lifford) 317
Gallagher, H. T. (Crown Prosecutor) 79
Gallagher, Hugh (Laghey/South Donegal) 138
Gallagher, James (Letterkenny) 177
Gallagher, Joe (Ardara) 318
Gallagher, Joe (Mountcharles) 222
Gallagher, John (Letterkenny) 97
Gallagher, Joseph (Glenties) 79
Gallagher, Joseph (Killendaragh, Crolly/West Donegal) 221
Gallagher, Michael (Ardara) 183
Gallagher, Owen (Bundoran) 129, 174, 318
Gallagher, P. H. (Donegal town) 87
Gallagher, P. M. (Donegal town) 96, 194
Gallagher, Paddy (IRA Vol. and Sinn Féin Councillor Mountcharles) 138
Gallagher, Paddy (IRA Vol. Meenbanad, West Donegal) 61

Gallagher, Patrick (Crolly) 90
Gallagher, Patrick (Donegal town/South Donegal) 110, 183, 185, 222
Gallagher, Phil (IRA Vol. Meenbanad, West Donegal) 61
Gallagher, Sarah (Letterkenny) 67
Gallagher, William (Letterkenny/Donegal County Council) 50, 121
Gallen, John (Donegal town) 159, 165
Gallen, Patrick (Clonmany) 110
Gallinagh, Thomas (Ballydevitt/South Donegal) 200, 222
Gallon, Ned (Donegal County Councillor) 284
Gatins, John (Killybegs) 183
Gaynor, Liam (IRB organiser) 37
Gibbons, Jim (Letterkenny) 54, 97, 122
Gill, George (Gleneely/Inishowen) 226
Gill, William (Meenavogy/Inishowen) 257
Gillen, C. (Derry) 57
Gilmartin, Charles (North County Leitrim/Inishowen flying column) 253
Gilmartin, Willie (Cliffony) 143, 144
Gilmore, Tom (Birmingham) 126, 132
Gilvarry, Patrick (Bundoran) 94
Glackin, Henry (Dungloe) 296
Glackin, John (Glenswilly) 287
Glasbeggan (Dungloe/West Donegal) 150
Glebe (Inishowen) 221, 232
Glen (Creeslough) 37, 313
Glen, The (Mountcharles) 222
Glencar (Letterkenny) 164, 280
Glencolmcille (South Donegal) 21, 41, 85, 87, 104, 107, 130, 131, 225, 229, 242, 314, 318
Glendowan (South-West Donegal) 204, 238, 246, 256, 257, 260, 262, 264, 267, 280
Gleneely (Killygordon) 105, 154
Gleneely, (Inishowen) 226
Glenfinn (Cloghan/South West Donegal) 53, 67, 73
Glengesh (South Donegal) 242
Glenmaquinn (East Donegal) 176
Glenswilly (North-West Donegal) 27, 105, 130, 145, 167, 314
Glenties (South-West Donegal) 31, 33, 51, 64, 72, 79, 88, 90, 98, 154, 193, 205, 225, 240, 241, 242, 243, 247, 250, 264, 267, 269, 271, 285, 294, 301, 314, 318
Gola Island (West Donegal) 24, 25
Gordon, C. (Ballybofey) 317

343

Gorman, Jacob (Laghey/South Donegal) 138
Gorman, John (Glenties) 193, 318
Gormley, John, Dr (Cloghan/Stranorlar) 183, 232
Gortahork (West Donegal) 37, 97, 110, 138, 156, 185, 189, 220, 251, 291, 294, 312
Gortnasade, Kincasslagh 233
Gortnasillagh (West Donegal) 262, 267
Gortward (South Donegal) 177
Grant, James (Railway employee/South Donegal) 176
Green, D. (Glenties) 318
Green, Dan (Ranafast) 294
Green, James (Rathmullan) 137
Greencastle (Inishowen) 111, 313
Gribben, Hugh (Castledawson, Co. Derry) 42
Grieves, Jimmie (Glenmornan, Co. Derry) 42
Griffin, Albert (Mountcharles) 223
Griffith, Arthur (President of Sinn Féin) 13, 18, 19, 47, 49, 75, 77, 306, 307
Guallagh, Annagry (West Donegal) 221
Gull Island (South Donegal) 242
Gweebara Bridge (West Donegal) 267
Gweedore (West Donegal) 33, 64, 67, 76, 83, 84, 90, 104, 107, 130, 131, 138, 166, 180, 218, 219, 221, 228, 240, 248, 251, 295, 298, 311, 312, 316

H

Hackett Pain, Brigadier-General 109
Hamilton, Captain J. S. (Ballintra) 169, 276
Hannigan, Bernard (Rosnakill) 182
Hannigan, Jim (Ballybofey) 165, 317
Hannigan, Joseph (Ballybofey) 283, 284
Hannigan, M. (Brockagh) 317
Hannigan, Mrs (Killgordon) 289
Hannigan, Patrick (Killygordon) 289
Harkin, Paddy (Drumkeen) 266
Harkin, Patrick (Kiltoorish/Ardara) 286
Harkin, William (Buncrana) 182, 215
Harley, John (Frosses) 110
Harley, John (Mountcharles) 225
Harley, John Francis (Quigley's Point/Inishowen) 189
Harley, Mary (Mountcharles) 223, 225
Harron, James (Laghey) 138

Harvey, Charles J. (Donegal town) 200, 222
Haughey, Charles (Dunkineely) 198, 318
Healy, Tim (MP) 17
Heaney, Michael (Malinbeg) 226
Hegarty, Paddy (Derry city) 42, 43
Hennessey, Charles (Drogheda) 285
Higginbottom, Andrew (Mountcharles) 179, 222
Higgins, Thady (Inver) 194, 319
Hinnell, J. (Carndonagh) 319
Hobson, Bulmer (IRB organiser) 37
Hogan, Seán (Tipperary Brigade) 100, 101
Holmes, William (Drumoghill) 217, 238
Houston, Denis (Dungloe) 136, 192, 212, 297
Houston, Seán (No. 3 Brigade O/C) 225
Howel, John (Carndonagh) 221
Howel, Patrick (Carndonagh) 221
Howel, William (Carndonagh) 221

I

Illies (Inishowen) 253, 255, 257, 258
Inch Island (Inishowen) 73, 180, 198, 251
Inghinidhe na hÉireann 19
Inishboffin Island (West Donegal) 41, 185
Inishfree (West Donegal) 312
Inishowen (North Donegal) 21, 27, 34, 52, 63, 88, 91, 106, 136, 139, 148, 149, 158, 161, 169, 170, 178, 181, 184, 189, 226, 228, 230, 236, 247, 253, 255, 257, 259, 268, 272, 277, 278, 279, 287, 290, 293, 311, 313, 316
Inver (South Donegal) 33, 94, 160, 178, 179, 184, 190, 194, 198, 224, 244, 281, 311, 315, 318, 319
Irish Parliamentary Party (IPP) 14, 15, 17, 18, 20, 26, 28, 44, 49, 52, 63, 70, 72, 76, 77, 78, 83, 84, 85, 86, 87, 88, 89, 99, 306, 307

J

Johnston (RIC Constable) 161
Johnston, Dr (Stranorlar) 227, 232, 233, 262, 267
Johnston, Patrick (Pappy) (Bundoran) 56, 173, 174, 186, 239, 240, 258

K

Kane, John (Ballyshannon) 318

INDEX

Kavanagh, Seamus (Dungloe) 127
Kearns, James (Letterkenny) 27, 39, 57
Keelogs (Inver/South Donegal) 198
Keeney, Charlie (Dunkineely) 94, 109
Kelly, Charles (Letterkenny) 121
Kelly, Daniel (Castlenagore) 26, 27, 28, 37, 39, 40, 41, 43, 46, 56, 57, 66, 216, 217
Kelly, E. J. (MP East Donegal) 78, 80, 89, 90
Kelly, Harry (Bundoran) 85
Kelly, J. J. (Clady) 165, 317
Kelly, James (Culdaff) 61
Kelly, Master (Corkskrew, Doochary, West Donegal) 266
Kelly, Neil (Glenswilly/Churchill) 73, 137
Kelly, P. (Killygordon) 317
Kelly, Paddy (Mountcharles) 222
Kelly, Thomas (TD Dublin) 79, 99
Kelly's Bridge (Ballybofey area) 277, 282, 283, 284, 292
Kennedy, Ambrose (Donegal town) 110
Kennedy, Con (Ardara) 241
Kennedy, Fr (Frosses) 187
Kennedy, Francis (Ardaghey) 178
Kennedy, John (Donegal town) 131
Kerrigan, Dr (Killygordon) 111, 289
Kilcar (South Donegal) 33, 58, 85, 104, 107, 151, 194, 217, 278, 292, 314, 318
Killaghtee (South Donegal) 27, 104
Killea (Donegal/Derry border) 239
Killendarragh (Crolly) 221
Killeter (Co. Tyrone) 130
Killyaghtee (South Donegal) 72
Killybegs (South Donegal) 33, 58, 66, 72, 73, 81, 85, 104, 107, 108, 110, 126, 129, 145, 146, 151, 177, 183, 194, 222, 228, 241, 243, 264, 292, 294, 295, 311, 314, 316, 318
Killygordon (East Donegal) 73, 105, 106, 111, 112, 133, 154, 161, 164, 233, 315
Killymard (South Donegal) 85
Kilmacrenan (North-West Donegal) 27, 29, 76, 84, 107, 175, 248, 252, 254, 295, 313
Kilmainham jail (Dublin) 42
Kilrean (Glenties/Ardara Road) 269, 314
Kiltoorish (Ardara) 286
Kincasslagh (West Donegal) 56, 64, 76, 84, 115, 124, 220, 233, 312
Kindroyhead (Gleneely/Inishowen) 226
Kindrum (Fanad) 171, 182, 230
Kingarrow (West Donegal) 63, 72, 96
Kingsbridge station (Dublin) 32

Kinlough (South Donegal) 94, 169, 177, 315
Knather (Ballyshannon) 129

L

Lafferty, Leo (Carndonagh) 140, 141, 247
Lafferty, Mrs (Carrowreagh near Cardonagh) 221, 222
Lagan Valley (East Donegal) 23
Laghy (South Donegal) 315
Lanaghan, Hugh (Mountcharles) 179
Langan, Frank J. (Buncrana) 137
Langan, James (Letterkenny) 57, 74
Lanigan, Bernard (Carndonagh) 221
Lanigan, James (Carndonagh) 221
Larkin, John G. (Letterkenny) 121, 122
Larne (Co. Antrim) 14, 20
Laught (South-East Donegal) 78
Laurentic (Canadian ship sunk off Fanad Head) 172
Lavey, Christy (Milford) 137
Law, Hugh (MP West Donegal) 76
Leamagowra (Ardara/South Donegal) 131
Leaper, Samuel (Meenagrave/South Donegal) 237
Leck (Letterkenny) 239
Letterfad (South Donegal) 215, 236
Letterkenny 17, 19, 24, 27, 28, 35, 37, 39, 44, 46, 52, 53, 56, 57, 62, 65, 67, 68, 72, 74, 77, 81, 82, 89, 95, 97, 99, 102, 103, 105, 107, 112, 113, 114, 117, 121, 122, 130, 133, 137, 145, 148, 150, 151, 152, 158, 159, 161, 162, 163, 164, 166, 167, 168, 171, 175, 177, 178, 179, 180, 183, 188, 191, 193, 203, 215, 217, 222, 228, 240, 243, 244, 245, 246, 248, 252, 254, 255, 256, 257, 264, 265, 266, 267, 279, 280, 285, 286, 288, 293, 294, 295, 309, 311, 314, 316, 317
Lettermacward (West Donegal) 56, 76, 130, 131, 231, 295, 312
Lifford 117, 119, 133, 146, 170, 185, 259, 270, 313, 317
Liscooly (East Donegal) 112, 315, 317
Lishally (Co. Derry) 31
Liverpool (England) 125, 132, 172
Lloyd George, David 49, 50, 58, 70, 74, 75, 124, 197, 299, 300, 301, 302
Logue, William (Bomany, Letterkenny) 191
Loughanure (West Donegal) 56, 76, 96, 217, 218, 221

345

Lough Derg (Donegal/Fermanagh border) 283, 284
Lough Finn 301
Loughkeel (South-West Donegal) 313
Loughmult (Dunkineely) 198
Loughrey, Patrick (Rathmullan) 137
Lough Swilly 21, 151, 171, 172, 229, 287
Loutelle, William Lindsay (British army) 135
Lowry, Anthony (Donegal County Council) 98
Lowry, Robert (Speertown, Donegal town) 191
Lynch, James (Derry) 217

M

MacCartan, Dr (Irish Volunteers Leader) 27
MacDonagh, Thomas (Irish Volunteer Leader 1916) 31, 34, 35, 51
MacEntee, Seán (Sinn Féin GHQ) 62, 63, 64, 65, 66, 67
Mac Giolla Bhríde, Niall (Feymore/Creeslough) 32, 37
MacGuibhal, Seasamh (West Donegal Sinn Féin) 107
Mac Loingsigh, Séan (Convoy) 117
MacManus, Joseph (Mountcharles) 72
MacManus, Seamus (Mountcharles) 18, 188
MacMenamin, Seaghan (Kingarrow – West Donegal Sinn Féin Executive) 63, 72, 76, 81, 84, 87, 96
MacNeill, Eoin (Sinn Féin/Irish Volunteers) 26, 79
Mac Phaidín, Pádraig (Sinn Féin West Donegal) 107
Macready, General N. (General Officer Commanding British army) 135
MacShane, John (Derry) 130
MacSwiney, Terence (Cork) 186, 187, 189, 258
Magee, Patrick (Ballyshannon) 175, 252
Magheragall (Co. Antrim) 36
Magherameena (West Donegal) 135
Maguire, Fr James, (Ballyliffen) 58, 91
Maguire, James (Burtonport) 76, 193, 198
Maguire, Sergeant (RIC) 118
Malin (Inishowen) 63, 88, 149, 169, 247, 253, 290, 313
Malinbeg (South Donegal) 41, 87, 226

Malin Head (Inishowen) 58
Malinmore (Carrick) 87, 141
Mamore, Gap of (Inishowen) 31
Mangan, James (Ballintra) 224
Manorcunningham (East Donegal) 27, 167, 217, 239, 294, 313
Manorhamilton (Co. Leitrim) 72
Markievicz, Countess 75
Marley, F. (Killygordon) 317
Martin, Frank (Quartermaster 1st Northern Division) 229, 262
Martin, Hugh (No.1 Brigade Flying Column) 241, 242, 243
Maxwell, General (British army) 40
Mayne, William (Derry) 130
McAdam, Eileen D. (Ballyshannon) 217
McAteer, Fr (Drimarone) 187
McAteer, Patrick (Ballybofey) 277, 282, 284, 292
McBrearty, Edward (IRA Vol. East Donegal) 165
McBrearty, H. (Killygordon) 317
McBrearty, Hugh (Mountcharles) 188
McBride, Charles (Dungloe) 113, 114, 115, 117, 119
McBride, Mary (Dungloe) 205
McBride, Maud Gonne (Sinn Féin TD) 19, 85, 86
McBride, Micheal (Meenalae/Annagry) 221
McCafferty, Fr John (Letterkenny) 52, 53
McCallion, Alfie (Derry) 202, 208, 210
McCann, Seamus (Derry/No. 1 Flying Column) 130, 202, 203, 210, 238, 239, 256, 263, 265, 266, 274, 275
McCarron, Cllr John (Clonmany) 110, 136
McCarron, James (Jim) (IRA Vol. Ballybofey) 165, 233, 272, 276, 277, 317
McCarron, Owen (Buncrana) 293
McCarry's hotel (Letterkenny) 62
McClay, Willie (Stranorlar) 233
McCluskey, John (Director of Training 1st Northern Division) 229
McClusky, Dr (Carrigart) 104
McCole, James (Dungloe) 53, 76, 115, 116, 266, 279, 290, 296, 299
McCole, John (Gortahork/West Donegal) 156, 176
McCole, Patrick (Dungloe) 116, 210
McConalogue, William (Inishowen) 226
McCool, James (Letterkenny) 137
McCool, Manus (Fanad) 83
McCormack, Mary (Derry) 239

Index

McCormack, Paddy (Tipperary Brigade) 101
McCormack's farm (Glendowan) 246
McCreadie, M. A. (Milford) 137
McCullough, Denis (Dinny) (IRB, Irish Volunteers, Sinn Féin) 27, 29, 36, 37, 43
McCullough, John (Gleneely) 154
McDaid, Charles (Glenswilly) 287
McDaid, Charles (Tullynaha) 138, 215
McDaid, Edmund (Letterkenny) 121
McDaid, John (Donegal town) 200, 222
McDermott, Éamon (Derry) 117, 118, 119, 123, 133
McDermott, John (Donegal town) 138
McDermott, Patrick (Letterkenny) 167
McDermott, Seán (IRB, Irish Volunteers, Sinn Féin) 36
McDevitt, Joe (Kilcar) 58, 84
McDwyre, Francis (Killybegs) 183
McElany, Owen (IRA Vol. Cardonagh) 253
McElhinney, John (Raphoe) 317
McElhinney, Thomas (Milford) 137
McElwee, Anthony (Milford) 159
McElwee, Paddy (Donegal Railway employee) 175
McFadden, Agnes (Cumann na mBan Letterkenny) 67
McFadden, James (Letterkenny) 137
McFadden, John (Gweedore) 221
McFadden, Patrick (Creeslough) 37, 76, 81
McFadden's hotel (Donegal town) 186, 189
McFeeley, Willie (Donegal Railway employee) 175
McGahern, James (Donegal town) 138
McGarry, Sean (Lincoln jail escapee) 108
McGarvey, Mrs (Letterkenny) 57
McGarvey, William (Milford) 137
McGee, James (Gortahork/West Donegal) 156
McGee family (Lough Keel) 211
McGettigan, Patrick (Milford) 159
McGill, Hugh (West Donegal) 76
McGinley, Anthony (Dungloe) 113, 114, 117, 119, 125, 136, 192, 210, 211, 296
McGinley, Bernard (Creeslough) 46, 104, 254
McGinley, Conor (Donegal/Irish Volunteers Dublin 1916) 40
McGinley, Dr J. P. (Letterkenny) 46, 56, 57, 62, 64, 69, 73, 77, 82, 84, 88, 105, 107, 112, 114, 115, 117, 118, 121, 122, 123, 133, 135, 161, 163, 165, 168, 171, 172, 175, 176, 183, 194, 203, 238, 258, 309
McGinley, Eunan (Donegal/Irish Volunteers Dublin 1916) 40
McGinley, Patrick (Gola Island/Howth Gun-running) 24, 25
McGinty, Thomas (Stranorlar) 232, 233
McGlinchey, John (Donegal Board of Guardians) 44
McGlinchey, Patrick (Killygordon) 154, 165
McGlinchey, Rev. James (Dean of St Columba's College, Derry) 82
McGlynn, Thomas (Carricknashane/Castlefinn) 78, 111
McGlynn, Tom (Liscooley) 317
McGoldrick, P. J. (TD) 83, 258
McGoldrick, Willie (Buncrana) 319
McGowan, Henry (Ballybofey) 164, 165, 167, 212, 232, 233, 234, 237, 252, 276, 282, 283, 284, 317
McGowan, Patrick (Ballybofey) 282, 317
McGranaghan, James (Killygordon) 289
McGranaghan, Mathew (Killygordon) 106
McGranaghan, Susan (Cumann na mBan Letterkenny) 67
McGrath, Hugh (Letterkenny) 162, 165, 171, 264
McGrath, Joseph (Dublin/Ballykinlar Camp Commandant) 195, 282
McGrath, Michael (Councillor) 121
McGready, Neil (Frosses) 184
McGregor (British army captain) 167, 276, 277
McGrenra, Patrick (Churchill) 137
McGroarty, John (Killygordon) 111, 164, 165
McGroarty, Willie (Mountcharles) 222
McGrory, Bernard (Mountcharles) 224
McGrory, Daniel (Buncrana) 232
McGuinness, Charlie (Derry) 241, 242
McGuire, Sis (Cumann Na mBan/Glenties/Ardara) 270
McGurk, Jimmy (Gullaghduff, Co. Derry) 42
McHugh, Joe (see James McKee) 246
McHugh, Patrick (Donegal town) 183
McIntyre, John J. (Kilcar) 318
McKay, Frank (Churchill) 171
McKay, Hugh (Churchill) 171
McKay, Willie (Churchill) 203

347

McKee, James (Ginger) (Armagh) 202, 203, 205, 206, 210, 246, 247
McKelvey, James (McKelvey's/Brockagh) 219, 256
McKenna, James (RIC Constable) 235
McKeown (British agent) 297, 298
McKinney, W. G. (Letterkenny) 121
McLaughlin (RIC Constable/IRA agent) 253
McLaughlin, C. (Dunfanaghy) 138
McLaughlin, Charles (IRA Vol. Buncrana) 182, 215
McLaughlin, Charles (IRA Vol. Carndonagh) 140, 197
McLaughlin, Daniel (Doe, Buncrana) 232
McLaughlin, Hugh (Carndonagh) 287
McLaughlin, J. D. (Ballybofey) 317
McLaughlin, John (IRA Volunteer/Councillor) 121, 165
McLaughlin, Joseph (Buncrana) 253
McLaughlin, Joseph (Joe) (Buncrana) 131, 278, 286
McLaughlin, William (Letterkenny) 165, 171
McManus, Joe (Mountcharles) 188, 223
McManus, Rose (Lettterkenny) 177
McMenamin, Dan (Irish Party Candidate 1918) 86, 88, 89
McMenamin, James (Ballintra) 224
McMenamin, Patrick 224
McMenamin, Tom (IRA Vol. Ballybofey) 233
McMenamin, William (Letterkenny) 57
McMonagle, Hugh (Glenswilly) 73
McMonagle, J. P. (Glenswilly/Churchill) 73
McMonagle, James (Letterkenny) 65, 95, 103, 163, 164, 165, 168, 176, 193, 196, 197, 317
McMonagle, John (Letterkenny) 54
McMonagle, Patrick (Packie) (Letterkenny) 164, 165, 171
McNally, James (Buncrana) 137
McNee, Colonel (Moville) 278
McNelis, Donncha (Carrick/Cork Volunteers 1916/IRA Vol. Donegal 1921) 41, 229, 230, 296
McNelis, Michael (West Donegal Sinn Féin Executive) 76
McNulty, Anthony (IRB Dungloe) 53
McNulty, James (Creeslough) 46, 76, 104, 255, 289, 292
McNulty, John (Creeslough) 138, 255, 292, 293

McNulty, Shane (Dunfanaghy) 138
McShane, Con (Teelin, Glencolmcille) 318
McShane, Johnny (Raphoe) 37
McShane, Thomas (Dunkineely) 138
McShea, Thomas (Bundoran) 56, 94, 129, 139, 140, 144, 174, 186, 239, 240, 258
McSorley, Ray (Trillick, Co. Tyrone/Donegal based IRA Vol.) 156
McTigh, Dan (Ardara) 270
Meehan, D. (Inver) 318
Meehan, George (Donegal town) 318
Meehan, Joe (Bundoran) 94, 129, 174, 258
Meehan, Joseph (Frosses/South Donegal) 236
Meehan, Manus (Drimaherk/South Donegal) 236
Meehan, Patrick (Frosses/South Donegal) 236, 318
Meehan, Peter (Ballymacahill) 72
Meenabrock (Dunkineely) 94
Meenacross (West Donegal) 56, 76, 84, 131, 135, 208, 312
Meenagrave (South Donegal) 237
Meenatinney (West Donegal) 263
Meenavogy (Inishowen) 257
Meenbanad (West Donegal) 60, 61, 88, 208, 209, 210, 211, 218, 298, 309
Meenglass (Ballybofey) 237
Meenmore (Dungloe/Burtonport) 61, 144, 176, 205, 256, 265, 266
Meentagh (Ballyliffin/Inishowen) 110
Melly, Edward (Donegal Board of Guardians) 44, 138
Middletown (West Donegal) 181
Midleton, Lord 300
Milford (North-East Donegal) 27, 62, 72, 137, 155, 159, 174, 183, 230, 239, 254, 297, 314
Mill Road (Dungloe) 229
Milltown (Dungloe/Burtonport) 160, 176
Milroy, Seán (Sinn Féin GHQ) 55, 85, 108, 109, 117, 118, 133
Mín Doire Slua (Annagry, West Donegal) 221
Molloy, John (Dungloe) 116, 198
Molloy, John (Dunkineely/Ballykinlar internee) 318
Molloy, Mary (Derry) 216
Molloy, Patrick (Glenties) 79
Monaghan, Brian (Mountcharles) 77, 222
Monaghan, Hugh (Donegal town) 224
Monaugh (Buncrana) 232

INDEX

Montgomery, Alexander (Donegal town) 169
Montgomery, Rev. (Methodist minister Donegal town) 165
Moohan, James (Letterfad/South Donegal) 236
Mooney, John (RIC Sergeant) 146
Moore, District Inspector 56, 65, 68, 109
Moore, Major R. L. 90
Morgan, F. J. (Ballyshannon) 318
Morrison, Hugh (Derry) 130
Mountcharles (South Donegal) 18, 19, 27, 48, 72, 77, 94, 104, 138, 158, 166, 169, 175, 179, 188, 189, 222, 223, 225, 236, 281, 315
Mountjoy jail (Dublin) 54, 123, 127, 133, 134
Moville (Inishowen) 27, 63, 111, 181, 230, 278, 287, 311, 313
Muckish mountain (West Donegal) 21
Muff (Inishowen) 112
Mulcahy, Richard (Chief of Staff IRA) 191, 193, 195, 200, 204, 227, 234, 245, 246, 256, 263, 267, 271, 284, 285, 288
Mulhern, Daniel (Glenties) 154
Mullaghduff (West Donegal) 56, 90, 312
Mullaghmore Castle (South Donegal) 143, 144
Mullan, John (Glendowan) 137, 178, 256, 280
Mullanmore (Glenties) 273
Mullins (Donegal town) 215
Mulroy Bay (Milford) 171, 172, 254
Murdock (RIC Constable) 255
Murlogh 73, 105
Murphy, Jim (Letterkenny) 57
Murphy, John (Bundoran) 188
Murphy, John (County Councillor Inishowen) 121
Murphy, Nan (Letterkenny) 67
Murray, Charles (Mountcharles) 222
Murray, Francis J. (Kilcar) 218, 318
Murray, Joachim (Kilcar) 217
Murray, Joseph (Bundoran) 56, 83, 85, 94, 283, 301
Murray, Neil (Milford) 137
Murray, Seán (alias used by Denis (Donnacha) McNelis) 229
Murrin, Michael (Croaghlin) 58

N

Newmills (Letterkenny) 239, 287, 288
Newtowncunningham (North-East Donegal) 27, 203, 313
Noonan, James (Letterfad/South Donegal) 215

O

O'Boyle, Bernard (Rutland Island, Burtonport) 110, 111
O'Boyle, Domhnall (Ballyliffin) 110
O'Boyle, Éamon (Carrick Battalion Vice-O/C) 142
O'Boyle, Éamon (Gweedore) 83
O'Boyle, Mrs (Rutland Island, Burtonport) 110, 111
O'Boyle, Neil, Plunkett (Lackenagh, Dungloe) 199
O'Brien, Conor (owner of the *Kelpie*) 25
O'Brien, Francis (Kilcar) 218
O'Brien, James (Bundoran) 239, 240
O'Brien, James (Limerick/Birmingham) 123
O'Byrne, Patrick (Killybegs) 183
O'Callaghan, Michael (Commissioner of the Peace – resigned 1920) 159
O'Connor, Batt (Dublin) 285
O'Connor, Fr (IRA sympathiser, Birmingham, England) 132
O'Connor, Patrick (IRB) 29
O'Doherty, Fr Philip (Buncrana) 58, 88, 118, 254, 258
O'Doherty, Hugh (Solicitor) 118
O'Doherty, John (IRA Vol. Bundoran) 174
O'Doherty, Joseph (Joe) (Derry/Sinn Féin TD North Donegal) 42, 54, 81, 82, 83, 88, 89, 113, 114, 123, 133, 147, 149, 216, 258
O'Doherty, Patrick (IRA Vol. Bundoran) 174
O'Doherty, Philip (IRA Inishowen) 189
O'Doherty, Philip (Irish Party Candidate 1918 General Election) 89
O'Doherty, Roisín (Cumann na mBan nurse 1st Northern Division) 256
O'Doherty, Vincent (Derry) 42
O'Donnell, Barney (IRA Vol. Cloghaneely) 57
O'Donnell, Bernard (Fanad) 190
O'Donnell, Biddy 263, 266

349

O'Donnell, C. V. (Buncrana) 215
O'Donnell, Daniel (Tondiff/Buncrana) 232
O'Donnell, Edward (Carndonagh) 287
O'Donnell, Frank (Meenmore/Dungloe) 76, 115, 136, 156, 157, 159, 176, 198, 204, 206, 208, 210, 235, 266
O'Donnell, Hugh (Dungloe) 227
O'Donnell, J. (Buncrana) 57, 286
O'Donnell, J. B. (Nationalist Councillor Milford area) 137
O'Donnell, James (Letterkenny) 57
O'Donnell, Joe (Meenmore/Dungloe) 209, 210
O'Donnell, John (Councillor South Area) 121
O'Donnell, John (Mín Doire Slua, Annagry) 221
O'Donnell, Owen (Ballybofey) 283
O'Donnell, Pat (Doochary) 204
O'Donnell, Patrick (Annagry) 76, 221
O'Donnell, Patrick (Kit) (Dungloe) 115, 209, 210, 211
O'Donnell, Patrick (Letterkenny) 123
O'Donnell, Patrick (Tondiff/Buncrana) 232
O'Donnell, Peadar (Meenmore/O/C 2nd Brigade 1st Northern Division) 202, 203, 204, 205, 206, 208, 210, 211, 217, 220, 228, 234, 238, 239, 241, 245, 246, 248, 256, 259, 260, 261, 262, 263, 264, 265, 266, 273, 274, 275, 280, 281, 288
O'Donnell, Peter (Donegal town) 215
O'Donovan Rossa, Jeremiah (Fenian) 29
O'Duffy, Eoin (IRA GHQ staff) 285
O'Duffy, Hugh (Beltany, Gortahork/Gaelic League organiser) 84, 110
O'Duffy, Liam (Adjutant No. 4 Brigade) 94, 143, 183, 184, 185, 199, 207, 216
O'Duffy, Liam (Donegal town) 94, 143, 183, 184, 185, 199, 207, 216
O'Dwyer, Bishop 51
O'Flaherty, John (Castlefinn) 133
O'Flaherty, John (Letterkenny) 137
O'Flaherty, Sam (Castlefinn) 50, 57, 67, 78, 81, 82, 90, 106, 111, 161, 163, 164, 165, 237, 258, 279, 283, 284
O'Gorman, John (IRA flying column) 198, 210, 296, 297
O'Gorman, Joseph (IRA Vol. Bundoran) 174
O'Hagan, John (Buncrana) 286
O'Hanlon, Hugh 77
O'Hara, John (IRA Vol. Kilcar) 194, 318

O'Mahony, P. C. (Sinn Féin organiser) 67, 71, 107
O'Malley, Dan (IRA Vol. Birmingham, England) 126
O'Malley, Ernie (IRA GHQ organiser) 93, 94, 111, 112
O'Neill, Denis 200, 222
O'Neill, Mrs E. (Publican) 185
O'Neill, Patrick (Armagh) 123
O'Rahilly Sinn Féin Cumann 61
O'Sullivan, Gearoid (IRA GHQ Adjutant General) 244, 281
Ó Dubhthaigh, Aodh (IRB West Donegal) 37
Orange Order 46, 65, 66

P

Parke, R. S. (South Area Councillor) 121
Pearse, Pádraig (1916 Leader/Signatory to the Proclamation) 29, 31, 32, 33, 35, 39, 40, 51, 57, 93
Pearse, Willie (Irish Volunteer/Executed 1916) 31, 35, 57, 96
Pennyburn (Derry) 112
Pettigo (Donegal/Fermanagh border) 94, 104, 143, 228, 283, 315, 316
Pim, Herbert Newman (IRB/Irish Volunteers organiser) 28, 29, 37
Plunkett, Count (Sinn Féin) 46, 47, 49, 91, 98, 100
Plunkett, Joseph Mary (Irish Volunteer/executed 1916) 31, 32
Portadown (Co. Antrim) 29
Port Bridge (Letterkenny) 133, 203
Porter, John (Sinn Féin Councillor Inishowen) 121, 286
Porter, Patrick (Sinn Féin/IRA Vol. Inishowen) 114, 117, 118, 121, 286
Port Road (Letterkenny) 52, 74
Portsalon (Fanad Peninsula) 31
Price, Eamon (IRA GHQ Director of Organisation) 281, 288

Q

Quay Road (Dungloe) 296
Quay Street (Donegal town) 200
Quigley, David (Malin) 253
Quigley's Point (Inishowen) 189
Quinn, James (Railway employee/South Donegal) 176

INDEX

Quinn, Joseph (Ballybofey) 77

R

Ramelton (North-East Donegal) 24, 179, 239, 295, 297, 314
Rampart (Dungloe) 115, 159, 192
Ranafast (West Donegal) 76, 90, 294, 312
Raphoe (East Donegal) 24, 27, 37, 53, 57, 64, 65, 68, 78, 99, 105, 106, 111, 133, 295, 313, 317
Rathmullan (North-East Donegal/Fanad Peninsula) 29, 73, 137
Ray (Fanad) 314
Redmond, John (Irish Parliamentary Party) 26, 27
Reegan, Charles (Ballyshannon) 174
Reelin Bridge (Ballybofey) 232, 233
Reilly, Mrs (Glendowan) 256
Reilly, Patrick (Kiltoorish) 286
Rickey, Captain (Ballybofey) 237
Rooney, Thomas (Ballyshannon) 192
Rosbeg (Ardara/South Donegal coast) 241, 243, 285, 314
Rosnakill (Fanad Peninsula) 83, 96, 114, 138, 182, 230, 249, 254, 311, 314
Rosses (West Donegal) 33, 56, 90, 107, 228, 241, 291, 315, 316
Roulstone, Robert (Unionist) 137
Royal Irish Constabulary (RIC) 16, 20, 21, 22, 23, 28, 29, 32, 40, 41, 49, 52, 60, 61, 65, 66, 68, 69, 74, 79, 81, 82, 93, 95, 100, 102, 103, 104, 105, 106, 114, 115, 116, 117, 120, 121, 126, 128, 129, 130, 132, 133, 135, 136, 140, 143, 144, 145, 146, 147, 148, 149, 151, 153, 155, 156, 157, 158, 159, 160, 161, 162, 163, 164, 165, 166, 168, 169, 173, 174, 175, 176, 177, 179, 180, 183, 186, 187, 192, 193, 198, 199, 200, 203, 204, 211, 213, 214, 215, 219, 220, 222, 223, 224, 225, 229, 230, 231, 232, 233, 234, 235, 236, 237, 239, 244, 246, 248, 249, 250, 251, 253, 254, 255, 257, 259, 263, 265, 268, 269, 271, 272, 276, 282, 286, 288, 289, 294, 295, 296, 303, 308, 309
Ryan, Bernard (Bundoran) 71
Ryan, Binny (Bundoran) 318

S

Scalp Mountain (Inishowen Peninsula) 31

Scottish Highlanders 43
Sentry Hill (Letterkenny) 72, 73
Shamrock Hall, Bogside (Derry) 202, 238
Shanagh, Ballylar (Fanad Peninsula) 190
Sharkey, Willie (IRA Vol. Milltown, Burtonport) 156, 157, 206, 210, 211
Shaw, William, John (County Councillor Laghey area) 138
Sheer, Michael (Derry/1st Northern Division) 241, 242
Sheeran, John (Ballyshannon) 173, 174
Sheeran, Joseph (Ballyshannon) 174
Shiels, Manus (Fanad) 83
Shiels, Patrick (Paddy) (Derry) 42, 123, 238, 260
Shore Road (Burtonport) 176
Sion Mills (Co. Tyrone) 111
Slieve League (South Donegal) 21, 226
Slieve Snaght (Inishowen Peninsula) 21, 257, 258
Sloane, Patrick (Co. Westmeath/Ballykinlar internee) 195
Smith, John (IRA Vol. Ballybofey) 276, 282
Smith, Louis (Derry Jail 1916) 42
Solohedbeg (Co. Tipperary) 100, 101
Speer, J. P. (Letterkenny) 121
Speertown (Donegal town/South Donegal) 191
St Eunan's Cathedral 35, 72, 193
St Eunan's College 73, 280
St Johnston (East Donegal) 53, 313
Stafford jail 40
Stack, Austin (Dáil Éireann, Minister for Home Affairs) 226
Stevenson, John (County Councillor Donegal town area) 138
Strabane (Donegal/Tyrone border) 28, 39, 150, 175, 176, 228, 258, 311, 313, 316
Straboy (Glenties) 241
Stranorlar (South West Donegal) 27, 37, 66, 68, 78, 112, 168, 199, 212, 228, 247, 254, 267, 276, 277, 292, 301, 314, 316
Summerhill (Donegal town) 191, 318
Sweeney, Anthony (Meenbanad) 61
Sweeney, Bernard (Bernie) (Burtonport) 60, 115, 176, 193, 198, 210
Sweeney, Charles (Killybegs) 183
Sweeney, Dan (Gortahork) 156, 176
Sweeney, Hugh (IRA Vol. Castlefinn) 165
Sweeney, J. E. (County Councillor Letterkenny Rural) 137

351

Sweeney, Joe (Joseph) (Burtonport/O/C No. 1 Brigade/O/C 1st Northern Division) 40, 53, 60, 61, 76, 81, 83, 84, 87, 89, 90, 104, 115, 127, 136, 193, 198, 204, 206, 208, 209, 210, 211, 212, 217, 218, 219, 220, 225, 227, 231, 232, 235, 240, 244, 245, 250, 256, 258, 260, 262, 263, 266, 268, 269, 271, 273, 275, 279, 280, 283, 284, 285, 290
Sweeney, John (Burtonport) 33, 84
Sweeney, John (IRA Burtonport) 210
Sweeney, John (Railway employee/South Donegal) 176, 177
Sweeney, Nellie (Cumann na mBan, Derry) 239
Sweeney, Philip (Annagry) 221
Sweeney's hotel (Dungloe) 64, 176, 198, 206, 211, 262

T

Tamney (Fanad) 96, 131
Tawnawully (South Donegal) 72, 104
Teelin (South Donegal) 87, 107, 142, 278, 314, 318
Termon (Kilmacrenan/West Donegal) 51, 73, 76, 99, 107, 179
Timoney, John (Donegal Board of Guardians) 44
Timony, Phil (Ardara) 183
Tirconaill Street (Donegal town) 224
Tolan, Denis (Keelogs/South Donegal) 198
Tor (Gweedore) 298
Tormy, Joseph (Co. Westmeath/Ballykinlar internee) 195
Tory Island (West Donegal) 31, 32, 312
Tralee Bay (Co. Kerry) 31
Treacy, Seán (Tipperary Brigade) 101
Trim (Co. Meath) 187
Trusk Lough (Ballybofey) 276, 282, 292
Tullaghan (South Donegal) 94, 315
Tullinteane (South Donegal) 242
Tullydish (Buncrana) 214
Tullynaha (South Donegal) 215

Tyler, James (Derry city) 202, 210

U

Ulster Volunteer Force (UVF) 14, 20, 23, 24, 25, 73, 95, 111, 169, 178, 306

W

Wakefield prison 42
Wallace (RIC Inspector) 116
Walsh, Archbishop 115
Walsh, Dan (Gortahork) 156
Walsh, Daniel (Dungloe) 296
Walsh, Jim (Mutt) (Cork – Donegal Flying Column) 202, 209, 210, 239, 256, 266
Walsh, Michael (Gortahork) 156
Walsh, Paddy (RIC Inspector/IRA agent) 168, 265, 309
Waltsteads, The (Letterkenny) 265
Ward, (Frank) Francis (IRA Vol. Bundoran) 174
Ward, C.H. (Barnesmore) 191
Ward, Charles (No. 1 Brigade/West Donegal) 210
Ward, James (Loughanure) 61, 218
Ward, Jimmy (Susan) (Cloghglass) 60
Ward, John (Killybegs) 110, 183
Ward, Michael (Letterfad/South Donegal) 222, 236
Ward, Seamus (Ballyshannon) 72, 94, 318
Ward P. J. (Killybegs/Donegal town/TD/Vice-O/C No. 3 Brigade South Donegal) 81, 85, 87, 89, 94, 96, 104, 108, 109, 126, 183, 184, 187, 222, 224, 258
Waterloo Place (Donegal town) 200
Waugh, Thomas (Letterfad/South Donegal) 223
Welchtown (Ballybofey) 112
West End (Bundoran) 85, 86, 188
White, William (Donegal town) 165
Wilkinson, Andrew (Creeslough) 104
Wilkinson, J. (Letterkenny) 152
Wilson, Hubert (Longford) 197

Lightning Source UK Ltd.
Milton Keynes UK
UKOW04f1845081215

264378UK00001B/30/P

9 781856 356329